NEW YORK

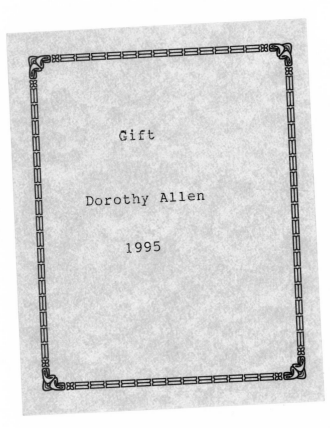

Gift

Dorothy Allen

1995

THE TRAIL OF THE
BLACK WALNUT

To My Wife

FLORA

for her help and encouragement
in the completion and publication
of this manuscript

THE TRAIL OF THE
BLACK WALNUT

BY

G. Elmore Reaman

McLEAN COUNTY
GENEALOGICAL SOCIETY

CONTENTS

vi

ILLUSTRATIONS

MAPS AND CHARTS

FOREWORD

I HAVE been more than a little astonished at the wealth of material Dr. Reaman has been able to glean in what was once an almost barren field, and I am glad, therefore, of this chance to pay tribute to a splendid feat of research. He has not only made the Pennsylvania Germans who came to Ontario in an early age familiar to us as a class which played a large part in the settling of the province, he has succeeded as well in turning a light on one of the blank spots of Canadian history. Little indeed has been known of Upper Canada in the years between the cession of North America to Great Britain and the war of 1812. On tracing back what little I knew of this period I find that I was under the impression (a nebulous one without reason or foundation) that the population was made up of a garrison or two and a few British and French settlers scattered about here and there on the great lakes and along the waterways. This has been, I think, a rather general impression.

By presenting the proofs of the important part these settlers of Teutonic origins played in the earliest days, Dr. Reaman has performed an important service. Now that he has broken the ground with straight and solid furrows, it is reasonable to expect a gradual clearing up of the obscurity. New facts will be uncovered and a full picture of Ontario in one of the first stages will emerge as time goes on.

He has performed one of the primary functions of the historian with clarity and vigor.

T. B. COSTAIN

A NOD FROM PENNSYLVANIA

WITH the presentation of Dr. Reaman's analysis of the influence of the Pennsylvania Germans upon the settlement and development of Ontario comes the realization that Canadian culture has entered upon its refining stage. In the pattern of all history one finds the stages of discovery, pioneering, rolling back frontiers, social and economic adjustment. All of these must take their turn before dynamic societies may turn a backward glance to survey the conquered territory.

Citizens of the United States became conscious of their local history near the close of the nineteenth century. Most historical societies of ancient vintage here, date their origins since 1890 or a century and a half after the last of the thirteen original colonies (Georgia, 1733) was founded. By 1956 Ontario could record one hundred and fifty years of its history, or the refining processes resulting from the services of seven or eight generations of men and women.

The study of the Pennsylvania German element in the founding of Upper Canada and in making Ontario great is properly one of the first projects of its kind. It is proper because these people were among the first to carve a great province out of an uncharted wilderness, and because of the indelible stamp which their culture, particularly their agriculture, has left upon the economic welfare of Ontario at mid-century.

We, in Pennsylvania, are delighted to note that the scholar who undertook this labor of love is one so eminently qualified in our eyes and so uniquely endowed with the necessary talents as is Dr. George Elmore Reaman. His frequent visits to Pennsylvania; his familiarity with the sources of information; his wide acquaintanceship with the scholars in the field and his unflagging devotion to his own country all combine to blend the objective and subjective approach to his study. His skill as a writer and his standing in the field of letters add

ix

authenticity, charm and beauty to his contribution as recorded in this volume.

For a number of years we, in Pennsylvania, have regarded Dr. Reaman and Dr. B. Mabel Dunham as the outstanding personalities in Canada in the field of Pennsylvania German studies. One of the greatest pleasures experienced by this writer was to be guided by the scholars, jointly, on a tour of the Markham-Kitchener-Haldimand-Thamesville area of Ontario and, in their company, to note the vestiges of a culture which was transplanted from Penn's province to Governor Simcoe's. Dr. Dunham has thrown the story on the canvas of fiction; Dr. Reaman has recorded it, factually, for posterity.

ARTHUR D. GRAEFF

Robesonia, Pa.

PREFACE TO THE SECOND EDITION

FURTHER research concerning the earliest settlers in Upper Canada has brought to light many new and significant facts, particularly regarding the French Huguenots and Six Nations Indians. In the sections included at the end of this book, certain highlights taken from two extended studies have been included.

Since no study has ever been made in Canada of Huguenots, it was found necessary to go elsewhere for information about them. This being the case, I went to Europe, where I met Huguenot historians and was given access to Huguenot libraries in London, Paris, Leyden, Bonn, Berlin, and Geneva. In the United States, I was able to get information from several of the thirty state Huguenot Societies. In Canada, I wrote to one hundred and fifty newspapers asking readers of Huguenot ancestry to communicate with me. A large number of them replied, giving me many valuable details. The results from this investigation have been very gratifying, for they have shown the great contribution made by French Huguenots to Canada in general and Ontario in particular.*

The Six Nations Indians have suffered for their allegiance to the Crown in several ways. Not only did they lose their homes but what has been written about them has, in the main, originated from French sources and is therefore biased. Like the white settlers in the English colonies who sought refuge in Canada after the American Revolution, they lost everything, including their independence; but they have never been given the same recognition by historians as the United Empire Loyalists. Logically, if they wished —which they do not—they could lay claim to the same designation.

* See *Trail of the Huguenots*, G. Elmore Reaman. Book Society of Canada.

xi

For this reason, if no other, they deserve a place in studies of those who followed the trail of the black walnut. They came to Upper Canada to find a new home and many of their descendants have found a place in our society and made a worthwhile contribution. We should remember that Francis Parkman called them "the Romans of the New World."

AUTHOR'S PREFACE

SOME ten years have passed since I began this study with the purpose of investigating the contribution of the Pennsylvania Dutch to agriculture. My researches had not however progressed far when certain facts became apparent which necessitated an entirely different approach to the subject, and resulted in its expansion into a fuller study of the whole way of life of these people.

First I discovered that the term Pennsylvania Dutch was a misnomer, indeed more of a nickname, their correct name being Pennsylvania Germans. Next, these people had migrated to Upper Canada very early, many of them soon after 1776, and the earliest group came, not from Pennsylvania, but from New York State. Thirdly, the Pennsylvania Germans did not come alone, for closely associated with them in their migration were French Huguenots, English Quakers, and Puritans from New Jersey. In religion the Germans included not merely Mennonites and Dunkards, but also Lutherans, Reformed, and Moravians. In point of time these three groups—German, French, and English—were the earliest settlers in Upper Canada. They came in large numbers, and many brought money, chattels, and animals, together with the experience and knowledge necessary to make good in a pioneer situation. Lastly, not only had these people made a significant contribution to agriculture, but they had also contributed much that was distinctive to the cultural life of the province.

To make these discoveries was one thing, but to justify certain contentions to the satisfaction of sceptical historians was quite another matter. The problem was complicated by two factors: few of these settlers ever held office of any kind because of reasons which will become obvious—hence historical records were not available or at best tantalizingly incomplete, and no studies of them had ever been made except as religious groups. Extensive searching through archival repositories re-

xiii

vealed little material, and primary sources were very few in number. In fact, the most fertile field I found was documents and family histories in the possession of private individuals. Thus I have been forced too frequently to rely on secondary sources as the only records available, not only to supplement the primary material, but occasionally to determine the agreement or disagreement of certain points of view. Rather than give my own interpretation on such issues I have invariably quoted the author's words so that the reader may form his own opinion.

This work does not pretend to be a cultural study of these different folk. Rather it is an effort to understand them as an ethnic group, which, despite linguistic and national distinctions, was bound together by the bond of a common, basic religious tradition. And because they were the earliest settlers in Upper Canada under the British regime, more stress has been put on the period before 1812—particularly before 1792. Historians have given much research to the coming of British settlers after the War of 1812; consequently, less attention has been paid to this formative era.

Nor is it my intention to present this volume as a definitive study of any one or all of these groups. What I have attempted is a collation of available historical material and an interpretation of this evidence in support of the thesis that the English Quakers, French Huguenots, and Palatinate and Swiss Germans deserve much more recognition as settlers and makers of Ontario than they have hitherto received from historians. Undoubtedly there is much more historical evidence on this subject which must be uncovered, studied, and interpreted. Such investigation will amplify, and, I believe, justify the conclusions arrived at in *The Trail of the Black Walnut*.

My indebtedness is great to many persons, but I should like to mention some who have been particularly helpful. Valuable advice and suggestions were given by Mr. Norman Fee, Assistant Dominion Archivist, Ottawa, and his staff; by Dr. Marius Barbeau, National Museum, Ottawa; and by Dr. George S. Spragge, Director of Ontario Public Archives, and his assistants.

To Mr. Thomas Reesor, Cedar Grove, and Bishop S. F. Coffman, Vineland, both recently deceased, I am especially grateful for background color and information about the earliest settlements in York County and the Niagara Peninsula. Bishop Ernest J. Swalm of Duntroon provided me with the authentic history of the Brethren in Christ in Ontario. Miss Sara Crysler of Niagara Falls gave me many facts about the settlements along the Niagara River. A special thank you goes to Dr. Harold S. Bender, Goshen College, Goshen, Indiana, for his careful reading of the manuscript to check on the accuracy of statements concerning the religious backgrounds of the Plain Folk.

Librarians have given every assistance and I should like to mention four in particular: Miss Dorothy Shoemaker, Chief, Kitchener Public Library, and Miss Grace Schmidt; Miss Margaret Ray, Victoria College Library; and Mrs. Elleine H. Stones, Chief, Burton Collection, Detroit Public Library. Dr. John S. Moir (Lecturer, Carleton College, Ottawa) was assiduous in his efforts to discover relevant material, and in his preparation of the index.

For taking time to read the manuscript and express opinions, I am grateful to Dr. Rufus A. Coleman, Professor of English, Montana State University; to Professor J. M. S. Careless, Department of History, University of Toronto; to Thomas B. Costain, author of historical novels; and to Dr. L. M. Klinck, President Emeritus, University of British Columbia.

Material assistance was given by Dr. S. F. Leavine, Kitchener, and Mr. Henry S. Hosking, Guelph. To Miss Margaret Y. Johnston goes my appreciation for much painstaking typing; also to Miss Susan Semevan of my publishers for her valuable editorial assistance.

To Dr. Arthur D. Graeff, Robesonia, Pa., must go the credit for being the first United States historian to interest himself in the Pennsylvania Germans who migrated to Canada. His visits and investigations created an awareness of our earliest racial backgrounds and without this awareness this study would never have been undertaken.

Finally, I should like to make acknowledgement of the fact that the publication of this manuscript was made possible by the support of the Pennsylvania German Society. In this connection I should like to mention Dr. Walter E. Boyer and Dr. Albert F. Buffington, Pennsylvania State University. The

Rev. William J. Rupp, Allentown, Pa., Editor for this Society, was untiring in his efforts to give assistance, and to him I tender my warmest thanks.

GEORGE ELMORE REAMAN

Waterloo College,
  Waterloo, Ontario
    May, 1956

INTRODUCTION

"The key to a nation's future is in her past. A nation that loses it has no future. For men's deepest desires—the instrument by which a continuing society moulds its destiny—spring from their own inherited experience. We cannot re-create the past but we cannot escape it. It is in our blood and bone. To understand the temperament of a people, a statesman has first to know its history." [1]

A SUB-TITLE for this study might be "Pennsylvania Germans and Plain Folk—An Ethnic Group." However, an explanation of this term is essential to a satisfactory orientation. Sometimes the groups to be studied are related racially, but in all cases historically, and, since they would seem to have a common and distinctive culture, the use of the term "ethnic" is permissible. The Pennsylvania Germans were not the only Germans to emigrate to Ontario; a number came from other states such as New York, New Jersey, Maryland, the Carolinas, and Vermont, and many came directly from Europe. Furthermore, the Quakers (known in Canada as Plain Folk) in most cases were not Germans but English or Welsh, and the Huguenots were French, yet these had much in common with their German neighbors in Pennsylvania. Some Germans came after a sojourn in Holland. The Lutherans, the Reformed, and the Huguenots were not strictly Plain Folk, although their beliefs had many similarities, and for our purposes they will be included under that category.

The extent to which this ethnic group has contributed to agriculture and the cultural life of the Province of Ontario is not generally known. This is so for several reasons: first, the Plain Folk were so self-effacing and avoided office-holding to such an extent that records of what they accomplished in the early days are practically non-existent. For this reason, historians and early travellers have made little or no mention of them, being content to speak of the "early settlers," without stating who they were or where they originated. Often the "early settlers" are referred to merely as United Empire Loyalists, the implication being that they were all English, Irish, or Scottish. Secondly, the studies which have been made of them have been for the purpose of appraising them as religious bodies, each religious denomination or sect being considered a separate entity with little relationship to other religious groups. Thirdly, with one exception—Waterloo County—descendants of these early settlers have lost their identity through intermarriage with other nationalities or acceptance of other religions. Lastly, because of lack of understanding of their cultural patterns and of what they have contributed to Canada's life, they have been viewed in a patronizing manner and considered interesting but "queer." Not infrequently this is the fault of persons who have forgotten, if they ever knew, that they themselves were descended from them. At any rate they are eating foods, using expressions, and following farm practices which had their origins among these Plain Folk.

The situation has been complicated by uncertainty as to who were included in the term "Dutch." It was often used to refer to the Hollanders as well as the Pennsylvania Germans. In this study the term "Dutch" will be applied to the Hollanders only, and the so-called Pennsylvania Dutch will be referred to as Pennsylvania German.[2]

It should be pointed out that the term Pennsylvania Dutch does not include the Amish in Canada, because the Amish in Ontario never saw Pennsylvania as they came directly from Germany and did not migrate until 1824, twenty-five to fifty years after the first settlers. Pennsylvania Dutch when used is meant to apply to those Germans, whether Lutheran, Reformed, Mennonite, Dunkard, or Moravian, who migrated to Upper Canada before and shortly after 1800. Furthermore, the term "Plain Folk" includes Quakers, Mennonites, and Dunkards, but not Lutherans and Reformed.

This study has been undertaken for the purpose of discovering, if possible, how and where these groups originated and what they have in common; then, to appraise the contribution they have made as pioneers in Upper Canada, and the extent to which we in modern times are indebted to them. This is an effort to speak, not for those "who could not speak for themselves," but for those in the past "who would not speak for themselves."

The history of the settlement of Ontario, or Upper Canada as it was first known, begins in the last quarter of the eighteenth century. An impetus for this settlement was very definitely given by the American Revolutionary War. Even before the close of the war, thousands of Loyalists began to swarm across the Canadian frontier to escape the persecutions which would follow them as long as they remained in the Colonies.

At that time Upper Canada was an unbroken wilderness—covered with mixed hardwood forests. A. W. Currie, in his *Economic Geography of Canada*, states: "The native forest cover of the St. Lawrence Lowland Region is mixed hardwood. The most common species are the sugar maple, ash, elm, beech, basswood, and some oak along with white pine, balsam fir, cedar, and a little spruce. In the southern part of Western Ontario and in Prince Edward County there are additional varieties not found elsewhere, such as black walnut, several types of oak, and even the red mulberry, cucumber tree and tulip tree." [3]

Thus settlers coming into Upper Canada found a problem of giant proportions. Before any grain could be planted the trees had to be cut down. The forest was inhabited by Indians and wild animals—a constant menace. Hence, only those inured to the hardships of pioneer life and endowed with indomitable courage were able to make any headway. A typical example of the futility of any other type of settler trying to wrest a livelihood from these early surroundings was the failure to establish the de Puisaye colony of French Royalists in the northern part of York County, Ontario.

To make good in Upper Canada in its virgin state, settlers had to have a knowledge of agriculture adapted to New World conditions, a willingness to endure hardships, and a love of the soil. Such persons were to be found among the Plain Folk, particularly those who lived in Pennsylvania and New York State, because, for the preceding hundred years, these people had met a similar situation there and had conquered it. Thus, to understand why these Plain Folk succeeded, first in Pennsylvania and New York, and later in Upper Canada, we must study their origins in Europe to see if their cultural patterns were the same there as in America, and if so, what brought these patterns into being; also, whether they remained constant in America.

It is now time to name the different groups which come into our study. They are, roughly in order of development in Europe: Moravians, Lutherans, Reformed, Huguenots, Mennonites, Amish, Quakers, and Dunkards. They divide into two groups—resisters: Lutherans, Reformed, and Huguenots; and non-resisters: Moravians, Mennonites, Amish, Dunkards, and Quakers. But whether resisters or non-resisters, one finds that, with the exception of the Quakers (who belonged to England), to a large extent they originated in Holland, South Germany, France, Rhine Palatinate, or Switzerland, and had important things in common: a love of the land, a thorough knowledge of agriculture, deep religious convictions, and a rugged individualism. These characteristics, developed in Europe, were carried into Pennsylvania and New York State and later into Ontario. For that reason it is important to discover under what conditions they came into being. To this group we should add the Six Nations Indians because of the part they played in the Seven Years' War and the American Revolutionary War. In point of fact they came to Upper Canada at the same time and for the same reasons as the groups mentioned above.

I

BACKGROUNDS IN EUROPE

SECTS denote a religious conflict in society which arises in opposition to an institutional church, based on the definite commitment of mature individuals to a definite set of principles. All faiths have been subject to this tendency. Chinese history has had various societies with religious interests, exclusive membership and revolutionary programs. Mohammedanism has given rise to numerous organizations of the sect type.

Christianity itself began as a separatist movement in Judaism, and in the Roman Empire it preserved its character as an exclusive society which not only forbade its members to participate in the popular worship and exercised strict discipline over their conduct, but also tended to separate them from the political and economic society; consequently, the early Christians became a relatively self-sufficient society within the empire, with resulting antagonisms.

From the third century to the eleventh there were sporadic developments of groups which directed their protests against the growing power of the clergy, the relaxation of discipline, and the substitution of doctrine for inspiration. Early Catholicism, however, was able to unite this sectarianism with the ecclesiastical movement and thereby negate the influence of the sects.

In spite of this, however, the early years of the twelfth century witnessed the rise of a number of sects. One group, the Waldenses, retained their sectarian character and professed beliefs. They sought individual perfection apart from the church, rejected the official clergy, abstained from oaths and from the use of force, and attempted in general to reintroduce primitive Christian fellowship and apostolic simplicity of living.

The Vaudois Valleys, or the Valleys of Piedmont, were the home of the Waldenses, or Vaudois, who, according to some historians, were converts of the faith preached by St. Paul. Proof of this cannot be established; however, the beliefs of these people have been widely accepted. In fact, members of this sect still exist, showing its vitality. According to James D. McCabe, Jr., they accepted and taught the doctrines of the Apostles and acknowledged the Bible, particularly the New Testament, as their guide.[1] The tenets of their religion were: (1) that oaths are forbidden by the Gospels; (2) that capital punishment is not allowed to the civil powers; (3) that any layman may consecrate the sacrament of the altar; and (4) that the Roman Church is not the Church of Christ but the enemy of Christ.

The Waldenses * carried on active missionary work among the barbarians to the north of them. "Their Pastors were designated Barbas [a term meaning uncle]. It was in the almost inaccessible solitude of the deep mountain pass that they had their school. . . . They were required to commit to memory the Gospels of St. Matthew and St. John, the general epistles, and a part of those of St. Luke. They were instructed, moreover, during two or three successive winters, and trained to speak in Latin, in the Romance language, and in the Italian. After this they spent one year in retirement, and then were set apart to the holy ministry by the administration of the Lord's Supper, and by the imposition of hands. They were supported by the voluntary contributions of the people.

"These missionaries always went forth two and two, to wit, a young man and an old one . . . they traversed Italy, where they had stations organized in many places, and secret adherents in almost all the towns. . . .

"Each pastor was required to become a missionary in his turn. . . . Besides this, the Barbas received instructions in some trade or profession, by which they might be able to provide for their wants. Some were hawkers, others artisans, the greater part physicians or surgeons, and all were acquainted with the cultivation of the soil, the keeping of flocks, to the care of which they had been accustomed in their early years." [2]

As the See of Rome became supreme, the isolation of the Vaudois Church ceased to exist and for several centuries the

* This sect is supposed to be named after Peter Waldo, a wealthy merchant in Lyons, France, who took upon himself the vow of poverty and gave leadership to it until he died in Bohemia in 1217.

Waldenses were bitterly persecuted yet were never completely conquered. The ideas for which they stood spread into Hungary, Bohemia, France, and England. Some historians go so far as to state that the Albigenses, a sect of Cathari in Southern France in the eleventh, twelfth, thirteenth, and fourteenth centuries, whose struggle with Rome was very bitter, were proselytized by the Vaudois missionaries, and that the teachings of the Vaudois heralded, if they did not hasten, the Reformation in Germany and Bohemia. Be this as it may, the effect of their teachings and their emphasis on the New Testament was far-reaching.

In the fourteenth and fifteenth centuries John Wyclif (1324–1384) in England, who translated the Bible into English, and John Huss (1373–1415) in Bohemia, built up movements that looked to the formation of a separatist community. This meant that they incensed not only the Roman Church but also the state authorities and in the end suffered greatly.

A modern commentator, Henry John Randall, considers that the "Waldenses may be regarded as one of the earlier forerunners of the reformers . . . they were anti-clerical and they reduced the sacraments to two—baptism and the mass. In the fourteenth century came Lollardy to England, and in the fifteenth the Hussites to Bohemia. The movement initiated by Wyclif was scholarly and somewhat aristocratic rather than a movement resting upon the masses. His main proposals were a Church independent of the State, without ordained priests, and without wealth, cults, or political influence. The Hussite movement, on the other hand, was more political and more revolutionary. The doctrines of Huss were founded upon, and even abstracted verbatim from, the works of Wyclif; but he attempted a greater measure of organization and drew conclusions from the Scriptures as to social relations that Wyclif had refrained from emphasizing." [3]

Out of the defeat of the Bohemian movement, however, a definite sect, the Moravians or *Unitas Fratrum* (1415–1648) emerged, which reverted to the tenets of the Waldenses. "This group accepted the ethics of the New Testament not as a program to be forced upon civil society but rather as the constitution of a separate religious community. It rejected all forms of violence, required its members to withdraw from public life and trade, to content themselves with agriculture and manual labor and to develop among themselves a fellowship of love." [4]

In 1501 the Moravians edited the first hymn book; later, the Bible was translated into Bohemian, and this translation is still used in Bohemia. Thus we see that when Luther came on the scene and in 1517 nailed his ninety-five theses on the church door, the time was ripe for a widespread secession from the Roman Catholic Church. It is said that at that time there were some 200,000 Moravian Christians. By 1526 Germany was divided into a Protestant and a Romanist party, and the Protestant party into the followers of Luther, Zwingli, and the Anabaptists. The spirit of reform was abroad in the land but expressed itself in several ways.

Briefly, Luther's (1483–1546) greatest contributions were made by his defiance of the Roman Church, his translation of the Bible into German, his polemical writings, and his revival of the essential gospel of salvation by grace, and justification by faith. He believed that the Church should be closely linked with the State, and his natural conservatism led him to retain most of the ceremonies, the vestments and the uses of lights on the altar, which had existed in the Roman Church, although he was careful to explain that their retention might be dispensed with if necessary. He insisted on the use of the vernacular and the supreme place assigned to preaching. Also, the people partook of the bread and wine in the sacrament of the Lord's Supper.

Zwingli (1484–1531) was a Swiss Reformer who preached and fought the power of Rome at the same time as Luther but quite independently of him. He began to preach "the Gospel" in 1519—that is, justification by faith—and to declare that Jesus Christ was the only mediator between sinful man and God. Like Luther he repudiated the medieval doctrine of transubstantiation, but he declined to accept Luther's teaching that Christ's words of institution required the belief that the real flesh and blood of Christ co-exist in and with the natural elements. Zwingli was the founder of the Reformed Church, which differed from the Lutheran in two outstanding particulars: Church and State were eventually to be entirely separate and there was to be no use of vestments or elaborate ritual.

The Reformed Church was really crystallized into a religious denomination by John Calvin (1509–1564), who was born in Picardy. Educated for the priesthood, he held several clerical positions and became a successful preacher until he began to study law. His brilliant mind reacted against the conservative doctrine of his day and he began to preach Reformed opinions which soon brought him into conflict with Church and State authorities. In 1534 he took a stand for Reformed doctrines and many followers flocked to his side. Because of his defence of the Reformed party he found himself in difficulties with Francis I, who was trying to suppress Protestantism in France, and he left for Switzerland, where he was persuaded to locate at Geneva. Here he became the acknowledged leader of the Reformed Church until his death in 1564, with the result that his followers, known as Calvinists, spread the doctrine of church control by preachers and elders throughout Europe. He also opposed the Catholic doctrine of transubstantiation and the Lutheran consubstantiation. The use of crucifixes and other symbols and ceremonies was rejected, while the separation of Church and State as advocated by Zwingli was sustained.

Coterminous with the movements initiated by Luther and Zwingli was that known as Anabaptism. Harold S. Bender, in his article *The Anabaptist Vision*, gives a modern interpretation of it:

"Before defining the Anabaptist vision, it is essential to state clearly who is meant by the term 'Anabaptist,' since the name has come to be used in modern historiography to cover a wide variety of Reformation groups sometimes thought of as the whole 'left wing' of the Reformation (Roland Bainton), the 'Bolsheviks' of the Reformation (Preserved Smith). Although the definitive history of Anabaptism has not yet been written, we know enough today to draw a clear line of demarcation between original evangelical and constructive Anabaptism on the one hand, which was born in the bosom of Zwinglianism in Zurich, Switzerland, in 1525, and established in the Low Countries in 1533, and the various mystical, spiritualistic, revolutionary, or even antinomian related and unrelated groups on the other hand, which came and went like the flowers of the field in those days of the great renovation. The former, Anabaptism proper, maintained an unbroken course in Switzerland, South Germany, Austria, and Holland throughout the sixteenth century, and has continued until the present day in the Mennonite movement, now almost 500,000 baptised members in Europe and America. (In Switzerland this group was called 'Swiss Brethren,' in Austria 'Hutterites,' in Holland and North Germany, 'Menists.' All these groups seriously objected to the name 'Anabaptists,' which was a term used to designate a punishable heresy and which, after the tragic Münster episode (1534–1535), was a name of odious opprobrium. The term 'Mennonite' came into wider use in the seventeenth century and was ultimately applied to all the groups except the Hutterites.) There is no longer any use for permitting our understanding of the distinct character of this genuine Anabaptism to be obscured by Thomas Münster and the Peasants' War, the Münsterites, or any other aberration of Protestantism in the sixteenth century." [5]

Anabaptism, which means re-baptism or adult baptism, has several interpretations: a forerunner of socialism, an ascetic semi-monastic continuance of the medieval Franciscan orders, a later brotherhood of Waldenses, or a missing link which keeps the members in line with the Waldenses back to Pentecost. Sometimes these people are considered as mystics, but Dr. Bender claims that a more acceptable interpretation and one which is securing increasing support is that "Anabaptism is the culmination of the Reformation, the fulfilment of the original vision of Luther and Zwingli, and thus makes it a consistent evangelical Protestantism seeking to recreate without compromise the original New Testament church, the vision of Christ and the Apostles." [6]

The genuine Anabaptist emphasized three major points: first, a new conception that the essence of Christianity was discipleship; second, that the Church was a brotherhood; and third, a new ethic of love and nonresistance. These principles of belief were acted out in the lives of the believers to such an extent that they were bitterly persecuted both by the Swiss Protestants because of their unwillingness to serve in the Swiss mercenary armies, and by the Roman Catholics because of their opposition to the Church of Rome. Their principle of nonconformity invited persecution, something they seemed to expect and which increased rather than decreased their numbers and importance. Their emphasis on brotherhood denied the right of private property: one branch of them, the Hutterites, came to practise a form of Christian

6

communism. The other sects, although they believed in brotherhood, nevertheless did not extend it to private property.

Harold S. Bender speaks of nonresistance as follows: "In this principle of nonresistance, or Biblical pacifism, which was thoroughly believed and resolutely practised by all the original Anabaptist Brethren and their descendants throughout Europe from the beginning until the last century (Mennonites of Holland, Germany, France, and Switzerland gradually abandoned nonresistance in the course of the nineteenth century. The emigrant Mennonites in Russia and North America have maintained it. The Mennonites of the United States furnish forty per cent. of all the conscientious objectors in Civilian Public Service in World War I, and the Mennonites of Canada a still higher per cent. of the conscientious objectors in that country), the Anabaptists were again creative leaders, far ahead of their times, thus antedating the Quakers by over a century and a quarter. It should also be remembered that they held this principle in a day when both Catholic and Protestant Churches not only endorsed war as an instrument of state policy, but employed it in religious conflicts." [7]

Thus we see that two outstanding characteristics of the present-day Plain Folk have an historical explanation: their tendency to withdraw from the world and associate as little as possible with it, and their policy of nonresistance.

About the same time as the early beginnings of the Swiss Brethren in Switzerland (1525), a similar group, the Mennonites, came into being in Holland. The chief leader of this group, Menno Simons, was born in 1496 in Witmarsum, Friesland. Educated for the Roman Catholic priesthood, he became a priest in 1524 and lived the easy-going and carefree life of his class. Like many other religious leaders his change of heart came about in a vivid and personal manner. One day when celebrating mass, a doubt crept into his mind as to whether the bread and wine actually became divine. To settle his doubts he resolved to study the New Testament. Although he never became a Lutheran, two truths from Luther's writings impressed him: a violation of human commands cannot lead to eternal death; also, that the ultimate authority in all matters of faith was the word of God, and nothing else. Two special events influenced him: in 1531, a

7

Hollander was executed because he was re-baptised, and four years later, his own brother, having adopted a different faith, was killed. In 1536, realizing that what he had come to believe and what he practised as a priest were incompatible, he renounced his Roman Catholic faith and adopted the Anabaptist. He married and carried on preaching and organizing work in Holland until driven out by an Imperial Edict in 1542. From then on until his death in 1561 he led a life of persecution and struggle.

Because of Menno's leadership, his congregations became known as Mennonites. Accepting many of the tenets of the Waldenses, they strove for religious toleration and separation of Church and State. Two outstanding beliefs characterized them: withdrawal from the world, and opposition to war.

The persecutions of the Mennonites in Holland were even more severe than those suffered by the Swiss Brethren. As their numbers increased, persecutions became more intense and many fled to England from Amsterdam. Later, the Holland Mennonites enjoyed a much greater toleration than their Swiss Brethren, who continued to suffer bitterly as late as the eighteenth century.

Because of their rugged individualism, the Mennonites experienced several divisions among their members. Chief dissenter among these was Jacob Amman from the Canton of Bern or Alsace. Whereas some of the Anabaptists had become very extreme and radical, Amman turned in the opposite direction and became very conservative. He considered that the Swiss Mennonites had departed from the truth; there was laxness of discipline and especially a failure to apply *Meidung*—avoidance or ostracism—to excommunicated members. This was a doctrine advocated by the conservative Holland Mennonites (including Menno Simons) and accepted by the Swiss Church but, like several other practices, not followed. It meant that if a member had offended in any way the tenets of his religion, he would be brought before the church fathers, reprimanded, and assigned punishment. If he failed to submit, he was "avoided"—that is, no contact was had with him in any way until he conformed.

This movement was quite successful, attracting many followers in Switzerland and Alsace. Unfortunately, bitterness developed between the Amish (followers of Jacob Amman) and the more liberal-minded Mennonites in Switzerland.

8

Both sects were cruelly persecuted, and the Amish group, at the invitation of the Holland Mennonites, went to Holland to settle. Many of this group later emigrated to America.

The early Moravians dressed in a uniform manner, and there was much in common between them and the Anabaptists. With the Mennonites, dress took on a significance which has changed little up to modern times. A possible explanation for the garb of some of the Plain Folk may be found in their abhorrence of war and their refusal to take part in military exercises. There is an interesting though not authentic explanation that the most conservative during persecution times, to show their disdain for the soldiery, adopted a manner of dress and appearance which was the exact opposite to the soldiers. Whereas closely cropped hair, shaven chin, smart moustache, colorful coat with many buttons, and a small hat were distinctive of the soldier, they wore their hair long with a broad-brimmed hat, shaved the upper lip, grew a long beard, and wore clothes of sombre hue and hooks and eyes instead of buttons. The women wore bonnets as they were not considered pious if their heads were bare. By this manner of dress they challenged the authorities and seemed to invite persecution.

This persecution of the Mennonites and like sects by Protestants in Switzerland was based on economic and political grounds as well as religious. The Swiss government financed itself largely by hiring out its mercenary soldiers to other nations. Since these sects would not fight, no income was forthcoming from them in this way. Furthermore, these people were excellent farmers, hence their refusal to fight was often used to deprive them of their farms. Thus, greed as much as religion was responsible for much of the persecution they experienced.

The Huguenots * were called the Protestants of France.

* The origin of the name Huguenot is as follows: The outstanding leader of the Genevese in their revolt against the Savoyards and in their union with the Swiss was Besançon Hugues, whose ancestors (Hug) hailed from Zurich. Because of their close relationship with Swiss Confederates or Eidgenossen, the liberals of Geneva were "Eidgenots," but later a nickname emanated from a combination of the two words Hugues and Eidgenots—Huguenots. At first the appellation had only a political meaning, but after the Huguenots had accepted the Calvinistic faith and became leaders in this movement, the nickname acquired religious significance. With the spread of Calvinism, this name followed over the border into France, and from 1550 on the Protestants of France became known as Huguenots.

9

Protestantism, arising in France early in the sixteenth century, received a great impetus from Lutheran ideas and was immediately persecuted in spite of the comparative tolerance of Francis I, whose sister, Margaret of Navarre, was a leading protector of the Protestants. The Huguenots increased in proportion as persecution increased, until in 1559 there were enough to hold a national synod. This set up a church with Calvinistic doctrine and Presbyterian government, and its unity was one of the principal causes for the success of the Huguenots in fighting against overwhelming odds. Opposition continued until the Massacre of St. Bartholomew's Day in 1572 and was continued until 1598, when, by the Edict of Nantes, freedom of worship was permitted. This was revoked by Louis XIV in 1685, and the Huguenots were forced to accept Catholicism or exile. Many fled to England, the Netherlands, Germany, Switzerland, and America (especially the Carolinas, Pennsylvania, and New York).

Dunkard is a nickname which has come into general use for two sects whose official names are Church of the Brethren (Germany and United States) and Brethren in Christ (Canada). Two other names are often applied to these two groups that have reference to their form of baptism: Tunker and Dunker. The Church of the Brethren is the parent body which grew out of the Pietist movement in Germany. Eight persons, led by Alexander Mack in 1708 at Schwarzenau, in Hesse-Cassel, organized the first congregation. Others followed, but soon persecution drove them from Germany. They were distinguished by their opposition to oaths or affirmations, alcohol, tobacco, and warfare. They rejected infant baptism and observed the washing of feet and the Holy Kiss as religious ordinances. They believed in trine immersion, the candidate kneeling and bending over three times, once for each person of the Trinity. Their ministers were selected by congregational vote.

Two movements of far-reaching importance in the seventeenth century were Quietism and Pietism. Quietism, a complicated movement that swept through France, Italy, and Spain, originated in the Roman Catholic Church through a Spanish monk, Juan Falconi. Essentially a reaction against the bureaucratic ecclesiasticism, it was always latent within the Church of Rome. Because the Quietists wished to look beyond the Church and enter into immediate personal relations with their Maker, they fell back on a doctrine of immediate inspiration of the individual conscience. The first duty of a Quietist was to be "passive." The self-conscious will was to be killed while the individual was to be indifferent to his fate in this world or the next.

When Falconi died in 1632, a disciple, Molinos, took the doctrines to Rome, where they received general acceptance until the Jesuits objected. They took their case to Louis XIV, and Molinos was consequently imprisoned for life.

The Quietist drama was carried on in France by Fénelon until disputed by Bossuet in 1697. However, there was a large following, although Quietism required the extinction of the will, withdrawal from worldly interest, and passive meditation on God and divine things. Quietism developed in England as Quakerism.

The other movement, which should be considered because it ties in with the doctrines of the Waldenses and was a very potent religious force in the eighteenth and nineteenth centuries, is known as Pietism, and arose in the Lutheran Church at the same time and for the same reasons as Quietism did in the Roman Church. Since the Lutheran Church in its teachings had become very formalized, and its clergy despotic, and since even the Reformed Church which gave the people a share in church life had developed a dogmatic realism which threatened Christian freedom, Philip Jacob Spener (1635–1705) originated a movement which combined Lutheran emphasis on Biblical doctrine with the Reformed tendency to vigorous Christian life. Born in Alsace, Spener early came to believe that there was need for a moral and religious reformation of the German Church. Pietism, as a distinct movement in the German Church, began by religious meetings at his house—*collegia pietatis*—at which he repeated his sermons, expounded passages of the New Testament, and induced those present to join in conversation on religious questions which arose. This gave rise to the name "Pietists" about 1670. Spener published six proposals as the best means of restoring the life of the Church: (1) the earnest and thorough study of the Bible in private meetings; (2) the Christian priesthood being universal, the laity should share in the spiritual government of the Church; (3) a knowledge of Christianity must be attended by the practice of it as indispensable and supplemental; (4) instead of merely didactic, and often bitter attacks on the heterodox and unbelievers, a sympathetic and kindly treatment of them; (5) a reorganization of the theological training of the universities, giving more prominence to the devotional life; and (6) a different style of preaching, namely, in the place of pleasing rhetoric, the implanting of Christianity in the inner or new man, the soul of which is faith, and its effects—the fruits of life.

These doctrines made a great impression in Germany, but our interest in them comes from their influence on the revival of the Moravian Church in 1727 by Count von Zinzendorf, Spener's godson and pupil.

As already mentioned, the Moravian Church or *Unitas Fratrum*, founded in the early part of the sixteenth century, was the precursor of the Luther Reformation. Its growth was rapid until 1630, when wars rapidly depleted its numbers. It was almost extinct until, in 1722, a group that had been kept alive among the Waldenses settled on Count von Zinzendorf's estate. The Count being an ardent Lutheran Pietist, the Moravian Church soon (1727) came again into being. Before long, persecution having broken out, the Count sent a band of emigrants to Georgia. Although Zinzendorf's conception did not aim at Church extension, settlements on the estates of friendly noblemen, brethren and sisters' houses were erected, and a quiet type of spiritual life was cultivated.

Our brief study of the sects in Europe shows that religion left to itself tends to become artificial and a matter of observing rules and regulations set down by Church authority. The greater the authority required and administered by the Church, the less freedom the individual comes to possess with a lessening of the interest he takes in religion. Furthermore, any direct relationship which the Church has with the State seems to foster dogmatic power on the part of the Church.

As one studies the history and development of these sects, he sees a recurring cycle of a church denomination arrogating to itself certain prerogatives, following which there is a splitting off of certain groups which proclaim the rights of the individual. At one time these groups took an extreme stand and in most instances were bitterly persecuted. As always happens, persecution, instead of destroying these groups or sects, kept them alive, together with the principles for which they stood.

Time and time again the new sect, emphasizing the simplicity of religion, went back to the Bible for its inspiration. There was an emphasis on the direct relationship between the individual and his Maker; also, there was always a recognition of each individual's responsibility for others—each was his brother's keeper. War or conflict of any kind was considered entirely unchristian. Let us see if these principles explain the "queerness" of the Plain Folk.

In the first place, the Plain Folk by their very cognomen suggest simplicity of dress and manner. Their sobriety may be explained by their belief that such is demanded of them by Bible teaching and also as a reaction against the worldliness of their times. Their literal interpretation of the Bible is responsible for their refusal to take oaths ("Swear not at all") and for such religious rites as foot-washing and saluting each other by a brotherly kiss. Because Christ taught the doctrine of "turning the other cheek," they were pacifists and abhorred anything which had to do with fighting. The statement, "Come out from among them and be ye separate," they interpreted as requiring each person not to mingle with the "world"—that is, with unbelievers. This was an injunction which prevented them from holding public office or gaining publicity of any kind. Because of being one another's keeper, they felt themselves both religiously and financially responsible for everyone belonging to their community. This explains why insurance of various kinds has not been popular with them. Situations requiring monetary help were taken care of within the group. The injunction "Be diligent" has always been taken seriously by them, small children even being taught the necessity of being industrious. Hard manual work is never avoided, with the result that seldom does one find a member of the Plain Folk unsuccessful financially. To this end, the care of soil, animals, and property generally has been considered not only a right but a duty; hence, these people have always been excellent farmers.

All the foregoing characteristics—and there are many more —have been an outgrowth of their beliefs as based upon a literal interpretation of the Bible. The persecutions these people have endured in order that they might practise these beliefs have fixed them indelibly on their natures, particularly noted in their dogged persistence under all conditions. Hence anyone attempting to understand why throughout the centuries they have appeared different from others—and, in fact, still are—must find the reason in their religious beliefs. One more feature may be noted: the tendency to split up into small groups. The Mennonites are now divided into five main groups of over 5,000 members each, and about seven smaller groups of less than 5,000 members each. This has usually come about through the attempt to interpret the Bible literally. Since many of the statements found therein lent themselves to various interpretations, just so were there many variations in belief. Although there was this strong tendency towards a literal interpretation, the emotional side of man's nature was often given free rein, a freedom which explains the excesses of some of the groups. Composed of persons easily swayed by "every wind of doctrine," these groups, however, were never very long-lived.

Niebuhr sums up his article on Sectarianism in this manner: Sects are "recurrent phenomena which have led to a number of important consequences. They have called back the Church from its accommodation to existing social customs and conditions and have been more important in the indirect influence which they have exercised in this way than in the effectiveness of their own organizations. They have provided, in the second place, for the rejection of religious sanctions of social customs which had become onerous and thus have helped to pave the way for radical reforms. Finally, the sects have emphasized individual conviction in religion and ethics and have offered a counterbalance to the system of collective dogma and authority." [8]

With this background of understanding let us see how these Plain Folk reacted in new surroundings—in a country where persecutions no longer existed. Often races as well as individuals, when outside coercion no longer exists, tend to lose the very characteristics which held them together as an ethnic group. Great in adversity, they disintegrated when freedom and prosperity became their lot. But in emigrating, they faced an additional test—a new country and different races with which to associate. The history of the settlements in Pennsylvania and later in Canada will show how they reacted to the test.

II

MIGRATION TO AND SETTLEMENT
IN AMERICA

QUAKERS

SINCE Quakerism was an important factor in our ethnic group, let us begin with its development in England. Dorland has written that it was greatly influenced by Quietism.[1]

George Fox, the son of a weaver in Leicestershire, was the founder of the Society of Friends who in law and general usage are commonly called Quakers. Beginning his ministry in 1647, he, like most religious reformers, did not set out to form a separate religious body. In 1652, through his emphasis on the importance of repentance and personal striving after truth, he attracted a sufficient following to set up an organization. The movement spread rapidly, its great contribution being the insistence on an inward experience.

Actually the word Quaker is a nickname, the one usually preferred being the Society of Friends. The nickname was acquired, so the story goes, when on one occasion the king summoned some of their leaders to explain why they did not doff their hats in his majesty's presence. (It was part of their belief not to remove their hats in the presence of persons of high authority.) As the spokesman for the Society of Friends stood shaking nervously before the king, he laughed in scorn at them and remarked, "See them quaking there."

Another explanation which sounds more plausible is as follows: "Until the year 1650, the followers of George Fox were called professors of the Light and children of the Light; but in that year they received the name they commonly bear. Fox at that time was imprisoned by the party (Independents) then in power, and Gervas Bennet, one of the justices who committed him, hearing that Fox had made the remark, 'quaking and trembling were necessary dispositions to hear the word of God with profit,' with some degree of profaneness took occasion from the saying to style him and his disciples

15

Quakers. The name took with the people, and was universally adopted." [2]

The Quaker doctrine was preached throughout Europe and soon spread to America. Until the Toleration Act of 1689 the Quakers were continuously persecuted in England, their leader Fox several times being imprisoned. Their refusal to take oaths such as the Oaths of Supremacy and Allegiance was used as an excuse to flog and imprison many of them.

The distinctive views of this sect included their refusal to take oaths, their testimony against war, their rejection of a professional ministry, and their recognition of women's ministry. In their public worship they met in silence, desiring that the service of the meeting should depend on spiritual guidance. Thus it was left to any man or woman to offer vocal prayer, to read the Scriptures, or to utter such exhortation or teaching as seemed to be called for.

Our interest in Quakerism centers around William Penn. Born in England in 1644 of a wealthy and influential family (his father being an admiral in the British Navy), he was educated at Oxford, where he came into contact with Quaker teachings. Because he rebelled against authority he was expelled from Oxford, after which he was sent to Paris. While at the Huguenot University at Saumur, he attended lectures teaching that war and Christianity were opposed to each other. For a short time he was a soldier, but in 1667 he became a Quaker, and was arrested and imprisoned several times for preaching Quaker doctrines.

In 1675 his thoughts were first seriously turned to America. Lord Berkeley and Sir George Carteret, who had received from the Duke of York the promise of New Jersey, sold the western half to two Quakers, John Fenwick and Edward Byllinge. When they had some difficulty between themselves in the settlement of their relative claims, they asked William Penn to arbitrate the matter. Byllinge afterward becoming financially embarrassed, he transferred to Penn and two others his interest for the benefit of the creditors. Thus when West New Jersey was opened for sale, it became an asylum for persecuted Quakers. Penn wrote to Richard Hartshorne, a settler whom he appointed as his agent, saying that they were laying a foundation for later generations to understand their liberty as men and Christians; that they might not be brought in bondage but by their own consent, for the power was invested in the people.

The colony prospered greatly under the management of Penn and his friends. In 1677, in company with George Fox, Robert Barclay, and others, he paid a religious visit to Holland and Germany and began that acquaintanceship with the Rhine Valley which resulted a few years later in a great migration to Pennsylvania.

In 1681 Charles II signed a deed in order to liquidate the £16,000 he owed Penn's father and made William Penn Governor and proprietor of "Pennsylvania," a vast tract almost as large as the whole of England, intended to be three degrees in latitude and five in longitude. It was described as bounded on the east by the Delaware River, on the west by Maryland, and was to extend as far northward "as plantable." He could sell the land on his own terms and to whom he would. He could establish government; make the laws (subject to the assent of the freemen); appoint magistrates and judges; levy taxes; control the military forces and grant pardons and reprieves, though in all these powers the Crown reserved a veto.

In 1682 Penn himself went to the colony, where he set up a liberal government, the best example of a proprietary government in America. He laid out the city of Philadelphia in the same year. He made friends with the Indians and signed a treaty with them in 1683. From his friend the Duke of York he acquired the "Three Lower Counties" (Delaware), which remained part of Pennsylvania until 1776. Although he owned a large tract of land, it was of little value to him unless he could sell it; hence he looked around for prospective settlers.

He knew from experience in New Jersey and Delaware that the English, Irish, and Scottish settlers had little skill in farming. He had, however, visited the Netherlands and the rich agricultural areas of South Germany and Switzerland, and was convinced that settlers from these areas would do well in America. He was also sympathetic to them because he knew that they had undergone religious persecution as had he and his Quaker brethren in England.

He therefore "published and distributed glowing advertisements in the form of pamphlets and posters in the English, Dutch, and German languages, describing the great promise that his new venture held. He described the abundance of fish, game, and wild fruits; he praised the fertility of the soil, declaring that crops yielded far more abundantly in Pennsylvania than elsewhere. He promised religious freedom to the persecuted and a new start in life for the despairing." [3]

The response to this invitation was not long in forthcoming. According to Dr. C. Henry Smith, the first German colony in America was founded at Germantown in 1683.[4] The first settlers came from Crefeld and the surrounding regions along the lower Rhine near the Dutch border, and consisted of one Mennonite and twelve Mennonite-Quaker families, all with Dutch names. Quakers, including both Fox and Penn, had visited northwest Germany and the Netherlands and, since there was much similarity of belief between the Mennonites and Quakers, the latter received a kind reception from the former, from time to time making converts to the Quaker faith. Thus it was only to be expected that when Penn made his appeal for emigrants he should seek out this group. The first transactions, according to Smith, are as follows: "In 1682, Jacob Telner, a Mennonite merchant in Amsterdam, who had visited New York several times, and who was acquainted with the London Quakers, together with five other Mennonites and Quakers from Crefeld and surrounding towns, purchased eighteen thousand acres of land in Pennsylvania for the purpose of founding a colony. About the same time, too, a group of Pietists from Frankfurt-on-the-Main, under the leadership of Francis Daniel Pastorius, established the Frankfurt Land Company which purchased forty thousand acres north and west of Philadelphia. It was from these two groups that the actual settlers purchased most of the land." [5]

Pastorius, having gone ahead of the immigrants, took them when they arrived to what was later known as Germantown. Thus Pastorius was the agent of the Frankfurt Land Company and not their leader, although he served the colony well and acted as their historian.

The first settlers were artisans and not farmers. William Rittenhouse, who arrived in 1688, built the first paper mill in America (in Germantown) and was also the first minister of the Mennonites. In Germantown were organized not only the first Mennonite, and the first and perhaps only German Quaker congregation in America, but also the first Dunkard, the first German Reformed, German Lutheran, and German Moravian.

"Soon after 1702 the available land about Germantown had largely been taken up, which necessitated the establishing of a second Mennonite colony along Skippack Creek, a tributary of the Perkiomen, about thirty miles above Germantown. This new settlement (called Skippack), begun by a Germantown colonist and several of his fellow immigrants a little later, became the center of a flourishing colony of Palatine Mennonites." [6]

"Germans and Swiss had a long and tedious way to go before embarkation, and many were the tribulations which they endured before facing the dangers of the sea. A journey down the Rhine from Heilbronn to Holland took from four to six weeks, and in the middle of the eighteenth century involved a stop at each of the thirty-six customs houses, where a toll had to be paid. The expense of this part of the trip averaged about £3, but it varied so greatly by reason of unforeseen delays or the dishonesty of agents that many emigrants found themselves on the borders of Holland without money enough left either to continue their journey or to return home." [7]

The one way out of this desperate situation was to indenture themselves to the captain of the vessel which would take them to America. The emigrant agreed to work for a stated length of time for his passage. This was a form of selling one-self into slavery for, when arrival was made, each person was auctioned off for a certain length of time to someone who would pay his passage. Overcrowding on shipboard, disease, lack of food and air, and the length of the voyage made the passage a hideous experience. Many did not survive. "In 1738," according to Abbot Emerson Smith, "it was written that out of the fifteen ships arriving that year at Philadelphia only two had come with those on board relatively well and 1600 had died. Sauer estimated that 2000 Germans died at sea in 1749, which was the heaviest year of immigration; on one ship in 1752 only 19 out of 200 survived, on another in 1745 fifty out of 400." [8]

The immigrant tide from Germany to America started for two reasons: economic and religious pressures at home, and a published invitation from Queen Anne of England for them to settle in the American colonies. Books and papers from England had been distributed in the Palatinate with Queen

Anne's picture on them. The title page of the book was in letters of gold, which gave it the name of "The Golden Book." These books and papers served their purpose in encouraging the Palatinates to travel to England. Some ten thousand of them (other estimates give as many as thirty thousand) accepted the invitation in 1708 and 1709 until it became necessary for the English to send legates to Holland and the Rhine to turn them back.

What to do with this large number of migrants was the great problem facing the Queen and her ministry. Army tents were supplied for some, and vacant warehouses were opened to shelter others. Queen Anne allowed them ninepence a day, and collections were taken up in the churches for their benefit.

Fortunately, a delegation from America came to England at this time, headed by Peter Schuyler, the mayor of Albany, and Colonel Nicholson, who had induced five Mohawk chiefs to accompany him. Coming across these homeless Germans, one of these chiefs, on his own account, presented to the Queen a tract of his land in Schoharie, N.Y., for their use.*

The next problem was to find ships to take them to New York. Several hundred stayed in England, while many Roman Catholics were persuaded to return to Germany. Some three thousand linen weavers were taken to Ireland, where a settlement was established near Limerick which is still flourishing. (This explains why some people in Ontario claim their ancestors to be Pennsylvania German even though they came from Ireland.) About six hundred were sent to the Carolinas, where a Swiss colony had been established in New Bern.

In 1710, ten ships set sail for New York. Of these, nine reached America, after some four hundred persons had been lost, together with much goods.[9] For a few months these emigrants were quartered on an island in the New York harbor until the governor could find land on which to locate them. No attempt was made to give them land offered by the Mohawk chief in England. The *Documentary History of the State of New York* quotes the governor as saying: "I have now settled the Palatines upon good land on both sides of the Hudson, about one hundred miles up, adjacent to the pines.

* Richard P. Bond, in his *Queen Anne's American Kings* (p. 11), claims that this statement is a legend, as the Palatinates had left for America three months before the arrival of the Indian chiefs.

I have planted them in five villages, three on the east side of the river upon 6000 acres I have purchased from Mr. Livingston about two miles from Rowlaf Jansens Hill. The other two on the west side near Sawyers' Creek." [10]

This arrangement did not work out satisfactorily. Conrad Weiser, an outstanding pioneer Lutheran who belonged to this group, wrote in his autobiography: "On June 13, 1710, we came to anchor at New York in North America, and in the same autumn were taken to Livingston's Manor at the expense of the Queen. Here in Livingston's, or as it was called by the Germans, Loewenstein's Manor, we were to burn tar, and cultivate hemp, to repay the expenses incurred by the Queen in bringing us from Germany to England and from England to New York. We were directed by several commissioners, viz.: John Cast, Henry Meyer, Richard Seykott, who were put in authority over us by Robert Hunter, the governor of New York. But neither object succeeded, and in 1713 the people were discharged from their engagements and declared free. Then the people scattered themselves over the whole province of New York. Many remained where they were. About 150 families determined to remove to Schoharie (a place about 40 English miles to the west of Albany). They therefore sent deputies to the land of Maquas to consult with the Indians about it, who allowed them to occupy Schoharie. For the Indian deputies who were in England at the time the German people were lying in tents on the Blackmoor had made a present to Queen Anne of the Schoharie, that she might settle these people upon it. Indian guides were sent to show the Germans where Schoharie was.

"In the spring of 1714 about 150 families removed from Schenectady to Schoharie in great poverty. The people settled in villages of which there were seven. The first and nearest to Schenectady was called Kneskerndorf; second, Gerlacho-dorf; third, Fuchsen-dorf; fourth, Hans George Schmidts-dorf; fifth, Weisers-dorf; sixth, Hartmans-dorf; seventh, Ober Weisers-dorf. So named after the deputies who were sent from Livingston's Manor to the Maqua country.

"Here now this people lived peaceably for several years. But they had taken possession without informing the Governor of New York, who, after letting them know his dissatisfaction, sold the land to seven rich merchants, four of whom lived in Albany; the other three in New York. Upon this a great uproar arose in Schoharie and Albany, because many people in Albany wished the poor people to retain their lands. The people in Schoharie divided into two parties; the strongest did not wish to obey, but to keep the land, and therefore sent deputies to England to obtain a grant from George the First, not only for Schoharie, but for more land in addition. But the plans did not succeed according to their wishes. In the end they got an order to the newly-arrived governor of New York, William Burnett, to grant vacant land to the Germans who had been sent to New York by the deceased Queen Anne. Governor Burnett gave patents for the land to the few who were willing to settle in the Maqua country, namely Stony Arabia, and above the falls, but none on the river as the people hoped. They, therefore, scattered. The larger part removed to the Maqua country or remained in Schoharie and bought the land from the before mentioned rich men." [11]

Leaving New York State in 1729, Conrad Weiser settled in Pennsylvania, where he was made official interpreter and mediator between the Indian tribes and the government. He is regarded as a very important factor in gaining the allegiance of the Iroquois for the British instead of for the French in the final French and Indian War, 1756–1763.

Because of their later connection with Canada, we are interested in the group that remained about Schoharie and the Mohawk. They lived at peace with each other and with their neighbors but for a few Reformed Hollanders of considerable affluence who regarded these poor Lutheran Palatinates and Swabians with contempt. This mild persecution was trivial, however, when compared to the events of 1757. In that year, the French with a group of Indians raided the north side of the Mohawk River, and the settlers were able to save their lives only by crossing the river. The following year the south side was devastated in a similar manner.

"Following the war with the French the Palatines took a neutral position under the leadership of Sir John Johnson. Philip Schuyler with a large force of men went to the Mohawk district in December, 1775, and demanded of Sir John Johnson that he and his followers give assurance of neutrality. This was readily given, but on the pretext that all arms had not been surrendered, Schuyler plundered the district. This action stirred up the wrath of the Palatines and

22

Sir John Johnson, with two hundred followers, started for Montreal. After many hardships the party arrived at their destination. Scouts were sent to the Mohawk to direct others to the British posts. Sir John Johnson was authorized to raise two battalions from among his followers, one of which was known as 'The King's Royal Regiment of New York' or 'The Royal Yorkers.' There were also a number of Palatines in Butler's Rangers. These battalions fought nobly and loyally on the British side until the end of the conflict. These German Lutheran Palatines are thus worthy of the title 'United Empire Loyalists.'" [12]

Quakers were found in America before any other of the Plain Sects. As early as 1663, a large number of them came with other settlers to New Jersey and Pennsylvania. Because of certain similarities with Mennonites, Dunkards, Moravians, and Amish, the Quakers lived in harmony with them, although in most instances the Quakers were English in nationality while the other Plain Sects were German, Swiss, French, or Dutch.

Although there was agreement in many points of belief between the Quakers and their neighbors, there were differences which were to have a later significance. The English Quakers owned slaves, and to this practice the Plain Sects, particularly the Mennonites, objected. As early as 1688—five years after their arrival—the latter memorialized the Quakers in the following words:

"Those who hold slaves are no better than Turks, for we have heard that ye most part of such Negers are brought hither against their will and consent, and that many of them are stolen." [13] Evidently this was bad publicity for further immigration from Germany. "For," the protest continues, "this makes an ill report in all those countries in Europe where they hear off, that ye Quackers do here handel men like they handel there ye cattle and for that reason have no mind or inclination to come hither." [14] Interestingly enough, these Plain Sects anticipated the events which were to take place a century and a half later and cause bitterness for still another century. Nothing very much, however, was done by the English Quakers regarding the abolition of slavery in America.

The second major difference was the refusal of the Mennonites and Dunkards to hold civil office. A unique situation developed in Germantown when, after being incorporated by special charter as a village in 1691, and the necessity arising to legislate for the welfare of the community, it was found that there were no men who would take office. This situation in 1707 cost the village the loss of its charter.

LUTHERANS

Immigrants, mostly Lutherans, after 1700 were routed to New York State, but they soon found that the land there had been pre-empted by Dutch settlers. Hearing about free land in Pennsylvania, they migrated into that state and founded Berks and Lebanon counties, following the earlier settlements in Montgomery and Lancaster counties by the Mennonites.

By 1727 so many immigrants had come directly to Pennsylvania that the English Provincial authorities became alarmed and a law was passed requiring all immigrants to take an oath of allegiance to the British Crown and to sign the ship's register. A head tax was levied on every immigrant and every ship's captain had to submit a complete list of all new arrivals after that date. This did not discourage immigration for, after 1740, there was a great influx which continued until 1776.

DUNKARDS

In 1719 fifty-nine families belonging to the Church of the Brethren (Dunkards) under Peter Becker left Greyfelt (Crefeld) for Germantown, Pennsylvania, where they established their first Dunkard church. In 1724 Christopher Sauer arrived. Securing a printer's outfit from Germany in 1743, he published in one large volume the first German Bible in America in the same year. He had also printed an ABC and Spelling Book and the first German Almanac in 1739. In the same year, too, he published the first German newspaper in America—a sheet of four pages, each page made up of two columns and measuring 13 by 9 inches.

In 1729 a large group of Dunkards arrived accompanied by their founder, Alexander Mack. Unfortunately, the usual differences sprang up among the Old Order, the Conservatives, and the Progressives who believed in higher education.

SEVENTH DAY BAPTISTS

An interesting offshoot of the Dunkards which became a separate church in 1728 was known as the Seventh Day Baptists—the only Protestant monastic society ever to exist in the United States. Conrad Beissel was its founder. One of their chief tenets was that the seventh day of the week, not the first, was the Sabbath. In 1733 a monastic society was established at Ephrata in Lancaster County. Separate buildings for the brethren and sisters were built of wood, clay, and straw. The food consisted mostly of vegetables and other plain dishes, but meat was avoided. They slept on bare boards with a square block of wood for a pillow. The narrow doors of the cloisters were meant to remind them of the straight and narrow way to heaven. Celibacy, though considered a virtue, was not insisted on. They were skilled craftsmen, making their own paper, printing their own literature, and making articles by hand. At one time three hundred persons lived in the cloisters and district. Because of their celibate life, their numbers have been diminishing until the order is now almost extinct. The property still remaining—the Sisters' House and Chapel—is now an historical site.

BRETHREN IN CHRIST

Another sect, Brethren in Christ (incorporated by that name in 1904 in Ontario, and frequently referred to as Dunkers, Tunkers, or Dunkards), had its origin on the Susquehanna River, Pennsylvania, around 1770. For this reason they have been known as River Brethren. Jacob Engle was looked upon as the leader of six brethren, of whom John (Hansley) Winger was one. Because the Church of the Brethren refused to baptise them, they formed their own group and began active missionary work. In 1788 John Winger emigrated to Canada and founded the sect there, and a year later Jacob Engle visited that country himself.[15]

Their beliefs have points of similarity both with the Mennonites and Church of the Brethren. They practice footwashing and baptism by trine immersion, are strict sabbatarians and simple in their manner of life, hold to nonresistance, and are keenly interested in higher education.

HUGUENOTS *

When in 1685 Louis XIV revoked the Edict of Nantes, thereby forcing the alternatives of Catholicism or exile on

*See page 195 ff.

the Huguenots, many of them fled to England, the Netherlands, Germany, Switzerland, and America, and especially to the Carolinas, Pennsylvania, and New York. The fact that a considerable number of them were befriended by England was an important factor during and following the Revolutionary War in America, when they had to choose between staying in the Colonies or remaining loyal to the English Crown and emigrating to Upper Canada.

Two communities in New York State were founded by Huguenots—New Rochelle and New Paltz. The following is an extract from the diary of a man who accompanied one of the founders of New Paltz—Louis Bevier.

"Abraham Hasbrouck was a native of the town of Calais, and, finding the troubles and oppressions and persecutions coming on the Protestants in France (it being before the Revocation of the Edict of Nantes), his father moved out . . . into Germany, in the Palatinate; and there lived several years until in 1675 he undertook to come to America. And he with his family and friends went to Rotterdam and from thence to Amsterdam, and they embarked for England in April 1675— and from England they sailed to America, and arrived in the town of Boston, and from Boston they sailed to New York and arrived in Ulster County July 1675 where he found his brother who had been here two years and several acquaintances. Later he married a native of the Palatinate in Germany." [16]

This parallels the records of the marital ancestors of Laura Secord, the heroine of the battle of Beaver Dam. "Family documents show that in the reign of Louis XIV of France, a certain Marquis d'Secor was marshal of his majesty's household. A son of this marquis embraced the Protestant faith, as did younger branches of the family. During the persecution of the Huguenots that preceded the massacre of St. Bartholomew, several of them suffered at the stake and the family estates situated at La Rochelle were confiscated. The survivors escaped the massacre by flight to England, together with some other noble families. . . . Eventually five Secord brothers emigrated to America where they settled in New Jersey, purchasing large tracts of land and founding New Rochelle (Westchester County, N.Y.) in honor of their ancient home and engaging in lumbering." [17]

AMISH

Beginning in 1734 or 1740, at the time of the Palatinate and Swiss immigration several hundred Amish came to America and settled chiefly in Lancaster County. These were the most conservative of the Mennonites, but through the years they have shown the most outstanding results in their farming operations. Instead of going farther afield for their prosperity when they wished to acquire more, they took over the impoverished land of persons not so skilled as themselves. Before long the land's fertility was restored. Their family groups were very closely knit, which possibly explains why few of them ever emigrated to Canada.

MORAVIANS

The Moravians became a very important sect in America, particularly in the field of education, the first evangelist migrating to Pennsylvania in 1734. At that time they were a Plain Sect with such doctrines as the use of the lot, plain attire, and nonresistance except when attacked. Actually, the first settlement was in Georgia, but it was not successful and the colonists from there were moved to Northampton County in 1740. The Moravians were simply and broadly evangelical, living in harmony with other Protestant denominations on the cardinal doctrines of Christianity. Imbued with a fervent missionary spirit, they carried their efforts to the Indians as well as to the white settlers. (Reference to the Indians is important in this case because of their missionary efforts in Fairfield, Ontario.)

In 1741 they took over a school which the evangelist, George Whitefield, had purchased at the "Forks of the Delaware" and called Nazareth. The same year Count Zinzendorf organized a settlement at Bethlehem which, following the influx of a considerable number of colonists in 1742, became the center of the Moravian Church in America. Both at Nazareth and at Bethlehem a coöperative union was carried on until 1762. Though all labored for a common cause, there was no surrender of private property and no obligation which prevented the individual from withdrawing when he chose. The settlement increased by immigration, and the material benefits of it were appreciated by the authorities of Pennsylvania, while the spiritual activities prosecuted by the Moravians, although misunderstood and opposed by some, as was the case in Europe, were epoch-making in the religious growth of the country.

One real contribution that the Moravians made to the English cause was in the person of Christian Frederick Post, a missionary to the Indians. Unarmed and alone, he entered the villages of hostile Indians in the neighborhood of the Ohio River, carrying messages of good-will from the English authorities. So successful in winning their confidence was he, that the Indians deserted their French allies and the enemy garrison of Fort Duquesne was undermined and depleted of support to such an extent that in 1758 the French abandoned their stronghold without a battle. In this way the entire Ohio River valley was opened for British occupation.

SCHWENKFELDERS

Mention should be made of the Schwenkfelders, followers of Casper Schwenkfeld who emigrated in 1733 from Silesia to Montgomery County, Pennsylvania, after bitter persecution by Charles VI. Only a few members of this sect migrated later to Waterloo County in Canada.

HUTTERITE BRETHREN

The Hutterite Brethren were a body of Christians practising strict communism based on religious principles. In the sixteenth century, in Moravia, this group suffered persecution after their leader, Jacob Hutter, was burned at the stake. In the seventeenth century there were twenty-four communal households called Bruderhofs of the Hutterite Brethren in Moravia. Driven from Austria, they settled in Rumania, then in Russia. In 1874, in company with Russian Mennonites, they emigrated to the United States, making their center in South Dakota and expanding from there. Their doctrines and principles, aside from communism, are in accord with those of Mennonites in general.*

SETTLEMENT OF THE VARIOUS COLONIES

The Carolinas were first explored by Sir Walter Raleigh in 1584, but a settlement made in 1587 had entirely disappeared by 1591, perhaps because of the unfamiliarity with the

* Since their ideas of nonresistance are extreme, many of the Brethren moved to Canada during World War II as conscription there was less rigorously enforced. There are about ninety communities in the United States and Canada—approximately 10,000 persons.

28

physical conditions of the country. Because of successful settlements in Virginia, Charles I gave proprietary rights to Sir Robert Heath. The land south of the 26th parallel was named Carolina after the king. In 1663 Charles II gave extensive tracts of land to eight favorites and divided the state into North and South Carolina. Because of opposition on the part of the settlers to the taxation and mismanagement of the state, it became a royal colony in 1729. In the colonial period immigration was rapid. Many settlers came in from Virginia; there were settlements of Scotch-Irish, chiefly from Pennsylvania in the New Hanover district in 1756; large numbers of Scottish Highlanders came into the southeastern part of the state; Germans from the Palatinate settled in Craven County; and in 1766 a group of Moravians under Bishop Fries established Salem, which was later united with Winston.

Virginia, named for the Virgin Queen, Elizabeth, was the first permanent British settlement in North America. The London Company established itself at Jamestown in 1607. Several years of great privation followed, largely because the settlers were not accustomed to New World conditions. In 1619 the first representative assembly in the English colonies met there, and there the first negro slaves in the English colonies were sold.

The Dutch were the first white settlers of New York State, establishing in 1614, Fort Nassau, and later, Fort Orange, both near the present Albany, and New Amsterdam (New York City) on Manhattan Island. They introduced the patroon system, virtually feudal in form, to encourage agricultural development. New England colonists settled in Westchester County and Long Island, while the French established themselves in the central and northern parts of the state. Early in the eighteenth century, German colonists settled near Newburgh, many leaving later for Pennsylvania because they found it difficult to obtain deeds to their property.

Those who settled in New York State belonged mostly to the Lutheran, Reformed, or Huguenot faiths and were non-pacifists. Their sympathies were definitely towards England; thus when it became necessary at the time of the Revolutionary War to declare their allegiance, many of them unhesitatingly chose England, and of course suffered the consequences of being arrested if they stayed in the state, or of having their property confiscated should they leave. These people were always potential United Empire Loyalists, and when they did leave for Canada, did so not for religious reasons, but for reasons of loyalty to the English Crown.

Maryland was set up as a proprietary state in 1632 with Lord Baltimore as the feudal head. One purpose of the colony was to provide a refuge for persecuted Roman Catholics from England. Originally the state included what is today Maryland, Delaware, and part of Pennsylvania—a situation which caused endless friction until the southern boundary line of Pennsylvania was established by Mason and Dixon during the years 1763–1767. Lord Baltimore, in order to guarantee religious freedom, initiated the famous Act of Tolerance (1649), the first complete charter of religious freedom in the colonies. After William Penn acquired the land in 1682, there were struggles among the Puritans, the Catholics, and the Quakers following the changes in power in England. Baltimore, established in 1729, by degrees passed into the hands of the people of the state.

New Jersey, taken over by the Dutch from the Swedes in 1655, was seized by the English in 1664 as part of a grant to the Duke of York. Later it fell into the possession of William Penn, became a royal colony in 1702, and was administered by a governor sent from England until 1776.

A considerable number of Quakers settled in New Jersey, encouraged doubtless by fellow-members like Fenwick, Byllinge, and William Penn, who sought to own and govern it. In 1677 some 230 Quakers arrived from London and Yorkshire. Probably descendants of this group came to Upper Canada a century later.

SETTLEMENT OF PENNSYLVANIA

For the purpose of this study we may consider Pennsylvania largely as the parent state for the transplants in Upper Canada, hence it is desirable to understand the part the Plain Folk played in this state as a background for their emigration from it.

The first white man to come to Pennsylvania was Henry Hudson in 1609. Other explorers from the Dutch East India Company later established trading posts, followed by the Swedish West India Company, which between 1638 and 1655 founded some permanent settlements. The Dutch returned to exercise control in 1664, until ten years later when the English first took possession.

Though in Europe there was much intolerance in regard to religious worship, in England the State Church persecuted those whom it considered as dissenters. Thus when William Penn, after acquiring his property in Pennsylvania in 1682, invited Quakers and other Plain Folk in Europe as settlers, his offer was readily accepted.

Our interest does not lie in Penn's problems in controlling his lands in Pennsylvania, but we are concerned with those emigrants who accepted his invitation. As has been stated before, the Dutch and German Mennonites settled in Germantown, where William Rittenhouse built the first paper mill and where the first varieties of garden products were grown, a factor which played a part in the later development of Philadelphia.

Quakers continued to pour into the state, most of them establishing themselves in trade in the growing towns or settling upon farms in the three original counties of Bucks, Chester, and Philadelphia. Welsh Quakers brought their families, first settling on the west side of the Schuylkill in Montgomery County, later in Berks and the northern counties.

In 1722 Sir William Keith, Deputy Governor of Pennsylvania, while attending a conference of colonial governors at Albany, New York, learned of the sorry plight of the thousands of German settlers from the Palatinate who were being forced off their farms in the rich Schoharie Valley, near Schenectady, New York, because rich Dutch farmers wished these lands for themselves. Knowing what good settlers these people were, he invited them to come to Pennsylvania. In 1723 the first families took advantage of this invitation, to be followed in the next twenty-five years by thousands of their friends living along the Rhine. The ships' lists from 1727 to 1776 contain more than 68,000 names of persons coming to Pennsylvania who took the oath of allegiance to the English Crown.

French Huguenots in the seventeenth century, because of persecution, fled to all countries of Europe. They often changed their names and migrated as belonging to the country in which they had sought refuge. Many came to Pennsylvania.

31

Schwenkfelders (followers of Casper Schwenkfeld), after bitter persecution by Charles VI, started a mass migration from Silesia to Pennsylvania in 1735, settling in Montgomery County. This group, strongly in favor of education, had a real interest in the fine arts. They resembled the Plain Folk in their beliefs except that they were willing to fight in self-defence. Only a few emigrated to Canada.

Moravians migrated in congregations, settling in Bethlehem, Nazareth, Emmaus, and Lititz. They were noted for their missionary work among the Indians, their love and development of music, and for founding in 1742 the first seminary for girls in the New World—the Moravian Female Seminary.

Most important for our study were the Mennonites from Switzerland and the Dunkards from Germany. Since these sects have been described elsewhere, mention that they came in large numbers throughout the entire eighteenth century is all that will be made here.

From the foregoing brief description of the mixture of races in these colonies, we can see many possibilities for friction. Some of the Quakers, Huguenots, Mennonites, Lutherans, and Reformed were sympathetic towards England because they had been granted asylum there and later in America. Others, such as the Puritans and Scotch-Irish,* were not too kindly disposed towards England. However, so long as they were not interfered with, they remained loyal. The situation was further complicated by the pacifist character of the Quakers and the Plain Folk Germans.

One more fact must be recorded. To quote Dr. Graeff: "The political alliance between the German and Scotch-Irish elements in Pennsylvania proved to be a vital factor in aligning Pennsylvania on the side of those colonies that favored a declaration of independence in 1776. It will be remembered that the vote on Lee's immortal resolution 'that these united colonies are, and, of a right, ought to be, free and inde-

* Another important group were the Scotch-Irish. This term is used because they were Scottish Protestants in origin who were induced to go to Ireland by Queen Elizabeth in the sixteenth century in order to help convert the Irish Roman Catholics to Protestantism. When they migrated to Ireland they were promised that they could worship as Presbyterians and that their exports would not be taxed. Since succeeding monarchs in England refused to recognize these privileges, many of them went to America, where thousands of them lived in Pennsylvania at the time of the Revolutionary War.

pendent states' stood at six colonies for and six against the resolution until Pennsylvania cast the deciding vote. . . . From 1740 to 1776 the Germans held the balance in power between the Scotch-Irish and the Quakers." [18]

Unfortunately, the winning of the Revolutionary War was but the beginning of other political worries. Firstly, there was the setting up of a new constitution not only for the United States but for the different states. The heirs of William Penn were paid one-half million dollars to resign their title to their estates. Anti-slavery having to be considered, the Quakers and others were urged to free their slaves. The Whiskey Rebellion broke out when an excise tax was levied on tobacco, liquor, and other manufactured articles, an impost which especially hit the farmers. In 1798 a tax was levied on land, houses, and negro slaves, one which naturally fell heavily on owners of houses and farms.

Thus we can see that the years from 1776 to 1800 were unsettled, both for those who had been English sympathizers and those who were opposed to war. Besides, as the Plain Folk were mainly farmers, the increased taxation was not to their liking. The situation resembled too acutely the conditions they had experienced in Europe; hence they were in the frame of mind to migrate to any country which promised peace, an opportunity to have religious liberty, and one which promised economic advantages.

One racial characteristic has been an important factor with the Swiss and Palatinate Germans: when they migrate they tend to do so in groups of twenty or more families. This has several advantages—the group is large enough to keep up morale, and it provides a variety of occupational training which, when used on a coöperative basis, has high economic value. Finally, and perhaps as important as the foregoing, the group is large enough to establish a church fellowship, for it must never be forgotten that these emigrants had strong religious tendencies.

Although these people were highly individualistic, their individualism was of a special kind. So long as they had a leader in whom they had every confidence, they followed without much question. However, should they lose this confidence, their individualism came to the fore and seldom was a compromise possible. There was usually a complete break which tended to weaken rather than strengthen the sect.

Up to now, primary consideration has been given to the pacifist group which became important more from the economic point of view than from the political. Attention must be paid to the Lutherans, Reformed, and Huguenots, because they surpassed, particularly during the years 1756 to 1776, the Plain Folk in numbers of immigrants. Furthermore, they were non-pacifists and willing to take their part in the political affairs of the state.

Following the Seven Years War (1756–1763), the former alliance between Germans and Quakers was not renewed. Originally, Pennsylvania was what is known as a proprietary province—that is, it was owned by William Penn and his sons who, incidentally, were not Quakers. When Benjamin Franklin and the Quakers tried to make Pennsylvania a royal province—that is, belonging directly to the English king—the Germans renewed their alliance with the Scotch-Irish or Presbyterians. The Germans felt that they should remain loyal to Penn because it was he who had invited them to emigrate. The Scotch-Irish in many cases were sons of covenanters, and when the Intolerable Acts of 1774 were passed they were reminded of the dreadful acts of the soldiery in the homeland. The Germans, too, had an ingrained hatred of oppression by princes and kings, and when Pennsylvania held the deciding vote as to whether they could claim independence, the combined weight of the Scotch-Irish and Germans swung the vote in favor of fighting for independence. Once war was declared, the non-pacifist Germans—Lutherans, Reformed, Huguenots—took an active part as in the Seven Years War when regiments were recruited by and from them. Conestoga horses and wagons carried the sinews of war in the form of food, sulphur, and saltpetre (the basis of gunpowder), and lastly, it was the German craftsmen from Pennsylvania who made the Kentucky rifles. These men had learned in South Germany how to rifle weapons—that is, to cut spiral grooves within a gun barrel to give the bullet a rotary motion and thus render its flight more accurate and enable it to travel twice as far as the guns with a smooth bore. (Because of these rifles during the Revolutionary War, General Howe had to evacuate Boston and retire to Nova Scotia until he could secure some Hessian soldiers who were equipped with this type of gun. It was not until after the Napoleonic Wars that similar rifles were made in England.)

Those who had immigrated prior to 1756 had witnessed up to 1800 the Seven Years' War, the War of Independence, Shay's Rebellion (which threatened the Confederation), and the Whiskey Insurrection (which tried the strength of the federal union under Washington). The Fries Rebellion in Eastern Pennsylvania caused a great deal of concern for President John Adams, as John Fries, although a Welshman, had his greatest following in Pennsylvania Germans living in Northampton, Bucks, and Montgomery counties.

At the beginning of our study we stated that one purpose was to discover if these different sects broke away from their religion and mores once they had become free and prosperous. We are now in a position to assess the situation, but first of all we must consider them as two groups: Lutheran, Reformed, and Huguenots, or "Church People," and the Plain Sects such as Quakers, Mennonites, Dunkards, Moravians, and Amish, or "Plain Folk." There were other sects as well as these, but since none of them came to Canada, no special reference will be made to them.

The "Church People," because of their similarities in Europe, did not find it difficult to work together in America. This was particularly true of the Huguenots and Reformed on account of their Calvinistic background. The Huguenots were bitterly persecuted in Europe, thereby making them strong, whereas the Lutherans and Reformed, suffering little from persecution, came to America in large numbers principally for financial reasons.

The Reformed Church flourished in America in New York State and in Pennsylvania. Actually both Lutheran and Reformed Churches were established in America before the coming of the Swiss and Palatinates, and the Quakers. The Swedes on the Delaware had instituted the Lutheran Church and the Dutch the Reformed Church, hence with the influx of the new settlers the former system of European control continued. Actually, the Reformed Church in Pennsylvania under the direction of the sponsoring Reformed Church of Holland was generally supported with preachers and money for some time. There was an effort to join with the Presbyterians but this failed. However, in recent years there has been a union with the Evangelical Synod of North America and a union with the Congregational Church is pending.

During the colonial period the Lutheran Church had a

status almost equal to that of the Church of England because of its recognition at the English court by Prince George of Denmark, the consort of Queen Anne. Also, outstanding preachers and organizers were sent from Germany, among them Heinrich Mühlenberg, who came out in 1742 to offset the wooing of Count Zinzendorf to join with the Moravians. It was he who not only saved the identity of the Lutheran Church in Pennsylvania but who was able to co-ordinate several branches of Lutheranism, set up a model for a church constitution, and compile a liturgy for use in the church.

In both the Lutheran and Reformed Churches the ministers were well educated and highly regarded by the people in general. Klees, in speaking of the Lutheran, Reformed, and Huguenot Churches, states: "By and large they have made the Pennsylvania Dutchman what he is today. They gave him his ways of celebrating Christmas and Easter; they give him his folk art, whether dower chests, *taufschein*, or barn sign; to a large degree they gave him his ardent patriotism; and to nine out of ten they gave religion." [19]

The Moravians, under the leadership of Count Zinzendorf, initiated communities at Bethlehem and Nazareth which were meant to be completely self-contained and independent units. Here, and throughout Eastern Pennsylvania, schools, even nursery and boarding schools, were established and a high standard of education was set. As previously mentioned, they were particularly noted for the establishment of higher education for women, their music, especially choral (Bethlehem Bach Choir), and for their mission work among the Indians.

Besides being hampered by European control, the Moravians were frequently in difficulty because of their pacifism. Finally, ceasing to look upon themselves as "peculiar people," they broadened out more or less, losing their identity but still maintaining a consciousness of the contribution they had made to American life.

Turning to the "Plain People," we find that they had different conditions to meet. In Europe they had increased under persecution, but in America, where they were not interfered with to the same extent, their problems lay chiefly in keeping separate from outside worldly influences. It is true that during the French-English struggle of 1756–1763 they found themselves occasionally in difficulties, but these were not too serious, since their contributions of food, horses, and wagons tended to give them considerable immunity. This situation was repeated during the Revolutionary War, when once again their religious observances were not interfered with.

The Quakers and Mennonites worked closely together. Both opposed war, objected to taking oaths, and believed in a plain religion and plain dress. They differed in that the Quakers would take part in governmental affairs with certain reservations and were not averse to having slaves, whereas the Mennonites were opposed to both. The Mennonites did not hold office in Europe until 1683 and not to any extent until 1840.

The meeting-houses of all the Plain Folk were plain both inside and out. Men sat on one side of the church, women on the other, with the older folk in front. There was no organ or musical instrument and all singing was in unison. With the Mennonites, attendance was almost one hundred per cent. Preachers were chosen by lot, and in the early days were not formally educated. The books available and read were usually religious, hence the outlook of these people was rather narrow. Men were usually clean shaven and their clothing was very plain; the women likewise shunned color and wore clothes of a simple pattern. They avoided lawsuits and were very socially minded in regard to their own people. They believed that each person should make some contribution towards alleviating the financial difficulties of his brethren.

The Amish, still the most conservative branch of the Mennonites, are divided into the Old Order and Church Amish. With the first, religious services are held in the various homes; among the second, they are held in regular churches. Services in both groups are very long and the Old Order use a mixture of High German and Pennsylvania German. The hymn book used by this group is one compiled in Germany and Switzerland. Among the Old Order Amish, telephones and motor cars are forbidden; however, they do not object to using someone else's phone or riding in a car owned by a non-Amish person. Though the men wear beards, they shave the upper lip and wear a style of dress which amounts to a uniform. Boys and girls are dressed similarly to their parents, all clothes being home-made. Haircuts are of a special character and so, all in all, the Old Order Amish person's appearance, whether male or female, old or young, is unique and striking.

The Amish have generally opposed education beyond the three R's, retaining an open mind only in regard to better methods of agriculture. They have prospered not by migration but by buying at a low figure land depleted by farmers who felt no regard for the maintenance of soil fertility. The soil has always been sacred to the Amish, and their practice of *Meidung* (ostracism) has been a big factor in helping them keep their solidarity and their interest in good farm practice.

Weddings and funerals have always been big events in the lives of these people—particularly the latter. Following the death of a member of the family, several neighbors took over, cleaned the house, brought food in and, after the funeral, attended by all the relatives and friends for miles around, a meal was served, usually in relays.

Another communal undertaking was the use of white or dull red paint and whitewash on buildings. Some say this was a means of gaining escape from repressed desires.

The Dunkards or Brethren resemble the other Plain Folk in their belief in nonresistance and in the simple life. As has already been noted, they believe in immersion (three times forward), performing the ceremony in the open streams. They have practised the love feast, after which an "experience meeting" is held, also the rite of foot washing. Some of their earlier leaders were educated, such as Christopher Sauer, who printed the first Bible published in German in America, and who invited Christopher Dock, a Mennonite, to write out his method of teaching for other teachers. Dock substituted persuasion for brute force. The Brethren ministers have been chosen by vote. This uneducated ministry has given way to an educated one, just as their plain dress, although still plain, no longer suggests a uniform. More individual freedom is to be found among the Brethren than among the other Plain Folk.

Finally, whether these sects were liberal or conservative, there was no fundamental change from the characteristics which had kept them alive during persecution days in Europe. In the main, their world was the homes bounded by the size of the community. Religion was just as essential to their well-being, and the soil was still held in veneration.

Ralph Wood put it this way: "In spite of the competition of Grange events, the automobile and the small-town movie, the Church has remained the center of community life in the Pennsylvania German countryside more than is usually the case in modern America. The visual proof of the hold the churches have on the people is the buildings themselves. Nowhere in America are there such large numbers of well constructed Protestant churches, some of them almost cathedral-like. . . . And church suppers and entertainments still attract many people. . . . In the basement social rooms, often as large as good-sized gymnasiums, sometimes larger, huge crowds gather to bear witness to the fact that Pennsylvania Germans not only worship in their churches, but enjoy themselves there." [20]

III

MIGRATION TO AND SETTLEMENT IN UPPER CANADA

REASONS FOR MIGRATION

FOR years the question as to why this ethnic group left the United States and migrated to Canada has been discussed. Doubtless it will never be completely answered, because migrations of people are never simple in motivation, there being always various reasons, some influencing one group, some another. Historians of British background have found a simple explanation by lumping these groups all together under the heading of United Empire Loyalists, thereby suggesting that these emigrants were largely English, Scottish, or Irish who, because of their allegiance to the English king, fought for him, were persecuted, and forced to flee the country. If it is pointed out that among these there were many pacifists, many not even British in race, an explanation is offered that they came for cheap land. While having an element of truth in them, both of these explanations oversimplify the situation.

Abbot Emerson Smith in his *Colonists in Bondage* makes an interesting comment on the migration of this ethnic group from Europe to America which would seem to help in an understanding of their later emigration to Canada. He writes: "German migration to the colonies during the eighteenth century was nearly always of a collective kind. The peasants of the Rhineland and the Palatinate, though not a little oppressed by their landlords, were much better off than those farther east. Their land was more fertile and their trade more brisk. From about 1685, however, their country was periodically ravaged by the armies of Louis XIV, and when the time of open warfare ceased in 1715, they were exposed, for the rest of the century, to the capricious tyrannies and outrageous exploitation of these petty princes, who sought to emulate the French monarch in the extravagance of their palaces and the numbers of their officials. Some of the Catholic potentates persecuted their Protestant subjects for religious reasons. There was reason enough for discontent, but except for the extraordinary hardships of Louis XIV's wars *there was no more reason for these Germans to leave their country than for the inhabitants of any other district in Europe to move; perhaps, in fact, there was rather less. Yet move they did, by the tens of thousands."* [1] (Italics mine.)

To some extent it was a case of history repeating itself in America. For the moment we can set aside those persons who actively supported England against the Colonies. It is quite understandable that following the defeat of England these people would find their situations untenable in the American Colonies and would seek to emigrate to a land like Canada, still under the control of England. But what of the Plain Folk who had taken little or no active part in the Revolution?

To answer this question one has but to consider three things: they were opposed to war in all its phases; they had suffered in Europe throughout the previous centuries because of their pacifist beliefs, often finding asylum in England from these persecutions; and they had come to America with the promise that England would give them freedom from army service and freedom of worship.

It does not require much imagination to picture the state of mind of these people. Because it was their custom to repress their feelings, one need not assume that they were oblivious to wars and rumors of wars. Many of the older generation knew that war brings out the worst in human nature, for they had seen plenty of evidence of it in their homeland. Fortunately they lived self-contained lives. They grew their own food, provided their own necessities of life and, as long as they were not interfered with, Stamp Acts and taxes on luxuries meant little to them. Living as they did in large communities, outside criticism could be ignored. Since economically they were self-contained, all they asked for was to be let alone.

On the whole, they were not greatly molested, due perhaps to their non-belligerent natures and to their community life. Though here and there it was inevitable that some super-patriots would annoy them, in all probability they were more influenced by the unsettled state of the country.

If, then, the Plain Folk were not molested to any very great extent, why did they emigrate to Canada? Why did they not all go into Ohio? Dr. Harold S. Bender has expressed the opinion that as a group these people were literalists and, having taken an affirmation of loyalty to the English king, they did not feel that they could swear fealty to another ruler. hence they made every effort to relocate in a country where this would not be necessary and where they would be free from war service. This, however, does not explain why so many remained behind.

Up to now no mention has been made of the economic aspect. All these Plain Folk were shrewd in money matters. By 1776 land had acquired considerable value in Pennsylvania. Since large families were customarily found consisting of several sons, and since to set them up on new farms required much money, the opportunity to get land for a minimum of investment appealed strongly to them.

Doubtless all of the above-mentioned motives were involved, but one should be mentioned which is suggested by A. E. Smith when he speaks of them leaving Europe when others stayed. There is no doubt that the Palatinate and Swiss Germans were born pioneers—they had an "itchy heel." This characteristic is still evident amongst them in modern times, because from Ontario many have gone to Western Canada and recently some have migrated to South America. Perhaps it explains why their descendants have pioneered in so many different activities in the nation. Once the land was cleared, they turned their attention to the world of ideas, with the consequence that many new schemes and enterprises have been initiated in Canada by pioneers of Pennsylvania German background.

Here we have one explanation for the migration of the Quakers. "The Quakers also suffered in both property and influence. The close of the Revolutionary War found them also divided and weakened and powerless to stem the tide of secularization....

"Thus the end of the war found the Quakers on the verge of open ruptures, that promised ill for the future, and prevented their exercising any large influence upon the political developments that were now absorbing more and more the interest of the country." [2]

Dorland, in referring to the Quakers, claims that a strong

motivation was "when conditions of life were too difficult or creditors too pressing, it was always possible to move into a new district and to begin afresh. There was also always 'the lure of the new and untried, the desire to work out their fortunes under new stars, the hope that a change of locality would bring into operation forces and powers for which they sought in vain in their habitual surroundings.' " [3]

There were two seemingly quite distinct streams of the earliest migrations to Upper Canada which eventually integrated to such an extent that the reasons for the migrations have either been misunderstood or lost. There was the group, later to be called the United Empire Loyalists, who, because they had fought on the side of England, had to flee the country, leaving behind them all their possessions. A large percentage of these came from New York State and were Huguenots (French) or Lutherans or Reformed (German) who had at one time or another been befriended by England. Among this group were English people belonging to the Quakers, who, although they did not fight for England, were pacifists and were looked upon as enemies by the Colonists, and, like those who fought for England, were forced to flee to Canada, leaving behind in many cases all their wealth.

Since all of the foregoing arrived in Canada without any means of subsistence, the British Government gave them free land and supplies for three years. Unfortunately, many were inexperienced in agriculture. Canniff affirms: "Many of the old soldiers had not the slightest knowledge of the duties of pioneer life, while others had but an imperfect idea. Some scarcely knew how to fell a tree." [4] Cruikshank bears this out when he says that only eleven of the thirty officers in Colonel Butler's Rangers were listed as farmers or farmers' sons. [5]

The second group was composed of all Germans and pacifists—Moravians, Mennonites, or Dunkards. Practically all settlers belonging to this group were farmers and brought money and farm supplies with them by which to establish themselves without much support from the government. Their custom was to send ahead two of their number to spy out the land. When these men found what they wanted, they staked it out or bought it, in many cases locating land for their friends and relatives. They then returned to bring back their families.

A third group might include those who came from the New

England States and New Jersey. As far as can be discovered, there was only a scattered migration from these states into Upper Canada, as many journeyed on to the Maritime Provinces because of their proximity. There were, however, a number—mostly from the British Isles originally—who found their way into Upper Canada, some coming through New York State and some by way of New Brunswick. Because the early settlers in the New England States and New Jersey had come to America for religious as well as commercial reasons, they found our ethnic group quite congenial and soon were assimilated with them in Upper Canada. This group was on the whole non-pacifist and had opposed the Colonists, thereby earning their ill will and losing their wealth and property.

Because of the complexity of these migrations and in order to get a clearer picture of the settlements in Upper Canada, chronological divisions will be made as follows:

(1) The period 1776 to 1792—that is, from the beginning of the Revolutionary War until the coming of Simcoe. This period will be called "The Squatters' Era" because land was selected and held with or without location ticket.

(2) The period 1792 to 1796 when Governor Simcoe promoted immigration and systematic land surveys. This will be named "The Simcoe Regime."

(3) From 1796 to 1812 there was a great influx of settlers and this period can be called "The First Great Migration."

(4) "After 1812." Following the war of 1812–1815, migrations from south of the border slackened materially, while there were many immigrants from the British Isles and the Continent.

The Squatters' Era (1776–1792)

Migration to Upper Canada during this period was made at three different points—Niagara, Detroit, and from Dundas County to the Bay of Quinté in Eastern Ontario. Of these three, Niagara was the earliest, Detroit next, and the Eastern section last. It should be noted that Fort Niagara was on the east side of the Niagara River and remained a British possession until 1796. Such forts as Oswego, Niagara, Detroit, and Mackinac were busy places because they were the centers for the fur-trading with the Indians. They were also a problem for the administration on account of the difficulty in getting

Secord house in Jordan Station—built in 1777

First schoolhouse in Waterloo—built in 1820

Humsberger Photos, St. Jacobs, Ontario

supplies to them. After 1776 their problem was increased by the number of refugees that poured into them.

The first record we have of persons reaching Upper Canada after the outbreak of the Revolution is found in Canniff's *History of the Province of Ontario*: "In 1776, there arrived at Fort George, in a starving state, Mrs. Nellis, Mrs. Secord, Mrs. Young, Mrs. Buck, and Mrs. Bonnar, with thirty-one children, whom the circumstances of the rebellion had driven away." [6] From other sources we learn that the Secords were of French Huguenot descent, that the Nellises (or Nelleses) were also French; Bonnar is probably an anglicized form of Bonheur; Young for Jung, whereas Buck is definitely German. Thus we see that the first women we have record of coming to Canada were non-English. This particular group probably came from New York State, for that is where the Secords and the Nelleses had located. Earlier mention has been made of the coming of the Huguenots to America; let us now consider two of these families, the descendants of which were among the first recorded emigrants to Canada.

Mrs. Elizabeth Bowman Spohn, in a letter (1861) to Egerton Ryerson and included by Dr. Talman in his *Loyalist Narratives from Upper Canada*, states that her grandfather, Jacob Bowman, emigrated from Germany to America in the reign of Queen Anne, and after having fought for the British in the French War, was granted 1500 acres on the Susquehannah River. Here he was carried off by the colonists, leaving his wife and his eleven-year-old son Peter almost destitute. The mother and her child then made their way to the Mohawk River. Some time later, the commander of the British forces at Fort George heard of their plight and sent Indians to guide them, as well as the Nelleses, Secords, Youngs, and Bucks to the Fort. From here they were sent to Montreal, and then on to Quebec, where they were given subsistence. [7] Peter and his younger brother later joined Butler's Rangers. After the war Peter married the daughter of Frederick Lampman and they settled near the fort.

Ernest Green gives the following additional facts about the Secord family: "The ancestor of the Secord Family, Amboise Secord, came with his five children from La Rochelle to New York in 1681. He with other French emigrants founded the town of New Rochelle in 1689.* Many of the Huguenots sympathized with England during the Revolutionary War because England had given them asylum from their persecutors on the Continent and helped them to emigrate to America. Family documents of this same family note that on the breaking out of the Revolutionary War the family divided; certain of them anglicized their surname by placing the 'd' of nobility (d'Secor) at the end, thus making it Secord, and others dropped the letter entirely, making it Secor. United Empire Loyalists of the strictest type, the Secords had warmly espoused the king's cause, and, as a consequence, the five brothers with their families had to fly early in the struggle, leaving their estates, and reaching Kingston and Niagara by way of New Brunswick as best they could. It is said that James Secord, who married Laura Ingersoll, thus giving her the name by which she is remembered, when a child three years old had accompanied his mother in her flight through the wilderness, with four other homeless women and many children. After enduring frightful hardships for nearly a month they finally arrived at Fort Niagara almost naked and starving." [8]

There seems to be some confusion as to whether they arrived at Fort Niagara or Fort George. Canniff states that it was the latter. Fort Niagara (now Youngstown) was the earlier and more important, situated on the east side of the Niagara River. Fort George was located on the west side; later it was known as Newark and finally as Niagara-on-the-Lake.

The following is an outline of the earlier history of the Nelles family: About 1618 the Nelles family, owing to religious persecution in France, moved to Bremen in Germany, where they were made welcome. Their name at the time was de Nélis.

The family lived in Bremen in the Province of Hanover for about ninety-two years. During the course of time the "de" was gradually dropped and their name became "Nelle." During the Thirty Years' War, like many other Protestants of the Palatinate, they sank into poverty. Some were driven

* Wm. Canniff, in his *History of the Province of Ontario* (p. 120), states: ". . . a town called New Rochelle in Westchester County, New York. This town or tract of land was purchased in 1689 expressly for the Huguenot settlement by Jacob Leister, Commissioner of the Admiralty under Governor Dongan of New York." Huguenots bought from him.

46

by distress to leave their native land and seek asylum in other Protestant states. Many came to England at the time of Queen Anne's reign. Among those who came to America were three brothers—William, Christian, and Johannes. On this continent, the family name became Nelles or Nellis—the latter spelling probably due to carelessness in forming the loop in the last "e."

They first settled on a tract of land in Dutchess County, but in the year 1712 with other settlers they hewed a road across the Catskill Mountains and came to the Schoharie River. Afterwards Johannes Nelles went to Pennsylvania and settled in the vicinity of Gettysburg. And in 1720 William Nelles, who was an army commandant under Queen Anne, settled with Christian in the Mohawk Valley. William later married a Miss Klock, and five children were born to them—Ludwig, Johannes, William Jr., Andrew, and Hendrick.

Hendrick Nelles served under Sir William Johnson as a lieutenant in a company of Confederate Northern Indians in the wars against the French in Canada. His son, Hendrick William Nelles (May 31, 1735–January 26, 1791), served as a first lieutenant in a company of grenadiers under Sir Henry Moore in 1763. He fought during the Revolutionary War as captain, came to Canada with his sons about 1780, and was the first settler in Grimsby, Ontario. He subsequently resided at York on the Grand River, where two of his sons had settled, and was in 1788 major commanding the 3rd Regiment of Militia of the District of Nassau, as that part of the province was then called. He had the following issue: Robert, William, and Abraham, all of Grimsby; John and Warner of York, Grand River; Peter, who returned to the United States; Andrew; and Anne, married to Charles Anderson.[9]

Regarding the settlement at Niagara, which had its beginning during the Revolutionary War, Cruikshank noted: "The Settlement at Niagara actually preceded that at the Bay of Quinté by nearly four years. The scheme of promoting a colony of farmers here had its origin in the great difficulty that had been experienced in supplying the garrison at Fort Niagara and its dependent posts with provisions."[10]

Witness the remarks of Colonel Bolton, commander at Fort Niagara, in a letter to General Haldimand. He considered that the expense of maintaining the posts was so enormous that he thought it a pity that they had not been abandoned to the Indians altogether and that they were costing old England far more than they were worth. The arrival of recruits for Butler's Rangers and other refugee loyalists, together with the demands of the Indians for provisions and other supplies, became more exacting and he dared not disregard them for motives of humanity as well as public policy.[11]

Haldimand,* then Governor of Canada, replied under date of October 1778: "The great expense and difficulty attending the Transport of Provisions to the Upper Posts make it much to be wished that effectual means could be fallen upon at them all for raising a supply within themselves that might relieve them from their inconvenient and sometimes distressing dependence upon what is sent them from below, and at the same time ease Government of part of the heavy charges to which it is now subject on this account.

"I must desire therefore that the Contractor at the Carrying Place and any other capable person you can find be urged to make use of every means to enable him, in which you will no doubt assist him all you can, to cultivate as much land next year as possible about the Fort; at least to lay a foundation of by degrees, supplying the Post with Bread . . . and the rearing of cattle is likewise possible, I should imagine to bring about in time. At present the excursions of the Indians might probably furnish something towards a supply of this article." [12]

During the fall and winter of 1778–1779 Colonel Butler had built a large range of log barracks (Fort George) on the opposite side of the river from Fort Niagara for the accommodation of his battalion of Rangers, which had increased to a strength of 300, and of their families, as well as of other fugitive families.

These "fugitive" families" evidently became a very serious

* Frederick Haldimand was a Swiss Huguenot who had had a career as a professional soldier, first with the King of Sardinia, then under Frederick the Great, later with the Swiss Guards in Holland. In 1754 the British were recruiting a regiment among Swiss and German Protestant settlers in Pennsylvania and Maryland, and Haldimand was asked to lead the regiment, known as the Royal Americans, located at Philadelphia. Serving in Canada, he was wounded at Lake George in 1758. Two years later he was with Amherst when he took Montreal, and because of his exploits was made a British subject. Being made a military governor at Three Rivers, he reorganized that area both socially and industrially, particularly the iron industry. After being sent to Florida as British commandant, he returned to New York to be in command there. Recalled to England in 1775, he returned in 1778 to succeed Governor Carleton as Governor-General of Canada.

48

problem to that garrison, for in June 1779 Haldimand again wrote Colonel Bolton: "I cannot but approve of your having forwarded Capt. Aubrey's Detachment to Detroit and the sooner you send down those men belonging to it that you mention might be unfit for service, from a confirmed state of bad health, the better, and here I must repeat to you my anxiety for having every useless mouth removed from Niagara for the reasons I have already mentioned to you, which is still as urgent as ever. All prisoners and idle people from the Frontiers I hope you have already sent, if you can find amongst the distressed families three or four who are desirous to settle upon the opposite side of the river, who are good husbandmen and who discover Inclinations for improvement of the Land only exclusive of every other view or pursuit, I would have you establish them there, affording them whatever assistance you may think necessary, whether by a little provisions or a few laborors. . . ." [13]

Evidently this proposal was approved by the British Government. "Authority was given for the issue of rations and simple tools to settlers, and it was understood that surplus products would find a market at the fort. In 1781 Lieut.-Col. John Butler declared that four or five families newly settled would require for seed sixty bushels of spring wheat and oats, twelve of buckwheat and a barrel of Indian corn. Peter and James Secord, two of the heads of families, were about to build a saw and grist mill. A census of the new settlement was taken by Col. Butler, its godfather, on August 25th, 1782 Besides the Secords already mentioned were George Stuart, George Fields, John Depuis, Daniel Rowe, Elijah Phelps, Philip Bender, Samuel Lutz, Michael Showers, Harmonious House, Thomas McMicking, Adam Young, McGregor Van Every, and Isaac Dolson. There were sixteen families consisting of eighty-three persons. One was a slave owned by McMicking. Cleared land made a total of 238 acres. . . ." [14]

Brief mention should be made here of the treatment of the Indians, whose title to the land was recognized by Great Britain. One historian writes: "The British Indian Department had behind it a long tradition of successful dealing with the Indians ever since the day when William Johnson had been appointed superintendent of the Six Nations in 1755. The Department had extended its activities to Canada after the Seven Years War, and after the American Revolution removed its main office to Montreal. In 1774 Colonel Guy Johnson was appointed to succeed Sir William (a cousin), and in 1782 Sir John Johnson, Sir William's son, was appointed superintendent-general of Indian affairs. The expanding needs of the service necessitated a division of responsibility and at the end of the eighteenth century the Department was divided, with the superintendent-general remaining at Montreal and a new office, that of the deputy superintendent-general, being opened at Fort George." [15]

Unfortunately when the treaty was signed in 1783, it included no mention of the claims of the Indians. The Indians claimed their lands were given away, henceforth they were never so kindly disposed to the English in spite of the fact that lands were given in the Bay of Quinté and the Grand River to offset their claims.

Thus, before these settlements could be made, the land had to be bought from the Indians. The grant of land attached to the Fort was a strip four miles in depth on the east side of the river extending to Fort Erie, and of two miles on the west side provided it was solely for the use of the Crown.

In 1780 General Haldimand had started proceedings to purchase land on the west side of the river. He wrote to Colonel Guy Johnson and instructed him to buy a tract of land from the Mississaguas "opposite to the Fort, bounded by the River Niagara, and what is called the 4 mile Creek, extending from Lake Ontario to Lake Erie in a parallel line or near it, with the river, taking advantage, wherever it can be done, of a natural boundary. . . ." [16] The land which Colonel Johnson purchased nearly a year later, however, was not parallel to the river, but bounded on the one side by the "Chippeweigh" River, and Lake Erie on the other. For this he paid three hundred suits of clothing.

It is of interest to note that Butler could not and did not wait for this purchase from the Indians to be consummated. This explains why the census of 1782 mentions 238 acres having been cleared. [17]

It would seem that not enough attention has been paid to the number of settlers who came into the province as squatters. "Many a soldier has arrived to claim his grant only to find resident upon it a 'squatter who may feel that he has an equal right to the soil through the improvements made on it.' " [18] Historians have relied upon census reports made by military officials, but such reports probably record only those who had been placed by them and received government help. Furthermore, it is difficult to understand why men like the Secords would build saw and grist mills if there were not settlers to make use of them. They must have had a tremendous confidence in the future developments if they built only for future business. Lloyd Graham states, without giving his authority, that the first country fair had already been held (1780) at what is now Niagara-on-the-Lake. In 1781 he claims that Buffalo had 481 men, 677 women, and 482 children (Indians).[19] Now whether or not this date for the fair is correct—and it seems a bit early—we do know that Simcoe in 1792 gave ten guineas to the Agricultural Society. Presumably by this time there must have been a large number of farmers in the Niagara Peninsula, although no settler had any deed to his property. We read in the Jarvis Letters: "Pimlico, 31st March, 1792 . . . I am told that at this moment there is not a single grant of land in Upper Canada but the lands are held by letters of occupation and that the grants are all to be made out by me after my arrival at which the secretary of L.C. is not well pleased as the letters of occupation have been issued by him for some years without fee or reward and by the division of the Province of Canada all the emoluments fall to my portion; there is, at this moment 12 to 20,000 persons holding lands on letters of licence in Upper Canada at a guinea only each, is a petty thing to begin with." [20]

In the Wentworth Historical Society Papers there is recorded the story of Robert Land: "Robert Land, living on the Delaware River near Coshecton, N.Y., decided to go to Canada. He arranged with a Quaker friend who had traded a good deal in that direction to accompany him . . . he arrived at the beautiful prairie valley around Burlington Bay when he took up a farm and built him a 'shack' in 1781, the first white man who made his home where this fair city stands." [21]

Here we have a settler coming to Canada without help from the government and selecting his farm site some distance inland without any prospect of obtaining a deed. The mention of the Quaker friend is interesting for two reasons: first, this man had "traded a good deal" in that direction; secondly, the Quakers were amongst the early settlers not only in Niagara but in Eastern Ontario and in York County.

One is led to believe that the people of New York and per-

51

haps Pennsylvania had a much more intimate knowledge of Upper Canada than historians have given them credit for. We do know that fur-trading had been carried on for a long time from such forts as Niagara, Oswego, and Detroit. Also, that these fur-traders in many cases were wealthy persons, consequently they lived well at the forts, enjoyed many of the amenities of life, entertained travellers, and travelled themselves. In addition, there were the military officers and their wives to give added color.

Let us look at the purchases for the family of Lieutenant Adam Crysler who settled in Fort Niagara in November, 1781. This family had accounts with a dozen or more mercantile houses and some of the purchases for that year as taken from old account books still in the possession of that family are as follows [22]:

	£	S.	P.
20 yds. of Irish Linen	9	7	6
4 pair Woman's Hose		6	
4 pair Woman's Pumps	2	2	
6 black ebony handled knives and forks	1	4	
6 wine glasses		9	
2 brass thimbles			8
1 large pair ear bobbs		4	
1 qt. de Canter		12	
$\frac{1}{2}$ gal. rum		8	
$1\frac{1}{4}$ yds. corded muslin	1	10	
3 yds. lace	1	10	
2 pieces nonsopretty		4	
$6\frac{1}{2}$ yds. chintz	5	4	
3 yds. muslin	1	10	
1 lb. Bohea tea		8	
1 pair silver shoe buckles	2	16	
2 pair silk mitts	1	4	
$40\frac{3}{4}$ lb. Casteel Soap	5	1	$10\frac{1}{2}$
1 pair silver knee buckles		14	
1 night cape		4	
12 bottles Madiera		7	
a fine hat	2	8	
21 pipes			6
2 packs Cards		4	
7 yds. Black Taffety	4	18	
a black feather		12	

From such a list taken at random from bills paid, one can see that these people were accustomed to most of the comforts and some of the luxuries of life. It is possible too that this family was representative of many of the people who lived in that district.

Another source of reliable information in regard to the financial background of some of these settlers is the statement of their losses laid before the British Claims Commissioners held in Montreal in 1787. These losses included lands, houses, barns, stock, furniture, clothing, and business undertakings such as grist and saw mills, carpenter's and blacksmith's equipment, and potash works.

In 1783 a petition from the merchants of the Fort was sent to the Commander of the Fort setting forth the facts that goods were being brought in from "the States of America" which had not paid the necessary duties. Furthermore, they were competing with the goods imported from Britain. This is probably the first recorded evidence of the competition between the United States and Britain for the Canadian market.

The grants of lands and assistance given to the early settlers in Niagara were not so magnanimous as they might seem. General Haldimand wrote to Colonel Bolton in July 1780: ". . . the above mentioned grant of land will be reclaimed at the expense of the government and of course remain at all times the sole property of the crown and annexed to the Fort. Those who settle upon it are not to consider they have the smallest right to any part thereof, the produce alone being their property. . . ." [23]

This last ruling raised a serious problem, and in a short time a number of farmers headed by Isaac Dolson and Elijah Phelps wrote to Colonel Butler claiming that only a part of the one year's provisions had been forthcoming. They further pleaded with Haldimand to grant them leases or some other security for their farms as they were obliged to sell the little produce they were able to raise at the prices the commanding officer thought proper. They were, on the other hand, willing to subject themselves to a rental for their farms after a term of eight years rather than remain in their position of being turned off their lands at the whim of the often-changing commanding officer.

This request was sent on to Governor Haldimand, who acknowledged it but did nothing about it. It was not until 1797 that deeds were issued. In the meantime there was much changing of ownership of property, since many of those given free land were either unable or unwilling to clear it and were quite anxious to sell to immigrants with money to buy it. It is just here where the pacifist Plain Folk enter the picture. Not many of them had been given free land, but in most instances they had money to buy. Where this did not obtain, they went farther afield, selected their own land, and became squatters.

Butler's Rangers have already been mentioned and their importance has been recognized as twofold: firstly, as a group of persons who fought against the American Revolutionists; and secondly, as providing some of the first settlers in Upper Canada, at a point along the Niagara River.

Colonel John Butler (1728–1795) was born at New London, Conn., the son of an Irish officer. He served in the expedition against Crown Point at Ticonderoga and at the capture of Cataraqui (Kingston) in 1758. He also commanded the Indians at the capture of Niagara in the following year. In the early autumn of 1777, he received authority from Sir Guy Carleton to raise a corps of rangers. Among the first to be enrolled were German farmers already actively employed on the frontiers. Butler later became Deputy Superintendent of Indian Affairs, a position he occupied with distinction until his death at Niagara in 1795.

Rarely did Butler's Rangers have the opportunity of operating as a battalion. During practically the whole period of their existence they were broken up into small detachments and employed in widely separated localities. They had the double duty of fighting the enemy and of controlling the bands of Indians so often associated with them in their expeditions.

Their very colorful activities in their daring raids on the enemy accomplished a great deal in protecting the Loyalists. In addition, when disbanded in 1783, they became some of the first farmers in the Niagara district of Upper Canada. By 1785, 258 Rangers had agreed to take up land opposite Fort Niagara, and the census of June, 1785, numbered the settlers as 770 men. women, and children.[24]

One of the terms of the Treaty of Paris, signed in 1783, provided that the Loyalists would either receive back their homes and lands or be compensated for them by the various State governments. This the States refused to do, claiming that the Federal Government had exceeded its powers when consenting to this stipulation in the treaty. The British Government then decided to grant land in British North America to these unfortunate people and to compensate them in other ways for the losses they had incurred.

To this end, in 1784 a second purchase of land in the Niagara district was made from the Indians. It included all the land lying west of Four Mile Creek along Lake Ontario to Burlington, and from there to the Grand River and down the river to Lake Erie. This land, called the "New Purchase" and bought at one-tenth of a penny an acre, was allotted to the members of Butler's Rangers which had been disbanded, each private receiving two hundred acres and each officer a larger amount.

For instance, in 1794, Lieutenant Adam Crysler and his heirs were given 2000 acres in the Township of Niagara. This Loyalist was of Palatinate background. His grandfather, Johan Philip Greisler, had lost his home and had accepted the offer of the British Government to transport him to America in 1710. Probably he brought some means with him to America, for he was able to support himself and family during the first winter and not resort to the camps. Also, his son was soon the possessor of a large estate which had been purchased. The family settled at West Camp, Green County, N.Y., but in 1740 moved to Schoharie, N.Y. A son, Adam, became a lieutenant in Butler's Rangers, leading many a foray into the enemy's country to destroy warehouses and supplies.

In November of 1781, Lieutenant Adam Crysler (Greisler) took his family to Niagara where, as previously mentioned they made their first purchases in December of that year according to old account books still in the possession of the Crysler family. A Loyalist brother, Henry Crysler, came to Niagara at the close of the Revolutionary War with his family. A government report in 1787 records that he had thirty acres of wheat.

Another family by the name of Bradt presents features which are not uncommon and often misleading. Coming from Holland to Albany in 1736 and married to a Dutch girl, Albert Andriessen Bradt might be considered to be of Dutch extraction. However, this is not a certainty. Possibly his fore-fathers for religious reasons had moved into Holland and married into Dutch families. It is known that they married into one Huguenot family, so perhaps originally they came from France. The family possessed a crest which showed that they belonged to the nobility somewhere in Europe.

When they came to New York, they settled among and intermarried with the Dutch there. Successive generations were active in the political life of New York State, but in the Revolutionary War Arent Bradt was a captain and later a colonel in the Canadian Militia. His son Andrew also became a colonel, both of them serving with Butler's Rangers. They were granted land in the Township of Louth, County of Lincoln.

There were also Holland Dutch who migrated from New York State to Upper Canada. For reasons stated above it is difficult to discover whether these persons were actually Dutch in ancestry or whether Holland was a country where they had found asylum from persecution and where they adopted Dutch names. What complicates the situation fur-ther is the fact that the point of sailing was usually from Rotterdam or Amsterdam, hence descendants state that their ancestors came from Holland, whereas that was the point of sailing, not the country of origin.

Mrs. Simcoe writes in her Diary: "This farm near Niagara was owned by Samuel Lutes or Lutz [obviously German] as it is also spelled." [25] In the first census of Niagara in 1782 Samuel Lutz is listed as having cleared eighteen acres of land, while in the list of farms on the Niagara River and back from it (near St. David's), mention of three farms belonging to Samuel Lutz is made. He is also identified as one of Butler's Rangers.

The Servos House at Four Mile Creek dates back to 1783. In 1779 Governor Haldimand gave Daniel Servos (of Prus-sian descent) a commission of lieutenant in Colonel Johnson's Company of North American Indians. In 1788, he received a commission from Lord Dorchester to be captain of the first regiment of militia in the district of Nassau. Mrs. Jarvis, wife of William Jarvis, Provincial Secretary (1792–1817), wrote of Four Mile Creek: "There is a great mill upon it, and the family that it belongs to are Dutch."[26]

Kirby, in his *Annals of Niagara*, states that "all owned land, for the king gave every man, woman, and child of the U.E. Loyalists two hundred acres of land in fee simple, and the surveyors could not lay out the land fast enough for the multitude of settlers who came in from 1783 to 1792."[27]

He further states that the Loyalists "as to origin and language were a mixed people. The majority of them were English speaking, but half of those who came to Niagara used the High or Low German and Dutch. All were Protestants, either of the Church of England, German Lutherans, or Dutch Calvinists....

"The first surveys were made under directions of Surveyor-General Smith, by Augustus Jones, who married the daughter of a Chippewa chief—the father of Rev. Peter Jones, Chief of the Mississauguas.

"The first complete survey of the town of Niagara and its division into lots was adopted on June 24, 1791."[28]

Presumably matters in regard to property were in a very confused state during the 1780s. This was so because surveying lagged far behind and because French civil law as to property and inheritance prevailed. "Until 1788 there was little or no governmental supervision. At that time Lord Dorchester issued a proclamation organizing Upper Canada into four districts and out of deference to the German population named them Nassau, Hesse, Lunenburg, and Mecklenburg, giving them civil jurisdiction and establishing English criminal law with courts and justices. Dorchester also empowered the General Sessions to construct and repair roads and bridges, and make provision for religion and the public peace and order.

"The four districts were still legally a part of the Province of Quebec and the French civil law as to property and inheritance was obnoxious to the free English spirit of the common law. As soon as the newcomers had time to consider their position they objected to the French laws and petitioned for a change until in 1791 Upper Canada was separated from and made independent of Lower Canada."[29]

In assigning German names to these districts it may have been the intention to honor the royal family, but G. C. Paterson in *Land Settlement in Upper Canada* agrees with Kirby "that the districts were so named 'out of consideration for the large German element in the United Empire Loyalist population.'"[30]

A visitor, Joseph Hadfield, who published in 1785 his diary under the title of *An Englishman in America*, wrote: "Niagara was the first Loyalist settlement in Upper Canada, lands on the west side of the river having been obtained from the Indians and a log barracks built for Butler's Rangers in 1778 paving the way. In the summer of 1780 the first five families moved in. They had entered into a contract with the government to sell all produce to the military commanders for use at the posts and to have no dealings with private traders. By 1783 the settlement boasted 46 families having 713 acres cleared with 123 acres under winter wheat and 324 acres ready for spring wheat. During the Revolutionary War the male settlers were enlisted in Butler's Rangers."[31]

"On the north you follow the course of the river. The lands for a few miles are cultivated and interspersed with a great number of farms and fine cornfields."[32]

Evidently settlers did not all concentrate along the Niagara River. Miss Evelyn H. C. Johnson, in her investigations of the Martin settlement, states:

"It is estimated that George Martin built his house about 1783–1784, shortly after the Mohawks removed to the Grand River. It stands today (1908) in excellent repair, on a high bluff commanding a magnificent view up and down the Grand River about two miles southeast of Cainsville. Martin, an Indian, married Catharine Rollston, a German girl adopted by the Indians. To them was born the family of children whose descendants include names of national celebrity; among whom are the late Chief George H. M. Johnson, Miss E. Pauline Johnson,* and from another branch, the late Dr. Peter Martin, known to the public in recent years as Oronhyehteka."[33]

"Daniel Claus, he married a daughter of Sir William Johnson, and served for a considerable time in the Indian Department of Canada, under his brother-in-law, Colonel

* Pauline Johnson's family tree: her parents were George Henry Martin Johnson and Emily Howell; her grandparents, John S. Johnson and Helen Martin; her great-grandparents, George Martin (an Indian) and Catharine Rollston (a German).

Guy Johnson. William Claus, Deputy Superintendent-General of Indian affairs, was his son." [34]

"The families of Bahl or Ball and Mann intermarried; all or a portion of either or both emigrated from Heidelberg, Germany, to Blofield, in the County of Norfolk, England.

"In the year 1690, during the reign of William and Mary, some members of the Ball family purchased from the Crown lands in the Mohawk Valley, at one York shilling per acre, emigrated to America and settled there.

"In the Revolutionary War the family remained loyal to the British Crown, and Jacob (the father), with his sons, Peter, Jacob, and John, came to Canada in 1782 and engaged in the war on the side of Great Britain in Butler's and Queen's Rangers. Jacob (the father), who was a Captain, was followed to Canada by the greater part of his company, who joined with him in the cause of the Crown. George, the youngest son, with the female portion of the family, came to Canada in 1784.

"Lands were granted by the Crown in the townships of Louth and Niagara—the family settled on the latter, about two miles from Niagara.

"George, the youngest son, went to the township of Louth, on the Twenty Mile Creek, that part afterwards known as Ball's Mills, where he erected a grist mill, saw mill, woolen mill, cooper shop, and general store. These were largely utilized by the military in the war of 1812—a portion of a British Regiment being stationed there for a considerable time to guard the mill and other property, whence a very considerable portion of their supplies was received." [35]

Ancaster owes much of its foundation to Jean Baptiste Rousseau, who married Marie Martineau of the parish of St. Michel, now a part of Montreal, on July 14, 1780, but this marriage was dissolved on June 23, 1786.[36] Probably a Huguenot in religion, he became a Mason and a member of Masonic Lodge 16 in the township of Barton. He married Margaret Klein, the ward and adopted daughter of Joseph Brant in 1787, and about 1790 settled in Ancaster, where he kept a store. In 1793 he built a grist mill in the village and did a thriving business.[37]

Sherk is a well-known name in the Niagara Peninsula. The original settler, who spelled his name Schoerg, came from Lancaster County in Pennsylvania in 1789, the revolutionists having burned his home because he had sympathized with the British and had harbored their officers. He bought his river farms (Lot No. 6, 1st Concession, Willoughby Township, containing 116 acres) from John Rowe, who was said to have been one of Butler's men. He afterwards received a Crown grant on the 2nd Concession, Lot 6, at the rear of his river farm.[38]

John DeCou's forefathers were Huguenots who fled from France to England on account of their religion and at an early date came to America and settled in Vermont, where John was born in 1766. Jacob DeCou took up residence in the Niagara District in 1790, later moving to Burford. The DeCous were Loyalists and were granted land as such.

John Winger (Wenger), one of the founders of the Brethren in Christ Church (Dunkard) in Lancaster County, Pennsylvania, came to Canada in 1788 as a minister of that church. The first member of this church in Canada, he settled in Pelham Township, Welland County. In 1799 he bought land at Black Creek, Bertie Township, where he lived until his death in 1827. He was recognized as an elder of the Tunkers (Dunkards) and in 1798 was authorized to solemnize marriages.[39]

Bernard Frey (Fry) came of a Swiss-German family which had settled in the Mohawk Valley as early as 1689. Here Bernard was born in 1754 and here he lived until he joined the forces of Guy Johnson in 1775. Two years later he received a commission under John Butler and shortly after was promoted to a captaincy. In 1778 he married Hannah McMichael, a rather militant person.

Serving with distinction during the Revolutionary War, he was granted 300 acres of land—Lots 112 and 119 of Niagara Township near the village of Virgil. Later he was given some 3000 acres of land in the Whitby district together with more land in Niagara. He enlisted in the War of 1812 and was killed by a cannon ball in November 1812. Because Bernard Frey came of a Quaker family, his service in the forces would preclude his continuing in that faith. Ernest Green states that he was an ardent Presbyterian.[40]

Philip Frey, a nephew, escaped to Canada in 1776, later going to Detroit where, because of his knowledge of surveying, he became a Deputy Surveyor of lands and in that capacity laid out much land in the neighborhood of Detroit. Because

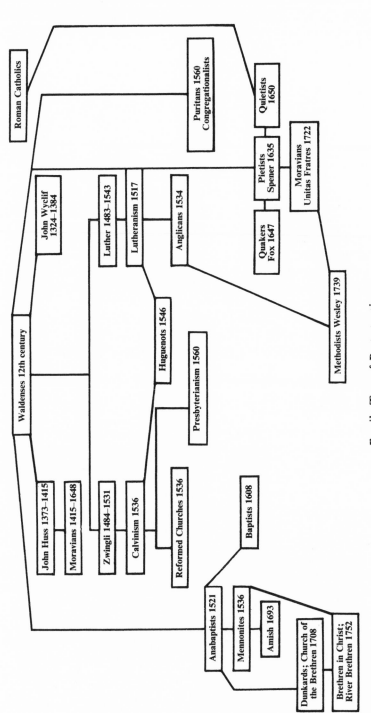

Family Tree of Protestantism

Plan of the organized part of Upper Canada, 1789

Department of Archives

of the confusion in land possession in the Niagara district, Frey was employed in that area until about 1789, when he returned to Canajoharie, New York, where his father lived and where Philip died in 1823.

Mrs. Simcoe, who frequently accompanied her husband on his trips, was a keen observer and narrates in her Diary of May 10, 1794: "We had not eaten since eight this morning. I was therefore desirous to get something for the children, and while some salmon we bought of an Indian as we passed Burlington Bay was preparing for our supper, we walked half a mile with the children to a farm house which we found inhabited by some Pennsylvanians whom Governor Simcoe had assisted last year at Niagara; we had there excellent bread, milk, and butter. . . . July 7, 1794, Forty Mile Creek —We walked through the village and beyond Green's Mills (five miles east of Hamilton on the Stoney Creek Road). Green ground the corn for all the military posts in Upper Canada. There are 100 people settled at the Forty and there have been but seven graves in five years." [41] (Green was a Loyalist from New Jersey who in 1788–1789 settled there.)

"August 31, 1795. A Moravian woman, married to a farmer near here, brought me a loaf of bread so peculiarly good, that I could not but imagine about it. She said that it was made with rennet and whey, without yeast or water, and baked in wicker or straw baskets which is the method taught at the Moravian School at Bethlehem (on the Lehigh River in Pennsylvania) in the States, where she was educated. The bread was as light as possible and rich like cake. . . ." [42]

Haldimand County, Rainham Township

In 1697 or 1699 Jonas Huber * (Hoover) emigrated from the Swiss Canton of Aargau to the Palatinate, thereby follow ing the example of many enterprising Swiss who took advan tage of the opportunities offered them in that region of the Rhineland which in 1688 had been devastated by the armies of Louis XIV. These industrious Swiss artisans were wel comed in the Palatinate as co-workers in the reconstruction of the ruined towns and villages. The reason for Jonas Huber's emigration from Oberkulen to the Palatinate, there

* The ancestor of ex-President Herbert Hoover. Herbert's father, Jesse Clark Hoover, a blacksmith, married Hulda Randall Minthorn, a Canadian by birth from Norwich, Ontario.

fore, was economic; it was not because of persecution, as is so often represented. The religious persecutions took place at an earlier date.[43]

Jacob Hoover and sons Abraham, David, Benjamin, and Daniel (Mennonites), who trace their ancestry to Jonas Huber, came from Pennsylvania in 1791 to settle in front of Rainham, where they purchased 2500 acres of land.[44] Later settlers before 1816 were Benjamin Stewart; Shank, a Mennonite preacher; Jacob Fite and Michael Sprangle, both Germans; and Peter Culver. Fisherville became the center of the German settlement, the settlers being mostly Lutherans.

Haldimand County, Walpole Township

Peter Klinger Smith, known as "White Peter," was probably the township's first white settler. Born in 1770 in New York State, he was carried off to Montreal district by the Indians, who adopted him. As a young man he made his way to Nanticoke (Winding Stream), locating first on the site of the Stone Quarry; later he moved to Lot 6, Concession 1, Nanticoke side road. He was twice married to Indian women. His first wife being drunken and quarrelsome, he left her; his second was from Montreal and a fine woman. In 1791, when the Hoovers had settled at Selkirk, he visited them and one of them recognized him as a long lost son of the Klinger family of New York State. Peter was persuaded to pay the Klingers a visit. This he did, but, although they were happy to welcome him, they refused to accept Molly, his Indian wife. For this reason he returned to Walpole Township. He and Molly were buried in the Nanticoke cemetery.

As it was most natural that settlers would follow the Lake Erie shoreline, the second settler to locate on Long Point Bay was John Troyer, a German who came from Somerset County, Pennsylvania, in 1789. John, a man of some means, belonged to a family which in the assessment list of Somerset County in 1783 owned 520 acres, John himself being assessed for 150 acres. A younger brother, Christian, probably preceded John in coming to Canada, as the former, in 1809, in petitioning for leave to locate on 200 acres in Vaughan Township, York County, said that he had returned twelve times to Pennsylvania and had been responsible for bringing some thirty-five people to Upper Canada, among them his older brother John.

John came to his location and bought out a squatter named Asa Holmes who had come from Detroit. In 1795, when he applied for his patent, he claimed that the Americans had taken all he had. From what has been stated above, we know he as well as his brother did own property in Somerset County. As John Troyer was a Dunkard he was exempt from military service but had to pay a yearly fine to the government. The Troyers were friends of the Ryerses and together they built grist mills.

John Troyer, frequently known as "Dr." Troyer, was a man of parts, since he built a vessel of thirty tons, could discover water by a willow twig, and act as a medical practitioner.[45]

Norfolk County

Norfolk County's first white man was William Smith, whose father, Abraham Smith, a German Amish, came from England and settled in New Jersey. In 1785 he came to Fort Erie by way of New Brunswick, where he stayed until 1793, when he located in Young's Creek Valley. E. A. Owen asserts: ". . . From the first settlement down to the present time, men and women through whose veins coursed the blood of some Dutch or German family have played an important part in making the county what it is." [46]

Welland County, Bertie Township

In the 1780s or later, the Tuffords, Culps, Konkles, Berridngers, Buchners, Corwins, Marletts, Clouses, Zimmermans, Adairs, Hares, Overholts, Sultzes, Houses, and Hawns settled the northern part below the mountain.

Commencing in 1788–1789 along Mud Creek and the "Twenty" were the Books, Teeters, Linderberrys, Freeses, Zimmermans, Dawdys, Hitchcocks, Bartrams, Dennises, Johnsons, and Cohoes from New York and New Jersey. In 1799 the Albrights and several of the Moyers were followed from 1800 to 1812 by the Grobbs, Hipples, Hunsbergers, Wismers, and other Germans from Bucks County. The Cohoes were the first to build a grist mill on the Jordan in 1790.

The founder of Beamsville, John Beam, located at the mouth of Thirty Mile Creek in 1790. He was a farmer in Sussex County, New Jersey, who had lost his property during the Revolution. Originally a Mennonite, he became a Baptist and made a gift of the present site of the Baptist Church, burying ground, and school at Beamsville. He is also noted for being the first to grow peaches in the Niagara Peninsula.

Quakers in the Niagara District

Two townships in the Niagara District, Bertie and Pelham, were settled by Quakers (Plain Folk). Dorland states: "Most of those who came overland to the Niagara District appear to have followed a pretty well defined route. Those from New Jersey and Pennsylvania went by way of Reading, thence across the Susquehanna River at Northumberland. From here they struck out in a north-westerly direction, through the great Genesee Tract, eventually finding their way to Buffalo Creek and Fort Erie, whence a ferry conveyed them to Canadian territory at Black Rock. The first Friends are credited with coming to the Niagara District as early as 1783. By 1792 quite a number of families had settled at Black Creek in Bertie Township and at Short Hills in Pelham."[47] Quoting from the *Journal of Joseph Moore*, he mentions some of the twenty-five or thirty families who settled there: Charles Wilson, Asa Schooley, William Lundy, Benjamin Paulin, John Taylor, Thomas Rice, Joshua Gillam, Joseph Havens, Obadiah Dennis, Abraham Webster, John Cutler, John Hill, Benjamin Hill, Jeremiah Moore, Abraham Laing, Benjamin Canby, Joseph Marsh, Adam Burwell, Daniel Pound, James Crawford, Enoch Serigley, Samuel Taylor, and Ezekiel Dennis.[48]

Kirby relates that "it was in 1791 that Prince Edward, the father of Her Majesty, Queen Victoria, visited the town of Niagara and Niagara Falls.

"One incident of his visit I will relate. During the privations of the 'Hungry Year' (1787–1788), the over-careful commissariat officers, who were under general orders to issue rations out of the military stores to the people, had in some cases charged in their books the price of the provisions given to certain settlers and now were demanding payment for the same. A number of these settlers, headed by David Schulter [Schultz?], waited on the Prince and stated their grievance to him in plain Low Dutch. The Prince heard them with sympathy, and calling in the commissariat officers ordered them to cancel every charge they had in their books against any of the settlers. 'My father,' exclaimed he, 'is not a merchant to deal in bread and ask payment for food granted for relief of his loyal subjects.' " [49]

Summing up this period, several things can be pointed out: into the Niagara District came two types of settlers— ex-soldiers and pacifist Plain Folk. Among the ex-soldiers are to be found a large number of persons of German or Huguenot background, most of them from New York State. Close on the heels of these ex-members of Butler's Rangers came the Plain Folk—those who were English in most cases being Quakers, and those who were German belonging to the Lutheran, Reformed, Mennonite, or Dunkard faiths.

The first group were penniless, having lost all to the Revolutionists; the second group in many cases brought money, household supplies, and farm animals with them, and bought land from the first group. A few of Butler's Rangers had been farmers in New York State, whereas all of the Plain Folk had had experience in selecting the best land and cutting trees, and were familiar with pioneer farming conditions. They followed the black walnut trail, viz. they sought the land on which grew the black walnut—the limestone soil.

It was customary for the Plain Folk to settle in communities. For instance, some twenty-five families of Quakers settled in Pelham Township to establish the first organized group of Friends in Canada. Eight families of Mennonites—John, Dilman, Jacob, and Stoffel Kulp, Franklin Albright and Frederick Hahn, Jacob Kulp Jr., and Conrade Tufford— came in 1786 from Bucks County, Pennsylvania, to settle near the Twenty. Any list of names of these early settlers will give a preponderance of either German or French extraction.

Furthermore, information about Upper Canada must have been quite widespread, else these people as soon as they found themselves in difficulties over the Revolutionary War would not have headed towards Niagara. Life at the forts must have bordered on the splendid, judging from the articles sold.

As stated before, the prevalence of grist and saw mills suggests that either these settlers were born optimists building for an anticipated population, or that there were far more settlers—squatters—dotted throughout the district than the census takers had any knowledge of. The latter reason would appear the more plausible.

Canniff reports that in 1783: "Besides the squatters around the military posts at Carleton Island, Oswego, and Niagara, there were a few inhabitants at Detroit and Sandwich, of French origin, where a settlement had sprung up in 1750." [50]

Eastern Ontario Settlements

The following appears in the 16th Report of the Ontario Archives (1920):

"It is important to note the different races that enter into the warp and woof of Ontario citizenship. Contrary to general opinion, the American immigrants who came to Upper Canada at the close of the Revolutionary War were not, as a whole or even mostly, of British stock, bringing with them and glorying in British traditions and as has been long supposed, founding time-honored British institutions in the forest clearings of Canada. This fact does not by any means detract from the genuineness of their professions of loyalty to the Crown, which were well tested and beyond doubt, while on the other hand it helps to explain the under-current of British policy on their behalf.

"The Loyalists traced their origin back to various European countries. The families, for example, which were spread over the district skirting the Bay of Quinté were mostly of Dutch or German origin, inheriting social and political opinions from the peasantry and burghers of the Netherlands and it is believed from the middle class of Saxony; the point of view of Von Tromp and Luther, rather than that of Blake or Cranmer.

"From the Mohawk Valley came the German Palatinates who did not forget Britain's hospitality in the days when persecution had rendered them destitute.

"There was a strong infusion of disbanded Hessian troops, cradled in autocracy, and handed over to the Hanoverian George by the landgrave of Hesse at so much per soldier. Their fealty while they fought was to their own ruler, their service to their foreign paymaster, who later became their liege lord.

"There was also a strong sprinkling of French Huguenots who had suffered for conscience' sake in their fatherland and had found refuge in New England after a recuperating sojourn in Great Britain and Ireland.

"The English element were chiefly descendants of Puritans more or less touched by Cromwellian republicanism.

"The Scottish Highlanders (Roman Catholic) who settled in Glengarry were comparatively few in number. They were mostly from the Mohawk Valley and had fought in one or other of Sir John Johnson's corps.

"This out of a total of 10,000 souls—men, women, and children—constituted what is known of the first Loyalist settlement of Upper Canada..." [51]

The first settlements in Eastern Upper Canada had something of a mass character and took place because of the tense situation in New York following the cessation of hostilities on September 20, 1783. During the years preceding this date many British sympathizers had taken refuge in New York, amongst them a Michael Grass,* who, during the French war, had been a prisoner for two or three years at Fort Frontenac. At the beginning of the American Revolution he was settled on a farm about thirty miles from New York. Having been an army man his assistance was sought by the Colonists, but when he refused to aid them, he and his family were forced to leave their home and take refuge in New York under British protection.

The British Governor was at a loss to place many of the refugees until one day, recollecting that Michael Grass had been a prisoner at Fort Frontenac, he asked him whether that part of the world was habitable. Upon receiving a reply in the affirmative, he was asked to lead a group of loyalists to Quebec and eventually Frontenac (Kingston). The result was that at least two companies, one under Captain Grass and another under Captain Van Alstine, together with other refugees in five vessels, set out for Quebec, where they re-

* Champlain Series (pp. 73–74): "Michael Grass came from Germany to America in 1752 and settled in Tryon County where he was a saddler and farmer. In 1777 he went to New York where he was made a lieutenant. Before the evacuation he was appointed captain of one of the Loyalist's companies going to Canada and was employed in settling about 900 persons at Cataraqui."
This account does not rule out the possibility of his having been a soldier in the French war. He would hardly have been given a lieutenancy in New York in 1777 had he had no experience in soldiering, nor would he have been put in charge of settling 900 persons if he had not had experience in handling people.

mained for the winter. In the following spring they proceeded up the St. Lawrence to Frontenac, where they pitched their tents and awaited allocation to promised lands.

Upon being given first choice, Captain Grass selected Kingston township (a continuing French settlement founded by Major Ross); Sir John Johnson, Ernestown; Colonel Rogers, Fredericksburgh; Captain Van Alstine, Adolphustown; and Colonel McDonnell, Marysburgh.[52]

James Croil, writing in 1861 and claiming that his information was obtained directly from the early settlers themselves, states: "There is no doubt that the disbanded soldiers of Sir John Johnson's regiment were the first settlers on the St. Lawrence between Cornwall and the west boundary of Matilda, and that they were located in the first, second, and third concessions. Jessop's corps,* belonging to the same battalion, were settled in Edwardsburgh and Augusta, while the second battalion went to the Bay of Quinté. These troops were not regular soldiers of the line, but volunteers, who had espoused the royal cause at the commencement of the Revolution. Johnson's regiment was 800 strong, and was called the Royal Regiment of New York. It was composed chiefly of Germans, with a few Scotch; the former mostly of the Lutheran, the latter of the Presbyterian faith. They were all natives of the old Johnson settlement on the Mohawk River, not far from Albany. At the close of the war, this regiment was stationed at the Île aux Noix, a fortified frontier post at the northern extremity of Lake Champlain. . . . Here they passed a whole year. . . . Late in 1783, the soldiers were joined by their wives and little ones."[53]

The disbanded soldiers and their families went in open boats through Lake Champlain, down the Richelieu to Sorel, thence to Montreal and on to Cornwall by way of the St. Lawrence. At Cornwall the rank and file drew their location of land from slips of paper in a hat and took up land on June 20, 1784, in the County of Dundas.

Each master of a family was given one hundred acres, and fifty acres for each member in his family. Fifty acres went to each single man, two hundred to each non-commissioned officer, and to every private in the army one hundred acres,

* Major Edward Jessop (1736–1816) was born at Stamford, Conn. In 1781 he organized and commanded the Loyal Rangers. Jessop, whose name was mentioned in the New York Confiscation Act in 1799, settled on the site of Prescott, Ontario. Jessop had Huguenot ancestry.

with fifty acres to each member of his family. In addition, each Loyalist field officer received 1000 acres, each chaplain 700, and each staff officer, subaltern or warrant officer 500 acres. In 1786 each settler was given an additional 200 acres if he had proven himself thrifty.

Cronmiller is of the opinion that the Lutheran settlers who landed in the County of Dundas on June 20, 1784, were the children of the German Palatinates who labored at Livingston Manor under General Hunter from 1710 to 1713. The list included such names as Garlough, Shell, Merkley, Becker, and Dillabough. These names are repeated often in the Lutheran Church Registers of Dundas County.[54]

Some forty Hessians settled in Maryburgh.[55] These soldiers had been brought from the German principality of Hesse-Hamburg on the Rhine to America under General Baron de Reidesel. They were equipped with bored rifles similar to the Kentucky rifles used by the Colonists. At Quebec they joined the British army and accompanied it to Ticonderoga and Saratoga, and when they were taken prisoners they were sent to Virginia. Released on parole they were given the choice of either returning to Germany or remaining in America, which meant leaving for Canada.

The majority of these soldiers were Lutherans and among them was one, Conrad Bongard, who brought with him a German Bible. Although they had fought against the Colonists, these Hessians were never considered as Loyalists. For this reason and because they spoke no English, their lot in Eastern Ontario for some time was not a happy one. They received land gratis, but as Canniff remarks, "When the title deed was given, a sum of £5 was demanded, being the amount of expense incurred at the time of their enrolment into the service." [56] They were to have three years' provisions, but for some reason received only two years'.

Smith's Bay was named after Charles Smith, whose father, Henry Smith, was its first settler and a German.

"It must be borne in mind," notes Herrington, "that Adolphustown was recognized as the most important center of civilization in Upper Canada at the time." [57] Major Van Alstine was the "first justice of the peace in the county to receive his commission; and in due course a similar honor was conferred upon Thomas Dorland, Nicholas Hagerman, Peter Ruttan, Michael Sloat, and Alexander Fisher." [58] Of these, Van Alstine * was of "Dutch descent and declared it in his build, complexion, and speech. . . . He was the leader of the first company of Loyalists who landed in Adolphustown and might properly be denominated the pioneers." [59]

Philip Dorland, who declined to take the oath of office as a member of the Legislative Assembly, was a Quaker. A brother, Thomas Dorland, originally a Quaker in Dutchess County, New York, had joined the Loyalist group. The Barkers and the Niles came to Canada because they too would not participate in the revolution.[60] Thus in 1784 there was a large Quaker settlement in Adolphustown.

The Ruttans, according to Canniff, were descendants of the Huguenots who emigrated to America in 1734 and settled at New Rochelle.[61] Henry Ruttan is the first founder of the Rotan or Ruttan family in America of whom we have any historical record.[62] He was the son of Jean Baptiste Ruttan, pastor of the Reform Church of Rochelle, who publicly disputed the dogmas of the Christian faith with an ecclesiastic of the Roman Catholic Church in 1693 at Sully's house in Nantes. Emigrating to New Rochelle in 1734, Jean and his brother Peter entered the army. They came to Adolphustown in 1783 or 1784. In 1788 Jean (or John) Ruttan married Margaret Street, by whom he had seven children. Henry, their third child, was born in 1792.

Two German Lutheran congregations were organized in 1783—one at Bath, and the other at Ernestown. The old Church Register of the Ebenezer Lutheran Church in Ernestown, which seems to have been the mother church, records 169 baptisms by the Reverend John G. Weigant from 1791 to 1807. Canniff, referring to the settlement of the second corps of Sir John Johnson at Ernestown, writes: "The next settlers, continuing westward, were Jacob Miller, Frederick Baker, Weigant (Lutheran clergyman), John Mabee, Joseph Huff, a wagon maker, Adam Peat, a tailor. . . ." [63] Another Lutheran congregation was organized in 1784 near Morrisburg and a church built at Riverside in 1788. This proved to be the first Protestant church built in Upper Canada.

* Although historians make little mention of immigrants of Holland Dutch origin, from time to time names which are evidently Dutch (such as those preceded by 'Van') do appear. This is quite understandable, since New York State had a large Dutch population. Thus it is quite probable that Van Alstine is representative of a number of immigrants of a similar background.

The Moravians, true to their belief in education, attempted to do some missionary work among the Mohawk Indians in the vicinity of Adolphustown across the bay from Prince Edward County. In 1748, a Moravian Church, presided over by Rev. Abraham Bininger, had been established in New York. His son, John, came to Canada in 1791 and moved to Mohawk Village from Adolphustown in the following year. Canniff quotes from letters which John Bininger wrote to his father from time to time.[64] From these it appears that there were a number of Moravian Loyalists who had settled along the Bay of Quinté. He mentions particularly Mr. John Carscollian and wife. Because the Moravians were pacifists, these settlers could not have been connected with regiments; probably they came from the Mohawk Valley. However, it must be noted that here was another group of Plain Folk who had settled in Eastern Ontario above the Bay of Quinté before 1790.

While an instructor to the Mohawks, John Bininger was in touch with David Zeisberger of the Moravians at La Tranche River. However, by 1797 the Mohawks did not appreciate the advantages of a school in their midst. Both the instructor and the school seem to have been financially supported by the Society for the Propagation of the Gospel in Foreign Parts until about 1802, when the school was closed.

A possible explanation for the disappearance of the Moravian settlement on the Bay of Quinté may be found in two factors: the zeal with which the Methodist Church was promoted, and the friendliness between the Methodists and Moravians. It should be remembered that John Wesley was said to have been converted by the Moravians; also, that the two societies were based on the Pietist belief. Apparently the Methodist Church absorbed the Moravians.

Dorland informs us that Quakers came from New York State to the Bay of Quinté with the original group of pioneers.[65] Occasionally a Quaker took an active part in the revolution, as for example Captain Allen, second in command under Captain Van Alstine, and Captain Thomas Dorland, of the same company. For doing so, both of these men were dropped from membership in the Society of Friends.

Canniff states: "Among the early settlers of the Bay [of Quinté] were a goodly number of the Society of Friends. Some of them were natives of Pennsylvania; but the majority were from the Nine Partners, Dutchess County, New York, where had existed an extensive community of the followers of Fox. The first meeting-house built by the Quakers in Canada was in Adolphustown upon the south shore of Hay Bay towards the close of last century." [66] Around 1790, Canniff goes on to say, two Quaker preachers of some note—David Sand and Elijah Hick—visited Canada, but it was not until 1819 that the first Canadian preacher, James Knox, appeared on the scene.[67]

Thus, by 1784 "the whole littoral of the River St. Lawrence, from Lake St. Francis to Lake Ontario, the shore of Lake Ontario as far as and including the Bay of Quinté, the neighborhood of the town of Niagara, then called Newark, and part of the shores of the Detroit River, were colonized by about 10,000 United Empire Loyalists who, assisted by government aid, took possession of land which had been laid out for their reception." [68]

Detroit Area

Between 1763 and 1774 the western portion of Upper Canada formed a part of the closed Indian territory into which settlers might now enter. Imperial legislation incorporated it in the old province of Quebec.

Detroit was probably as important a trading post as Niagara. Relations with the Indians were active both on the west—the Michigan side, and the south—the Ohio. Established about 1700 by the French, Detroit remained entirely French until 1760, when it was taken over by the English and an English population introduced. In 1778 a new fort was built which played an active part in the Revolutionary War.

From 1783 to 1796 the British and Americans were both established in the Detroit area. Britain retained control of Detroit and Fort Niagara because of the necessity to keep the good-will of the Indians. This good-will had already been jeopardized when they were not treated as allies after the signing of the treaty of 1783.

Because of its proximity to Upper Canada it was logical that settlers should use Detroit as a means of entry. Strangely enough, those who first came were white prisoners of the Indians brought for ransom. Many of those who arrived in this fashion were from Kentucky or west of the Alleghanies. Let us now consider some of the pioneers of South Essex and learn how that part of Upper Canada was settled during the Squatter Period.

Leonhard Kratz was born near Frankfort-am-Main in Germany in 1756.[69] Evidently he joined the Hessian soldiers hired by England, and came with them in 1776 to America to fight the Revolutionists. In 1777, as a member of General Burgoyne's army at the battle of Saratoga, he became a prisoner of war and was sent to Virginia, where he remained for two years. When the Hessians surrendered it was stipulated that they take no further part in the war. They were offered free passage across the Atlantic or they could remain and share with the Loyalists in grants of land.

During 1779 and 1780 many settlers left Virginia to take up free land in Kentucky. Among these were Leonhard Kratz who had elected to stay in America, and two families named Munger and Toofelmeyer. They located some twenty-five miles south of Cincinnati. In the spring of 1780 their district was raided by a force of British and Indians. The latter got out of hand and took all the whites as prisoners. Leonhard and his wife Mary Munger were separated, but after great privations on the part of each were reunited when ransomed at Detroit by General Coombs, the American commander. The price of their freedom was paid in blankets.

In the spring of 1781 the Kratzes settled on Hog Island, now Belle Isle. This island and Grosse Isle opposite Amherstburg were made available for refugees. To show the uncertainty of the state of affairs, one can point out that Kratz went from Hog Island to Michigan because of the Indians, then back to Grosse Isle. From there he went to the township of Gosfield in Canada only to find that the land had not been purchased from the Indians. Returning to Grosse Isle, he remained there until the land was purchased in 1792, after which he was able to settle at Gosfield again and become a British citizen. The name Kratz was eventually changed to Scratch by a schoolmaster with the name of McMurray.

The Wigle family in Canada had John Wendel Weigeli as an ancestor in Germany.[70] Born in 1753, he came to America as an indentured servant, sworn to work seven years for his passage. In Little York, Pennsylvania, he worked as a weaver and in 1776 married Julianna Romerin. Evidently a pacifist, he found himself in an uncomfortable atmosphere at the outbreak of hostilities. Consequently he set out for Canada with a number of others and stopped over at Detroit. They travelled by pack horse and drove their cattle before them. At Detroit they met Leonhard Kratz and the group travelled on to Michigan, then Grosse Isle, and finally settled at Gosfield in 1792. Here a family of eleven children was born to them. Here, too, the family name was changed to Wigle to suit the aforementioned schoolmaster.

Philip Fox (Fuchs) came to Maryland in 1772 from Baden County, Germany. Later he moved to Pennsylvania, but after hearing of free land in Canada he proceded to Detroit, where he met Leonhard Kratz and other Germans. At first he stayed at Grosse Isle as the others had done, but in 1791 he moved to an area six miles below Windsor in the neighborhood of Petite Côte. Three years later he settled permanently at Gosfield.

Jacob Iler, together with his wife Elizabeth Snyder and her father, John Snyder, came from Pennsylvania about 1790 to settle at Grosse Isle. From there they moved in 1808 to a place near the lake now known as Colchester (Lot 37). At that time, trouble was brewing between the United States and Great Britain, and moving was forbidden. He was taken to Detroit to be tried for violating the law in attempting to move to his new purchase, but was acquitted. A man by the name of Chittenden encouraged him to make another attempt, promising him assistance. In the dead of night, provided with sleighs by Chittenden, the Ilers moved all their goods and chattels across the river without detection and, once over, were safe from molestation.

A treaty with the Indians dated May 22, 1784, had secured for the settlers a legitimate title to their lands. The earliest settlers appear to have settled at Delaware. James R. Brown of Edinburgh, who published his *Views of Canada and the Colonists* in 1844 and who claimed to have received his information directly from some of the original settlers, states: "Shortly after the landing of the U.E. Loyalists in the Niagara District, a party of them left Ancaster for the west, with tobacco, whisky, calico, knives, and trinkets for the Indian trade. Striking La Tranche about the present site of Woodstock, they took canoes and followed the river down past the forks, and camped near the present village of Delaware, making it the headquarters of the traffic with the Indians. The location pleased them and they sent back word to their friends in Ancaster, some of whom speedily joined them and the foundation of the settlement was made." [71]

The Thames River Valley provided a natural means of communication between the Detroit area and Niagara for those who could not afford to travel by boat on Lake Erie. Fur-traders and Indians were doubtless familiar with this overland route, and we have the names of two families which came in by way of Niagara and who worked their way over to the Thames Valley. They were the Dolsens and the Fields, both from Wyoming, Pennsylvania. Having lost their farms and possessions through their unwillingness to join the Revolutionists, they later fought with Butler's Rangers.

George Field with his sons Daniel, Gilbert, and Nathan came to Niagara in 1778 from Northumberland, Pennsylvania, having been threatened with imprisonment because of their loyalty. Two of the sons, Daniel and Nathan, joined Butler's Rangers in 1778. The father died in 1787, and the mother and Gilbert were given land in 1791 in Ancaster Township, while Nathan took up land on the Thames. His brother Daniel went on to Detroit but later was given land in Raleigh.

Isaac Dolsen Sr., also originating in Northumberland County, Pennsylvania, was a man of property who fled to Niagara in 1778 with eighteen other Loyalists. His signature appears in a petition in 1783 to Colonel Butler asking for the right to sell their produce to others than the garrison, and also for leases. When this request was refused, Dolsen Sr. evidently became dissatisfied, since we find him in Detroit in 1784 and settled on a farm at Petite Côte next to that of Daniel Field.

Isaac Dolsen had seven sons: Isaac, Daniel, Gilbert, Matthew, Peter, Jacob, and John. One of these, Matthew, after fighting for a time with Butler's Rangers, came to Detroit in 1781 where he first became a trader, later buying a farm next to his father at Petite Côte. In 1789 he settled at Dover.

Another important pioneer of German or Plain Folk background mentioned by Hamil is Frederick Arnold Sr. [72] He is listed as a Dunkard who came from Germany in 1770 and settled in Redstone, Pennsylvania. Because he remained a Loyalist and his son joined Butler's Rangers, he came to

Detroit in 1784 and located in 1787 a few miles north of the present town of Amherstburg.

Captain William Baker was a Quaker who came to Detroit in 1789 and became a ship-builder. In 1794 he was given a grant of land on which he settled his daughter, who had married a son of Dr. Herman Eberts, a surgeon with the Hessians.

Peter Shonk (Shunk) is mentioned as having worked for Matthew Dolsen. In a survey he is listed as owning Lot 18 on the north side of the river, and his name is spelled Shunk, a common Pennsylvania German name.

Another interesting person who came from Pennsylvania was Sarah Ainse, an Indian.[73] Brought up on the Susquehanna River, she married Andrew Monture, Interpreter for the Crown. Several children were born to them, and in 1756 she and her husband separated. In 1766 we find her a trader on the lakes, first at Michilimackinac, then at Detroit in 1774. In 1787 she moved to the Thames, taking up land in Raleigh Township next to the Dolsens. The fact that the one son, Nicholas, whom she brought to Canada with her, was baptized in the Reformed Church at Albany, and that she herself eventually settled among Pennsylvania Germans, gives her a place in this study.

Nathan Bangs on his missionary visit to the Thames Valley made the house of Sarah Ainse his headquarters and found her a "good, simple-hearted, earnest creature who gave him comfortable lodging and served him his food in his room because she felt unworthy to eat with him. When he left, she gave him a dollar." [74]

Her son, Nicholas Monture, became a member of the Northwest Company and made a fortune in furs, spending his last days as lord of the seigneury of La Pointe du Lac in Lower Canada.

According to Surveyor McNiff, in the fall of 1790 there were twenty-eight log houses below the site of Chatham together with properties to the west and north in the names of Surphlet, Charon, Merry, Peck, Field, Newkirk, Williams, McCormick, Dolsen, Holmes, Meldrum, Park, and Sarah Ainse.

By 1790 the following soldiers had applied for land and provisions: Peter Shonk (Shunk), Jacob Quant (Quantz, Hessian?), John Wright, Thomas Parsons, Nathan Lewis, John Goose, William Hooper, John Embury, Hezekiah Wil-

Williamsburgh Lutheran Church;
first Protestant church in Eastern Upper Canada—built in 1788

Hunsberger Photos, St. Jacobs, Ontario

Pioneer Tower, Waterloo County

cox, Josiah Wilcox, Hugh Holmes, Gaspar Brown, John Hazard, Jacob Hill, and John Gordon. A number of these names have a German connotation.

Essex County

The background for the settlement of Essex County is to be found in the Detroit area. The following facts are taken from a manuscript by Quaife on Detroit History, 1783–1796:

"The Moravian missionaries came from Ohio in 1782 and settled upon land on the Clinton [then called Huron] River a short distance above the present city of Mount Clemens. There were six of the Moravian teachers and they brought with them all of the Christian Indians [Delawares and others] that they could collect and persuade to come. The greater part of the peaceful or Christian Indians had been murdered by the Americans at Gnadenhütten in 1781 and the survivors went into winter quarters on the banks of the Clinton in the fall of 1782. . . . Within a short time they had built 24 log houses besides stables, outhouses, and smaller buildings. . . . The land on which the village was built was claimed by the Chippewa Indians and was by them leased to the Moravians until the end of the war." [75]

Here they remained until 1786 when they sold their buildings at the request of the Chippewas to John Askin and Major William Ancrum for $400 and departed from Michigan— some to Ohio, and others to Canada.

Duperon Baby got a farm two leagues wide by five leagues in depth—some 57,600 acres, and others in like proportion. After the peace of 1783 it appeared necessary to establish a settlement at what is now known as Colchester for Detroit settlers who wished to retain British citizenship. It was called the "New Settlement" and soon land speculators stepped in, particularly one Jacob Sheiffelin. The deed of the latter was cancelled by the commander-in-chief, later with the approval of the Canadian authorities.

Others interested in real estate in the Detroit area were also prominent figures in Upper Canada history: Thomas Smith, surveyor; John Kinzie, the founder of Chicago and first white inhabitant of that place; Herman Eberts, a physician; John Askin Sr.; Philip Fry and Patrick McNiff, land surveyors. John Askin Sr. associated himself in large real estate deals with his half-breed Indian son, John Jr., Isaac

Todd (an Irish capitalist), and James McGill, founder of McGill University, Montreal.

These land transactions became so notorious that Brant complained in one of his letters that there was a swarm of land jobbers at Detroit buying land from the Lake Indians, continually giving them rum and not really doing any business with them. Apparently the earliest settlers at Detroit were the first to deal in these land events.

J. V. Campbell in his article on "Moravians in Michigan" gives an interesting outline of conditions in and around Detroit at the time of the Revolution which shows how well advanced they were, contrary to our usual conception. He writes: "In 1734 the Governor-General Beauharnois made a series of land grants. . . . Within the town of Detroit were many skilled artisans of various kinds, prominent among whom were workers in metal, including black and white smiths of all kinds, cutters, lock-makers, gold and silver workers, and the like. The Indian markets were good for all sorts of trinkets and implements. They were also excellent carpenters and masons.

"It has often been overlooked by most persons that the buildings of the early period were often not only well—but handsomely—built of the best material. In describing houses conveyed by deeds in the town of Detroit, they are sometimes described as built piece over piece, which may have been in the ordinary style of log houses, but which in the better days were timber or blockhouses of smooth finish. These were usually either of oak or cedar, the latter of which was brought from a distance. The Huron Church at Sandwich was built of very large timbers of white cedar, which never decayed. The very ancient French houses near Detroit of the better class are very generally of cedar. But there was a sawmill in the pine region near Lake Huron on St. Clair River at a very early day. Dates are not preserved, but the pinery was well known before 1742 and the mill and the lumber are mentioned in a public report of the resources of the post in 1749. During the Pontiac war, one of the first massacres was of Sir Robt. Daves and some companions who had gone thither.

"Quarries were also worked before 1749, and probably very much earlier at M—— and Stoney Island. In 1763 there were several lime kilns within the present limits of Detroit, and not only stone foundations but stone buildings existed in the settlement. During the siege of Detroit one stone building which must have been quite old was demolished for the sake of the stone to be used for other purposes.

"As Detroit was the only place where there were any land grants (except a small settlement at the Sault de Ste Marie in the latter days of French Dominion), most of our information concerning the doings of the French aside from hunting and trading is derived from that point.

"Agriculture was carried on profitably and supplies were exported quite early from that settlement, consisting chiefly of corn and wheat and possibly beans and peas. Cattle, horses, and swine were raised in considerable numbers, but salt was so expensive that very little if any meat was salted for sale. Salt springs were known near Lake St. Clair and on the River Rouge, and some salt was boiled in both plants—but not probably such as would have been available for packing.

"Farming was superficial and not thorough—although gardening and fruit raising appear to have been more cared for. The land required little manuring, and raised good crops for many years in succession with no special care. Apples and pears were good and abundant. Peaches also were in 1796 spoken of by Mr. Wild as of great excellence. Little mention is made of the smaller fruits, but cherries and currants were undoubtedly raised in many of the homesteads.

"There were several water-mills and numerous wind-mills all along the river near Detroit, most of which were grist mills. The lack of roads made the streams serve as common highways and these mills were very accessible."[76]

The two following accounts of Alexander McKee, an Indian agent, give an interesting glimpse of the transactions carried on by the British with the Indians, and show that they tried to be fair to both colonists and Indians.[77]

The Crown for Sundry Expenses incurred in several Journies into the Indian Country to promote His Majesty's Interests from 1778 to 1780 To Alexander McKee

Dr.

1778	Paid for four Horses died and lost upon service in the enterprise to Post Vincent with Gov. Hamilton and in returning	137	0	0

79

1779 July 3	Paid for a beef to a Delaware Indian killed by the warriors preparing to join Capt. Bird to go against the enemy	16	0	0
Oct. 4	Paid for a beef killed for use of our prisrs released out of the hands of the enemy and for sundry Indian chiefs	26	10	0
	Paid for 2 horses purchased to conduct prisrs taken by the Indians to Detroit	36	8	0
	Paid for 2 hogs for use of Indians	9	10	0
Nov. 20	Mr. Dawsons Acct for Com. delivered by him to the Indian Chiefs on their way to Sandusky	6	0	0
	Delivered 18000 Wampum at —— Meeting and to sundry chiefs at 30/	54	0	0
	To Messrs. —— Acct paid sundry Accts and drafts drawn by me for expenses made in the Indian Country & this place from June 1778 to the 29th	549	17	4
		835	5	4

The Crown for Sundry Expenses incurred in the Indian Country By Alexander McKee Deputy Agent for Indian Affairs

Dr.

1780				
April 15th	Paid for a Beef killed by a Party of Hurons on their way to join Captain Birds Expedition 4 Dollars	16	0	0
25th	Paid for One Beef 45 Dollars One Hog 10 Dollars delivered at a Council of the principal warriors of the several Nations	22	0	0

May 15th	Paid for 2 Hogs 20 Dollars & one Beef delivered to the Indians for war feasts	28	0	0
June 2nd	4 Horses purchased and used upon the Expedition with Captain Bird afterwards delivered to Capt. Hare on going to join him 170 Dollars	68	0	0
July 7th	Paid for Fat Cow kill'd by the Hurons who accompanied C. Hare	24	0	0
Septemb. 11th	Paid for One Beef 40 Dollars upon my arrival ware assembled	16	0	0
Oct. 10	Sundry Expenses to redeem Prisoners furnishing them with necessaries & sending them to Detroit from time to time	163	0	0
22nd	Paid for sundry Cornfields used by the Indians drove by the Enimy	93	4	0
Nov. 20th	Paid for a Horse delivered to a Shawanese Chief going to head a Party toward the Enimy to make discoveries	26	0	0
Dec. 29th	Paid for the hire of two Horses sent with a Party employed to gain Intelligence & watch the Enimy said then to be on the way	16	0	0
1781 January 26th	Purchased 1600 Strings of Corn a 3 strings per Dollar	213	6	8
		675	10	8

Note: The American Dollar did not come into use until 1792. The Dollar mentioned is probably the Spanish Dollar.

The Essex County Atlas states that most of Colchester's pioneers came from Pennsylvania, though some were of

European birth. Among them were the Cornwall and Huffman families. John Cornwall, a member of Butler's Rangers, came in 1779 from Connecticut along with other families. The Snyders located as early as 1784. Thomas Ferrers and his son Joseph came to the Township from Maryland in 1794. Phil Fox migrated to America in 1772, thence to Canada in 1791. Henry Toffelmire petitioned for 200 acres of land in 1790. Other families of German background were: the Brunners, Henry Racus, George Lichelstil, Fred Weizback, Henry Huffman, George Dice, and John Lipps.

Mention should be made of Simon Girty, a colorful and, until recently, a much-maligned character. Born in 1741 near Harrisburg, his father and stepfather were both killed by Indians when he was in his teens. He was taken captive by the Indians and brought up to be their leader. Like Butler he carried on border warfare, sometimes being able to restrain the Indians from massacring prisoners, sometimes not. Robert M. Fuller, who has made a careful study of the charges against Girty, stated in a radio broadcast: "Americans and Canadians should perform some distinctive act of devotion and try to correct the false impressions about the man who was, in my opinion, a warrior leader, a patriot loyalist, and a friend of the down-trodden savage." [78]

Simon Girty was with the Indian Department during the War of 1812–1814 at the age of seventy or so. He died in 1818 on his farm two miles south of Amherstburg—a farm given to him by the Indians, and the title confirmed by the government.

Matthew Dolsen, a member of Butler's Rangers, settled in Detroit about 1780. John Askin reports that a delegation of Quakers who visited Detroit in 1793 in the capacity of peace commissioners lodged with Dolsen and seemed to have conceived a real friendship for him. In like manner he cultivated friendly relations with the Moravians and enjoyed their confidence over a period of years. It seems probable that Dolsen later moved to the Thames River region, where he obtained a grant of land from the local land board in the spring of 1792.[79]

Kent County

It is difficult to determine the date of the arrival and the nationality of the first settlers of Kent County. Writing to the Surveyor-General in May, 1791, McNiff (the surveyor) states that in the Township surveyed on the River he found twenty-eight families settled on the front, some with con siderable improvements. This would indicate that the settlers had been there some little time, and it does not seem un reasonable to put 1775 or 1780 as the date of the first settle ment.[80]

"On the plan of the River Thames compiled from the sur veys of McNiff and Jones (the latter having made surveys last of the locality covered by McNiff's surveys), the locations of twenty-seven houses are shown between the present loca tion of Chatham and the mouth of the River, nineteen of these being on the south side, and eight on the north." [81]

THE SIMCOE REGIME (1792–1796)

The significance of the statement, "What William Penn was to Pennsylvania, John Graves Simcoe was to Ontario,' can be easily explained. When William Penn acquired his property in the Colonies he knew that its wealth could only be discovered and developed by farmers. From his actual knowledge of the Palatinate farmers, he felt that they were the right people to take over his lands. History has proved how right he was.

During the Revolutionary War, Simcoe, as head of the Queen's Rangers, was quartered one winter at Philadelphia Here he had a close-up view of the eastern counties of Penn sylvania as farmed by the Palatinate and Swiss Germans, and he realized what excellent farmers they were. Hence when he was appointed Lieutenant-Governor of Upper Canada he found a similar situation there as Penn did when he took over his lands in Pennsylvania. Simcoe realized that there might be money in fur-trading but that no great wealth could ever be achieved for the country in that way alone. He felt that wealth must come out of the soil and, remembering the farms he had seen in Eastern Pennsylvania, he determined to invite those who farmed them to come to Canada.

But the Palatinate and Swiss Germans were not the only Plain Folk valued. There were the English Quakers. Dor land, obtaining his information from Simcoe's letters, writes: "Simcoe, Governor of Upper Canada, evidently thought that Quakers were desirable colonists, and with a watchful eye to the welfare of his beloved province, was anxious to divert as many as possible into Upper Canada. . . . He discovered that they were a conservative, punctilious folk who were inclined to caution lest they should in any way depart from the good order of their Society or from their strict, political neutrality which they had always sought to maintain. Simcoe sought to convince them that they would enjoy the full benefit and protection of the recently established government of Upper Canada, especially 'exemption from militia duties which they have always met with under the British government.' The suggestion was even made—and this probably had Simcoe's approval if it did not actually come from him —that the Quakers might be granted the special favor of being exempted from taxation and from the taking of oaths as an inducement to settle in Upper Canada. This, however, was rejected by Dundas as unfair to the other colonists and impracticable, though he paid a very warm tribute to the desirability of the Quakers as pioneers in a new colony." [82]

Simcoe, according to Canniff, "held the opinion that there remained in the States a large number of Loyalists, and conceived the idea of affording them an inducement to again come under British rule, as they were British in heart." [83] Consequently, on February 7, 1792, Simcoe issued a proclamation which, amongst other things, offered 200 acres to each immigrant who could show that he was in a position to cultivate and improve land. The grantee was obliged to clear five acres of land, to build a house, and to open a road across the front of his land, a quarter of a mile in length.

Simcoe advertised this offer in the Philadelphia papers presumably to attract the attention of the German farmers in Eastern Pennsylvania.* Since during the preceding dozen years a number of German farmers had settled in the Niagara district, this offer was appreciated at its full value. However, when Simcoe was recalled in 1796 these terms were abrogated; nevertheless many immigrants had already taken advantage of them.

Although Simcoe remained only above five years in Canada, much credit must be given him for his vision and understanding of the needs of the province. Although an

* A Statute was passed in 1790 (30 George III C.27) in which Americans were invited to "come . . . with their families . . . to any of the Territories belonging to His Majesty in North America for the purpose of residing and settling there."

ardent "Britisher," he had a fine appreciation of what other races could contribute.

When Simcoe arrived in Canada in 1791, Lord Dorchester wished him to select Kingston as its capital. However, Simcoe chose Fort George, which he renamed Newark. Here he carried on his administration until 1796, when Fort Niagara across the river was to be given to the United States. Believing that the capital of the province was too near the guns of Fort Niagara, he moved to Toronto, renaming it York.

As he thought the capital should be farther west, he selected a site on the river La Tranche (Thames) and named it London. Going farther on, he chose a place, Chatham, to be the location of a navy yard. In order to connect these two centers with the eastern part of the province, he caused the Dundas Road to be cut through the forests. Lord Dorchester, however, opposed London as the capital of the province and selected York.

One of Simcoe's first acts in his parliament of July 16, 1792, was to give English names to the four districts into which Lord Dorchester in 1788 had divided the province: Lunenburg became the Eastern (lower Canada to Gananoque River); Mecklenburg, the Midland (Gananoque River to River Trent); Nassau, the Home (River Trent to Long Point); and Hesse, the Western (Long Point to Detroit). Nineteen counties were formed: Glengarry, Stormont, Dundas, Grenville, Leeds, Frontenac, Ontario, Addington, Lennox, Prince Edward, Hastings, Northumberland, Durham, York, Lincoln, Norfolk, Suffolk, Essex, and Kent.

As under the French tenure the settler held his land by certificate of occupation, land boards were established to issue the location tickets. These were composed of a Crown-appointed official through the Governor of Quebec, seven or eight principal settlers, and the district commanding officer. These land boards lasted until May 1, 1791. Upon Simcoe's arrival, he decided that three members of the Executive Council would deal with all petitions for land. In order to facilitate land settlement David William Smith was appointed Surveyor-General in September, 1792, and associated companies were set up to settle the township and act as middlemen. In 1797 "An Act for Securing Titles to Land in this Province" was passed as the culmination of Simcoe's efforts to bring some sort of order into land holding in Upper Canada.

Norfolk County

Settlers of Plain Folk origin who played important parts in developing Norfolk County and surrounding districts during Simcoe's regime were quite numerous. To name a few: L. H. Tasker in his studies of the settlers at Long Point states: "The Dedrick family were of German descent and early settlers in Pennsylvania. Lucas Dedrick was one of the Pennsylvania Loyalists but remained in his native State until 1793, when he came directly to Long Point.

"He built a log cabin on the high land overlooking the marsh, about a mile and a half west of the present village of Port Rowan. He was no doubt the second white settler in Walshingham, his predecessor being the noted Dr. 'Witch' Troyer (not a Loyalist) who had settled on the lake front in Eastern Walshingham. It was not till 1797 after the township had been regularly surveyed that Mr. Dedrick received the patent for the land on which he had settled." [84] In other words, he was a squatter or at best had a ticket of location for four years.

Peter Teeple, whose family were Hollanders living in New Jersey, married Lydia Mabee, whose father was a Hollander and mother a French woman. They came to Turkey Point in 1792 with Frederick Mabee—a cousin of Peter Secord and a prominent Quaker. They erected the first log cabin at Turkey Point.

The Ryerson family have also played an important role in the history of Ontario. Here is the story of their migration as told in a letter from George J. Ryerse to Egerton Ryerson, written June 23, 1861: "My father was a captain in the New Jersey Volunteers during the American Revolution; and at its close in 1783, having his property confiscated in the United States, he went to New Brunswick and drew lands according to his rank as captain. . . . But he determined to remove to Canada. In the spring of 1794 he went back to his family at Long Island and then started for Canada on foot and arrived at Niagara where his old friend, General Simcoe, greeted him and promised him 3000 acres of land as a captain, 1200 as a settler, and his wife and each of her sons 1200 acres and each of his daughters 600 acres. He brought his family, arriving at Long Point July 1, 1795."[85]

Another letter gives the following information: "It was in 1794 my father came here. . . . At that time there were but eight families residing within thirty miles of this place except Indians; no roads; the nearest mill 100 miles distant by water [at Niagara Falls]. My father purchased corn off the Indians at the Grand River, thirty miles from home, and carried it home on his shoulders. Afterwards he bought a yoke of oxen from the Indians, and on a toboggan sled put his son, and with his axe and compass made his way through the woods and streams to his beloved home. Two years afterwards he built a saw mill and afterwards a grist mill. These very nearly proved his ruin, not understanding the business, and very little to sustain them; they were badly built, and proved a bother to him, but still a great help to the settlement for a long time. . . ."[86]

Mrs. Amelia Harris, only daughter of Colonel Samuel Ryerse, carries on the story: "After one day's rest at Ryerse Creek, they re-embarked and went fourteen miles further up the bay, to the house of a German settler, John Troyer, who had been there two years and had a garden well stocked with vegetables."[87]

"A few days after, a party of pedestrians arrived, on the lookout for land, and they at once set to work and put up the wished-for log-house or houses, for there were two attached, which gave them a parlor, two bedrooms, and a kitchen and a garret. . . . They bought a cow from Mr. Troyer and collected their goods.

"Long Point now boasted four inhabitants in twenty miles all settled on the lake shore. Their nearest neighbor, Peter Walker, at the mouth of Patterson's Creek [now Port Dover] was three miles distant. But from this time, 1795, for several years to come, there was a constant influx of settlers."[88]

"The Ryerson family was of Dutch Huguenot origin. . . . The Canadian branch of the family is descended from Martin Reyerzoon, who with his brother, Adrian, migrated to New Amsterdam [New York] in 1647. The name was abbreviated to Ryertz, later Ryerse, and about 1700 anglicized to Ryerson."[89]

It is not often remembered that as well as white people from Pennsylvania there were transplants of Indians in Ontario. It is further true that this migration was fostered by Moravians and supervised by them from 1792 to 1903, an almost unparalleled piece of missionary effort.

Although this enterprise was largely related to the Indians who settled near Moraviantown in South Western Ontario, it had the blessing of Governor Simcoe. Doubtless, too, the influence of the Moravian missionaries had an important effect on the neighboring communities. In one particular alone, they are noteworthy: they were the means of introducing the first hive of bees into Canada.

To understand their very noble and self-sacrificing efforts we must go back to our studies of the Moravians, both in Europe and in Pennsylvania. It will be recalled that the Moravians were Pietists, pacifists, and the first religious body imbued with an active Christian missionary spirit. As this desire to make converts in Pennsylvania was directed towards the Indians and was quite successful, a number of converts from several tribes became known as Moravian Indians.

However, these Moravian Indians were a problem for the government of the State because they had no permanent abode. Wherever they settled, white settlers coveted their land. This situation prevailed until Brother David Zeisberger * moved the Indians, after a few years' location at Friedenshütten and Friedenstat, into Ohio, where they were welcomed by the Delaware Indians. Here from 1771 on, Zeisberger and Heckewelder guided their Indians in building four villages—Schoenbrun, New-Schoenbrun, Lichtenau, and Gnadenhütten. For several years these communities flourished under Zeisberger, Sensemann, and Yung.

Dr. Arthur D. Graeff recounts: "In 1781, the Delawares living in the Christian villages were prevailed upon by the British agents and some Indians to abandon their homes and move nearer the British fort at Detroit. Most of the Delawares found new homes in present-day Wyandotte County,

---

* David Zeisberger was born in Moravia in 1721. When seventeen he came to Georgia with his parents. He gave himself to missionary work among thirteen tribes of Indians and spent sixty years establishing the first Protestant missionary enterprise west of the Alleghanies.

one hundred miles west of Muskingum. Zeisberger referred to this village as *Captivetown*." [90]

One year later, in 1782, nearly one hundred Christian Indians returned to Gnadenhütten to harvest some crops. While there some two hundred Virginia and Pennsylvania militiamen fell upon these defenseless Indians and murdered them in cold blood.

Although the war officially ended in 1783, there was constant warfare in and around Captivetown. It must not be forgotten that the Moravian missionaries were opposed to bearing arms, consequently they had much difficulty in controlling their Indians and in keeping them from participating in the struggle. Zeisberger met this problem by moving his people westward until they came under the protection of the British at Detroit.

In June, 1791, the Delawares were visited by some Monsey Indians who had come up from Pennsylvania and settled near St. Thomas. They said that good land was available along the La Tranche River (Thames River). Zeisberger being acquainted with the Monsey Indians, as the Moravians had done missionary work among them, was not anxious to have the Delawares unite with them.

On the advice of Matthew Elliott, an Irish immigrant who had been a fur-trader, and Colonel Alexander McKee, Commandant of Fort Detroit for the British, Zeisberger waited until January, 1792, when the Canada Act was in force. Urged on by dissensions with other Indians over nonresistance, he sent Indian Samuel and five "young brethren" to investigate the possibility of getting satisfactory land in February, 1792. They reported favorably, and in April they set out for their Canaan.

The following excerpts from Zeisberger's Diary tell the story of the settlement in his own words:

"Tues. Feb. 28. . . . Then the Indian, Samuel, with five young Indian brethren, set out for Retrenche [La Tranche] River, to learn about the country, to examine the land, to seek out and determine a place where we can settle next spring, after they had first been prepared and instructed by us.

"Thurs. March 1. The brothers came back again, who had gone away to get information. After passing Detroit, they had met a man, Hasle by name, who came by land from Montreal, and told them he had spoken with the governor in our behalf, who would come here when the lake opened, when our business about the land would be put in order; that he had letters for Col. McKee, wherein everything was set forth, and which would soon be told us. . . . We heard also that the Monseys there, many of whom were here visiting last summer, had already made ready for us, a place a day's journey from their town. These Monseys came from Niagara some years ago and remained there.

"This matter was arranged on March 16 that they were to move in Easter holidays. They dealt with Sir Johnson. They left Detroit April 15 but encountered rough weather even when they came to the mouth of the Retrenche River. There they went ashore and stayed over night near a vacant house.

"Tuesday, April 17. We staged to Sally Hand [a colony composed of English, German, and French settlers].

"April 25, 1792. . . . The inhabitants whom we addressed were everywhere very friendly and serviceable, and if we wished to buy bread or any provision, they would take no pay, for they thought it mean to take pay from us. . . . The man who lives there was a well-read man in history.

"May 11, 1792. We sowed garden seeds. All the brethren were industrious and busy in clearing land.

"May 15–16. The brethren cleared, each for himself, built huts in town, and all had enough to do.

"May 19. They planted our three fields, which they had cleared for us, two acres perhaps.

"May 21. . . . Certainly this year more than a hundred acres will be cleared and planted.

"Dec. 31. . . . It was a perfect wilderness and the building site thickly grown with heavy timber, and now already [Dec. 31, 1792] nearly thirty good houses stand here, among them many dressed block houses. More than a hundred acres of land have been cleared and planted . . . there are in all 151 inhabitants here.

"Feb. 16, 1793. He [the Governor Simcoe] arrived in the forenoon . . . but stayed only a couple of hours, and then continued his journey to Detroit. He looked at everything, went into our meeting-house and the school-house, where we had fires in two chimneys; we entertained them at breakfast as well as we could and it tasted right good to them. He had nothing to remark against our settling here, but said that our town stood on Chippewa land, for on the north side of the river the land has not been bought farther than eight or ten miles from here; on the other hand, upon the south side, the river is the boundary up above the Monsey town, and thus towards Niagara....

"Feb. 25. In the afternoon came back his excellency the Governor from Detroit with his suite and passed the night with us.... About the land whereon we live, he had informed himself more carefully, and found that it was included in the purchase, that the government was well disposed towards us, and would give us land in consideration of our having suffered great losses, but he thought that a township fronting on the river took away from them too much land, since they intended to settle it thickly, and we could not make use of so much land. . . . The conclusion was that if the land should be surveyed and laid out, and it should be found necessary, one of us should be called to Niagara, and there we should be well considered and advised. We asked further if a deed for the land would be given and when he said yes, we said at once we should like to have it made out in the name of the Society's trustees in England, which he not only approved, having nothing to say against it, but was pleased with.

"April 7. After the surveyor had first examined the country, he laid out today the third township below us, and found that the boundaries of it would fall a mile and a half from here. As this is too near, it will be lessened, and some lots in the upper part be made over to us (a lot is three hundred acres) so that we shall have room. It is found that we have the best and greatest piece of land, in one body, upon the river.

"May 28. We planted vegetables, tobacco.

"June 27. The Indian Peter's hive of bees which he brought here from Pettquotting, swarmed today for the second time. There are none here in the bush in the whole neighborhood.

"June 28.... The Six Quakers, to whose ears the need and want of our Indians had come, and who had themselves spoken with our Indians, took compassion on them, and gave Dolsen an order for a hundred dollars' worth of provisions for them at their cost, a part of which they brought thence with them....

"July 9.... Many of our Indians went to the settlement to

work; those who were at home cleared land for sowing turnips and hay.

"Aug. 2. Br. Sensemann arrived early, well, and safe from Niagara. He got there at just the right time, for the Council was sitting, to which he submitted our plans and reasons, whereupon it was concluded and established that we should have land six miles in length, fronting on the river on both sides; how many miles inland could not be determined since the boundary line of the purchased land has not yet been run on the north side.

"Dec. 31, 1793. There live here now 159 Indian souls. . . .

"Jan. 9, 1794. The surveyor with his people surveyed today our township below as far as the town. He has orders from the Governor to give us six lots from the adjacent township, and to bid those *who have already settled on them* [italics mine] to go away, so that thus our town comes quite in the middle of the township. A township has twenty-five lots, but ours thirty-two, since it lies on both sides of the river, namely, sixteen on each side (9600 acres).

"Jan. 14. Since yesterday the surveyor finished surveying the upper part of our township, Br. Sensemann went with some Indian brethren up there, and blazed the line on both sides of the river. There are thus above us, up the river, nine lots, and below us eight, and the lot whereon our town stands, he has also given, so that in all eighteen lots on each side of the river are ours, that is, thirty-six. On the north side of the river we are probably the last on the purchased land.

"Jan. 18. We gave notice to a German, who settled in the autumn not far from us, and had built a house, that his lot stood in our township, and that he must go to some other place; this the surveyor bade us do.

"March. Towards evening his excellency, Gov. Simcoe, arrived with a suite of officers and soldiers, and with eight Mohawks, from Niagara by water, and remained over night. . . . He was glad to see so many houses built since he was here, also that our Indians had cleared much land, and he praised their industry and labor.

"Aug. 4. White people went through here for Detroit with cattle, who have begun a settlement forty or fifty miles up this river, thirty families strong, having lately come over from Europe. The land will be very thickly settled and grows perceptibly. We should have gained nothing then if we had

First Canadian Methodist Church, Adolphustown—built in 1792

Principal surrenders of Indian lands in Upper Canada prior to 1840

Department of Archives

PRINCIPAL SURRENDERS OF INDIAN LANDS IN UPPER CANADA PRIOR TO 1840

Scale 35 Miles to one inch

L. Christie, 1921

settled as far again up the river. At present there are living in Fairfield 165 Indian souls.

"Oct. 27. . . . Our neighbor, Kessler, ploughed for some Indians, and sowed wheat for them, as Bill Henry and his sons had worked in the harvest above us this summer.

"Dec. 24. . . . Two Germans went through here early for Long Point.

"Jan. 13, 1795. The brethren got timber together over the snow for a bridge over a deep ravine and brook at the east end of the town." [91]

Zeisberger and Sensemann laid out the village of Schoenfeld, or Old Fairfield as it is now known, in similar fashion to the Ohio village of Schoenbrunn—in a rectangular form with separate plots for all Indian families, for the chapel, for the schoolhouse, and other buildings. Since in the village there was an average of more than 150 persons, the land covered by the buildings would probably be as large as the original Schoenbrunn.

Heriot, in his *Travels through the Canadas*, gives a visitor's opinion: "A village of Moravians, under the guidance of four missionaries from the United Brethren, is placed twenty miles above the intended site of Chatham. They established themselves in that situation with a design of converting the Indians, and their conduct is peaceable and inoffensive; their chief occupation is in cultivating their corn-fields and in making maple sugar. A chapel is erected in the village. Not far from hence is a spring of petroleum." [92]

The Fairfield settlement, modelled after the Ohio village of Schoenbrunn, flourished between the years 1792 and 1798, when Zeisberger's diary suddenly ends. In that year he returned to Ohio, and although seventy-seven years of age built a new town, Goshen, near the ruins of Gnadenhütten. Here he labored another ten years, dying in 1808, the same year as Joseph Brant.

Following Zeisberger's death, the work among the Indians was directed by Michael Yung. "In the Moravian Archives in Bethlehem are the diaries of all the missionaries of that faith from Zeisberger's time to 1904." [93] In that year the Delawares in Canada were committed to the Methodists. A study of these diaries might give valuable information about early conditions in the Fairfield district.

The Old Fairfield settlement was destroyed in 1813 by General William Henry Harrison on the pretext that some of the Indians living there had participated in some massacres and that this was a preventive measure he was taking.

When peace was restored, the scattered Indians were brought back and the village of New Fairfield was built on the south bank of the Thames. Here in 1817 the present Moravian Church was built. Once each year a memorial service is held in the Moravian Church at New Fairfield, when the Delawares, Nanticokes, Chippewas, Wyandotts, and Monseys gather to pay honor to the Moravians who founded their community. In the area of the original Fairfield a park has been laid out to commemorate its founding in 1792.

The missionary efforts of the Moravians among the Indians in and about Fairfield are often thought remarkable, more for their persistence than for their success. They were battling with situations over which they could have little or no control. The Chippewa tribe were round about them, always trying to entice the Delawares into unlawful acts. The missionaries found it next to impossible to keep their Indians away from liquor, as the French traders did everything they could to encourage them. Another problem was the pacifism of the Moravians. This doctrine, which they tried to teach their Indians, created many problems during the War of 1812–1815, as it had during the Revolution.

In spite of all these difficulties, the Indians raised much corn and maple sugar, both of which found a ready market in Detroit. The missionaries also taught them to manufacture such articles as baskets, dishes, and brooms.

A careful study of the Moravian missionary efforts at Fairfield would indicate that their contributions to Upper Canada were much greater than have been thought. Their influence, although at all times primarily for the Indians, extended far beyond the confines of their Indian settlement and was most beneficial in several ways for the white settlers. They provided the only Protestant preachers in southwestern Upper Canada, hence they held religious services, baptizing, marrying, and burying the dead. They also encouraged agriculture, and as early as 1798 they had 300 acres of land under cultivation with an annual sale of corn to the Northwest Company of 2000 bushels, about one-third of the total yield of that section. Their canoes, baskets, and mats found ready sale, and nowhere in Canada was better maple sugar to be had. They raised large numbers of cattle for sale, as they preferred venison for their own use. The white people, who usually desired to live as far as possible from Indian settlements, were very eager to take up land and establish their homes in the vicinity of this mission station.[94]

Frederick Coyne Hamil amplifies the foregoing when he writes: "Nearly every Sunday white people came from the lower settlements to attend services in the chapel at Fairfield. Soon the missionaries were called upon to extend their work outside the town. Sensemann was much occupied with marrying couples and baptizing children. Sometimes this was done at Fairfield, but more often in the settlements. Often he went down to preach, or to visit the sick, and rarely left without baptizing several children. He was so beloved that in 1796 the inhabitants of the river wanted to choose him as their representative to the assembly, but this he declined. For years, beginning in February, 1796, Michael Yung preached every alternate Sunday at the house of Francis Cornwall, seven miles away. Like Sensemann, he frequently baptized children and conducted funerals. The demands on the missionaries were so great that they had to decline a request from a new settlement far up the river, that one of them should preach there." [95]

Hence we see the great contribution these Moravian missionaries made to the white portion of the nation living in that area.

County of York

This part of Upper Canada was well known in the early days of the fur-trade because the Humber River was a favorite waterway to Georgian Bay, then to Fort Michilimackinac. The Humber River afforded access to the ancient country of the Hurons in what is now the county of Simcoe. This route was frequently referred to by French writers as the "Pass by Toronto." A fort, built near the mouth of the Humber River, was called Fort Rouillé, but the name "Toronto" won out in the end.

Here from time to time a village flourished and was a point of call for troops going west to Detroit and for voyageurs. However, it did not gain significance until May, 1793, when Simcoe entered the harbor. Changing the name to York, after the King's son, Frederick (who was Duke of York), he took up his residence there that summer and brought most of his troops from Newark, making use of them in building operations and in making roads.

Yonge Street was laid out by Augustus Jones who began his survey in February, 1794, and continued it until it reached Lake Simcoe, some thirty miles north. The street took its name from Sir George Yonge, then Secretary of War in the Imperial Cabinet, while Lake Simcoe was named after the Governor's father.

Jones may have laid out Yonge Street but it was Berczy * who, with the settlers that he had brought from Hamburg to Canada by way of the Pulteney settlement, in New York State, hewed out a road from York to the southern part of Markham. The Berczy settlers have always loomed large in the history of York County, partly because they came as a group and partly because they were about the first to locate in that county of which we have any historical records.

William Berczy had attempted to settle them in the Genesee Valley, New York State, but they found that there they could only be leaseholders, hence when they learned that they could get 200 acres of land free in Upper Canada they decided to migrate. From a manuscript written by Fredric Sommerfield (in possession of Abraham Sommerfeldt, Ringwood) and quoted in *Historical Sketch of Markham Township, 1793–1950*, we learn that from the Genesee Valley they proceeded to Niagara where there was a long delay, after which they came on to Markham about Christmas, 1794.[96]

Another manuscript written by the Reverend Edward Ritter gives further facts which suggest that the sixty-four families might have had some additional ones with them. Two families are named Stephens, one Temple, and one Hall. It is known that Philip Eckhardt had long been established in Pennsylvania but came with them. Also, Melchior Quantz, a veteran soldier of a Hessian Regiment, had been in Markham two years before Berczy arrived, had taken Lot 2 in the 2nd Concession and had built the walls of a log-house but not roofed it. Quantz was outside the Township when he met

* Born in Saxony in 1748, William Berczy went to England in 1790 and undertook to act as agent in bringing out German settlers for an English association owning land in the Genesee Valley, New York.

96

the Berczy immigrants and returned to the Township along with the company and roofed his house, where some of the settlers found shelter. The total number must have been well over three hundred, although there is some question about this. An archives report states: "As a matter of fact twenty-one of these 'families' were unmarried men, some being boys not over sixteen years of age, and all too poor to have servants. Furthermore, of the fifty-four families remaining, four had joined the main body at Niagara and hence had not been brought into the country, while two heads of families had died. Of the forty-seven families remaining, twelve had left the province. Hence, only thirty-three families really were his settlers...." [97]

The center of this settlement was a village known as German Mills, which was located on Lot 4 in the 3rd Concession, Markham Township. Here were erected a saw mill, a flour mill, a distillery, a brewery, a malt house, a blacksmith shop, and cooper shop. It should be noted that the settlement of German Mills was not on the Rouge River, as is so often stated, but on a branch of the Don. The settlement declined because there was not enough water to create power for the projected industries. After several sales, the mills were finally closed.

It has been suggested that Simcoe hoped to make use of these immigrants to build his parliament buildings, since they were mostly artisans, but that when they arrived he was not able to go ahead with his building and so they were taken to Markham and settled on the banks of the Don River. Berczy was promised some 64,000 acres and the inducements held out to his settlers were quite generous, but he could not sell his land, and the settlers, little interested in farming, refused to stay. Only a few, such as Eckhardt, Sommerfeldt, Pingle, Stiver, Luneau, Quantz, and Helmke, remained. Philip Eckhardt built a flour and a saw mill in York County on Lot 4 in the 3rd Concession of Markham, later to be known as German Mills. Eckhardt's house, which he built in 1794 just north of Unionville, is still inhabited and is probably the oldest house in the county.

Berczy, because of financial losses and disappointments, left and settled in Montreal, later going to New York where he died in 1813. His son, William Bent Berczy, was later given a grant of 2400 acres and became the postmaster of Toronto from 1840 to 1852. Berczy painted the portrait of Joseph Brant in the National Gallery.

The land in York County had been purchased by Sir John Johnson from the Mississaugas in 1787, at a council held at Carrying Place. It comprised 250,880 acres, being bounded by the Etobicoke River on the west and the extreme point of Ashbridge's Bay on the east, and consisted of a rectangular block running twenty-eight miles northward, roughly to the northern boundary of King and Whitchurch Townships.[98]

Settlement in York County began shortly after the arrival of Simcoe at York in February, 1793. There must have been communication between Upper Canada and New York State, as Nicholas Miller, a mill-wright, was brought by the government from New York State to build some mills in York County. He erected in 1793 the first flour mill—an old-fashioned coffee mill on a very small scale.[99] In 1794, settling on Lot 33, Concession 1, of Markham, he built a small grist mill; also the first flour mill on the Humber.

John Lyons, coming to Canada from New York State in 1794, after living for a while in York, settled on Lot 32, Concession 1, in Markham. He later brought Lot 36, Concession 1, Vaughan, on which he built a saw mill. Asa Johnson and his wife Hannah had a daughter, Sally, who married Nicholas Miller. Evidently the Johnsons came to Canada about the same time as Miller, since he is credited with a patent for land in 1796, the first year patents were issued.

The question might well be asked if there was any connection between Nicholas Miller and John Lyons, who were reputedly asked by Simcoe to come from New York State to Canada, and the first families on Yonge Street such as the Cobers, Fishers, and Cummers. The answer may be found by referring to the Tax Lists of Somerset County, Pennsylvania. Nicholas Miller is listed as a taxpayer in 1776; in 1779 as owner of 400 acres, and in 1783 as non-resident.[100] John Lowan (Lines or Lyons) is listed in 1776. Mary Cober, a daughter of Nicholas Cober, who emigrated to Canada, married Henry Lyons as her first husband, hence persons by that name lived in that locality.[101] Jacob Fisher was taxed in 1772 for 200 acres, 12 cleared, and in 1783 for 300 acres. In 1784 there were 10 whites in his family. Peter Cober (father of Nicholas Cober) owned 200 acres in 1783. Other families which came shortly after were the Troyers, Keffers, and Wingers, who settled in Vaughan Township, all from Somerset County.

It would look as if Nicholas Miller and John Lyons came to New York State and from there in some way got in touch with Simcoe. Through them the Fisher family doubtless heard of the quality of the land in York County and emigrated at once. Here again we have people migrating who possessed good land in Pennsylvania. The Cummers * lived in Lancaster County, Pennsylvania, and yet intermarried with the Somerset County family.

Jacob Fisher petitioned the Governor on November 20, 1798, as follows: "That your Petitioner came into this Province in 1795 bringing with him his sons and sons-in-law with their families and his own, amounting to 22 persons. That your Petitioner served as a corporal in the 1st Btn. of the 68th Regt. in the French war of 1756–1763—that in 1763 the Indians took part of the Company's Book—whereby your Petitioner lost his pay for upwards of two years—which he never received—that your Petitioner has received 400 acres of land in this Province, yet as his family is large, he humbly hopes your Honor would be pleased to indulge him with such additional grant under the New Regulations as to your Honor may seem meet, and your Petitioner in duty bound shall ever pray." This request was granted at once "in consideration of the long Services & large family of the Petr. & also of his exemplary exertions as a farmer." [102] He was recommended for 400 additional acres.

Elizabeth, a daughter of Jacob Fisher, who married Jacob Kommer (Cummer), came to Canada in 1796, locating on 300 acres of land at Willowdale. Eva, another daughter of Jacob Fisher, married Nicholas Cober, and they came to Canada in 1796, settling on Lot 34, 1st Concession of Vaughan Town-

---

* Conrad Weiser was a neighbor of the Cummers, as the following translation from an original document found in the *Cummer Family History* will bear witness:

"Mr. Cookson

The bearer hereof Daniel Koomer by name prevailed on me to settle his account before he goes to you because he has no English and is a feared he cannot get an Interpreter to do for him. I believe you will find everything right.

I am
Sir yours,
C. Weiser."

ship between Richmond Hill and Thornhill in March, 1797. On their tombstone is the statement: "Of the first settlers on Yonge Street, they were the fifth family." Doubtless they came with the same party as did the Cummers, because in both cases the records state that they came with the bride's parents. Jacob Fisher's petition states that this group came in 1795.

Some further proof that the first settlers in York County were from New York State, though originally from Pennsylvania, is found in the statement that Isaac Devins, who came with Simcoe, had married Polly Chapman of Genesee, N.Y., and was said to be a brother-in-law of Nicholas Miller.[103]

The Ashbridges were Pennsylvania Quakers who had settled before the war in Philadelphia. After the close of the war, the father being dead, the mother and two sons, John and Jonathan, came to Canada. This was in 1793, and on arriving at York they stayed the night in the old French fort, subsequently making their way to what is now known as Ashbridge's Bay. Being U.E. Loyalists, they drew land from the Crown and settled on Lot 8, Concession 1, east of the Don.[104]

From all accounts, Simcoe probably was in touch with potential Pennsylvania immigrants when he was at Newark, because at that time Fort Niagara on the American side was still under British control. Nicholas Miller was apparently a prime mover in this first group of settlers. Having himself lived in Somerset County, Pennsylvania, he encouraged a migration from that county which continued for the next dozen years.

Mrs. Simcoe makes the following statement which is rather puzzling. She wrote: "Jan. 19, 1794. The weather was so pleasant that we rode to the bottom of the bay, crossed the Don, which is frozen, and rode on the peninsula; returned across the marsh, which is covered with ice, and went as far as the settlements, which are near seven miles from the camp. There appeared some comfortable log-houses, inhabited by Germans and some by Pennsylvanians. . . ." [105]

John R. Robertson in a note suggests that this was the Berczy settlement, but this could not have been so, because these settlers did not arrive until late in 1794. This is another bit of evidence that there were settlers and settlements in existence some time before we have any historical record of them. Mrs. Simcoe speaks of these dwellings as "comfortable," which suggests that they had not been recently built.

Etobicoke Township had Colonel Smith of the Queen's Rangers as owner of a large tract of land. No patents were issued before 1798 and only some six before 1801.

THE FIRST GREAT MIGRATION (1796–1812)

York County

As we have seen, immigration into Upper Canada began first from New York State and New Jersey. Later, Eastern Pennsylvania provided the source. As time went on, general economic conditions in the United States became a greater motivating factor than political considerations. The Whiskey Rebellion in Pennsylvania upset the farmers very much, particularly those west of the Alleghany Mountains. On March 3, 1791, Congress placed a tax of four pence per gallon on all distilled spirits. "This new law," states John C. Cassady in *The Somerset County Outline*, "seemed to affect the interests of the people who were living west of the Alleghany Mountains more than it did the interests of the people of any other part of the United States. Rye was the chief farm crop of this region, but there was only a limited home demand for it. It could not be carried across the mountains on pack horses and sold at a profit, except in the form of whiskey. A pack horse could carry only four bushels of rye to market, but he could take the product of twenty-four bushels in the form of whiskey and bring back a good supply of salt, sugar, and iron articles." [106]

A great number of the early settlers in southwest Pennsylvania, banding together, refused to pay the tax until a large body of militia was sent out by Washington. This state of affairs made economic returns so uncertain that towards the end of the century a migration began towards Canada. As the wonderful limestone soils of the Niagara peninsula had become well known in many parts of Pennsylvania and Maryland, the lure of a new country, coupled with the unsettled state of the country at home, increased the tide of migration.

For some twenty years settlers had located in the Niagara district, in Essex County, and along the shores of Eastern Ontario. But by the time Simcoe left for England in 1796, desirable and accessible land was either becoming expensive or difficult to get, hence incoming settlers started going farther afield for their land. Those who came in by way of Niagara spread along the shores of Lake Erie or by way of Lake Ontario to York. Where settlers located was partly determined by the fact that purchases of land from the Indians had been made by the government.

Probably a different situation obtained in York County and the surrounding districts from that which existed in the Niagara and Bay of Quinté sections. By the time York County was being opened up, speculators had come to see that there was money to be made by getting and holding large tracts of land which would increase in value. Simcoe's successors gave away many thousands of acres to their friends besides setting aside one-seventh of all the Crown lands as Clergy Reserves, amounting to 2,395,687 acres. This meant that those who came into York County had to possess enough means to buy land since there was little available to be secured from the Crown.

As has been pointed out, though Simcoe retired in 1796, during the short time he spent as governor of Upper Canada he did two outstanding things: he opened up the western part of the province by the Dundas Road and by Yonge Street, and he encouraged a great migration of farm settlers, mostly of German stock from the United States. By the time he left, this migration was just getting under way and it spread into two main districts—York County and Waterloo County.

York County received the first settlers, beginning, as we have seen, as early as 1793. The coming of the Berczy settlers in 1794 and the opening up of Yonge Street gave impetus to settlement. Actually, 1796 seems to have been the year when the great exodus into Upper Canada began from the states of New Jersey, New York, and particularly Pennsylvania. The invitations of Simcoe for settlers to take up land in Upper Canada began to be accepted, and word soon got back to the States concerning the quality and quantity of the land available.*

* John Ross Robertson, *The Diary of Mrs. Simcoe* (p. 161): "**Mon.** Apr. 15th, 1793: I dined at the Fort and caught cold by crossing the water this very cold day. In a newspaper from the States was the paragraph: 'His Serene Highness of Upper Canada gives great encouragement to settlers.'"

Of original land owners in the different townships of York County before and including the year 1801, we have the following numbers listed: York, 176; Scarboro, 71; Markham, 34; Vaughan, 79; Whitchurch, 15; King, 27; and Etobicoke, 44.[107] A total of 446 properties were registered, though doubtless there were a considerable number for which registration had either not been asked for or were not completed in 1801. This would show that York had received earlier settlers than is sometimes thought to be the case. As many a settler never bothered to get a deed for his property until he was about to die, the record of settlers is never very accurate.

York County had the distinction of having two migrations directly promoted by the government, neither one proving very satisfactory. The Berczy group described above were Germans who were located in Markham Township. The second group, composed of French refugees from the French Revolution under the direction of Count de Puisaye, consisted of forty individuals, several of them persons of distinction. They left England in 1798 and came first to Kingston, then to York, where they were given land in the townships of Uxbridge and Gwillimbury, a township in the rear of Whitby not yet named, and the ungranted part of Whitchurch—some 5000 acres in all. De Puisaye himself was to have 5000 acres. A residence of seven years was stipulated before they were given their deeds.

A village soon grew up and some land was cleared, but dissatisfaction developed, although the government provided seed wheat and barley as well as rations to the workmen assisting them. Evidently the conditions of life were so foreign to these people that the group soon began to dissolve. De Puisaye himself bought a farm in the Niagara district and moved there. De Chalus began another settlement at the head of Lake Ontario. By October, 1799, there were only twenty persons left at Windham (York County) and five at Niagara. De Puisaye returned to London and only thirteen of the original settlers remained in Upper Canada.[108] Mention has been made of these settlers from France to show that only persons inured to the hardships of pioneer life had any chance of survival in Upper Canada at that time.

There was one other group which made a signal contribution to York County—the Quakers. The leader of this group was Timothy Rogers, who originally lived with his wife and family at Danby, Vermont. Later he moved to Ferrisburgh in the same state, where he utilized a large waterpower source and built a mill. In 1800 he visited Canada and made arrangements with the authorities for forty homesteads of 200 acres each. The following year he located forty families in the neighborhood of what is now the town of Newmarket. A little later (1809) he settled in Pickering where he received a large grant of land. He built the first mill in the township and was the first of a considerable number to settle in this area.[109]

At the same time (1800) that Rogers was arranging for his land, two Friends from Muncey, Pennsylvania, Samuel Lundy and Isaac Phillips, had secured a grant of land for twenty more families in a district adjacent to him.

Quaker settlements developed very shortly in the adjoining townships of East Gwillimbury, Uxbridge, and Pickering—the last two in the present county of Ontario. In 1804 James Starr, a Quaker, removed from Roaring Creek Valley, Pennsylvania, together with his wife Sarah Kinsler, to the Friends' settlement near Newmarket.

Jonathan Heacock, also a Quaker, moved to St. Catharines district before 1800, later, in 1804, purchasing 100 acres of land—Lots 26 and 27, 3rd Concession of King Township.

The ancestors of the Bogart family came to Pennsylvania from Holland. Mary Bogart, widow of Martin Bogart, came to Canada with her son John and his wife Mary Opp Bogart in the fall of 1802 from Muncey, Pennsylvania, and located on Lot 31, 2nd Concession of Whitchurch. "Their home consisted of a log cabin 18 × 20 containing two rooms, one being floored by split basswood logs, the door of the cabin frequently did duty as a sleigh bottom on which to take the family to a Quaker meeting." [110]

Isaac Webb and Ann Clayton emigrated from Bucks County because of their Quaker beliefs and settled in Whitchurch, near Aurora, in 1806.

The Klinck family was one of the earliest to settle in Markham Township. The origin of the family is as follows: James Brown of Somersetshire, England, and Mary Marr of Pennsylvania were married in 1779. About 1800 a number of their children emigrated from Pennsylvania to Canada West. After staying at Niagara-on-the-Lake for a short time, the parents moved to Markham Township, where they obtained their patent in 1801. A daughter, Elizabeth Brown, was born in 1782, and married Calvin Grant of Niagara-on-the-Lake in 1802. Four years later, following the death of Calvin Grant, she married Leonard Klinck (1785–1852). Leonard Klinck was the son of George Klinck of Albany, N.Y. After their marriage, they took up land in Markham Township, where they resided until 1847 when they returned to the United States.

The Reesor family has played an important role in the life of York County. Tradition has it that Peter Risser (Reesor), who was about eighty years of age in 1796, made the trip to York in that year, but he never settled there. His son Christian, however, migrated in 1804, together with his sons and daughters and their families. They drove big Conestoga wagons pulled by four horses which carried each a ton and a half of goods. Cattle, pigs, and chickens were brought along too. Christian settled on Lot 15, 10th Concession, now known as Locust Hill. Peter, son of Christian, came in 1796 and returned in 1804.

In the Reesor family at the present time is a Zurich Bible, printed by Kristoffel Froschover, and a German-Swiss Bible published by the Reformed Church of Switzerland. Froschover began publishing his Bibles circa 1500. A commentary bound with the Bible, *Biblick Namen und Chronick Buch*, is dated 1579. Thomas Reesor, who had the Bible in his possession, was outstanding in giving direction to the Mennonites during the last two wars and in European Relief. He died in 1954.

Peter Reesor, Christian's eldest son, settled on the Little Rouge River next to his father. He was a shrewd business man, as the following story will attest. On his way to Pennsylvania he was approached in York by Frederick Baron De Hoen, an ex-army Hessian officer, who offered him six hundred acres for Peter's horse, saddle, and bridle. Because he failed to name the halter, Peter carried the halter with him back to Lancaster County, Pennsylvania.

Abraham Stouffer, a Mennonite, arrived with the Reesors in 1804 and located in 1805 eight miles north of Cedar Grove, later in the same year moving to land on part of which Stouffville is now located (named after the Stouffers).

There was a migration from Somerset County, Pennsylvania, in 1804. Doubtless these people came with the group that settled in Markham Township, but they themselves went on to Vaughan Township. All of this latter group must have possessed money because most of the land in Vaughan Township belonged to soldiers who were holding it for a price.

In our study of Vaughan Township we find that the Cozens family, consisting of Samuel, Joshua Y., Daniel, and Benjamin, came from the neighborhood of Philadelphia (where they had disposed of their property) and were granted 1200 acres of land in Vaughan Township, some of which was cultivated and some in a state of improvement. This was in 1796. Three years later they were granted 2600 acres more. This last grant was on Concessions 2, 3, and 4 in the neighborhood of Thornhill and Concord. Captain Richard Lippincott was given 3000 acres, mostly in Vaughan.

Nicholas Cober and his wife, Eva Fisher, migrated to the Niagara District in 1796. Here they stayed for a few months, then went on to Vaughan Township where they settled on Lot 34, Concession 1, between Richmond Hill and Thornhill.

Jonathan Baker came with his father, John Baker, to the township in 1801 and settled on Lot 29 in the 3rd Concession. In 1816, Lot 11, Concession 2, was purchased and a bank barn was built several years later. The barn is still in use and the land still in the possession of Baker descendants. This family possesses a Conestoga wagon which brought their goods from Somerset County in 1797.

John Reaman, emigrating from Somerset County in 1804, bought 200 acres of land, Lot 15, Concession 2, in Vaughan Township. In 1817 he bought 200 acres more—Lot 10, Concession 2. This property is still in the Reaman name. John's grandfather, Jacob, originally from the Canton of Aargu, Switzerland, came to Philadelphia in 1753, and his son, Gottlieb, left Berks County for Somerset County in 1768 where he acquired some 800 acres. When he died in 1804, his oldest son, John, sold his share of the property to his brother, George, and came up to Canada.

John Jacob Keffer * was born in Somerset County, Pennsylvania. He found the town of Berlin in 1784 and gave 40½ acres of land near Berlin, Somerset County, to be used for Lutheran and Calvinistic (Reformed) churches and schools. In 1792 he and his brother Michael came up to

---

*Two brothers named Tonnelier escaped from Paris in 1685, went to Germany and changed their name to Küfer (Kieffer, Keefer, Keffer).

Niagara district and from there went on to the Humber River in York County, where they selected Lots 8 to 14, comprising 1400 acres. Returning to Pennsylvania, they remained there until the death of their father in 1796. With their mother and their wives they set out for York County once more. Upon their arrival they found that a claim had been staked for their land and so they had to buy it. This they did for a shilling an acre. A day book belonging to Jacob Keffer states that "on April 22, 1802, I walked around my share of land, $161\frac{1}{2}$ acres for four dollars comes to 646 dollars, makes in pounds namely 2–42. Signed Jacob Keffe." We do know that Jacob Keffer settled in Vaughan Township on Lot 12 in the 3rd Concession in 1806. In 1811 he gave a plot of ground on the 4th Concession of Vaughan near Sherwood to the Lutheran Church. Eight years later a church was built on the property. A Lutheran church is still located there.

Evidently there were some Hessian soldiers who settled in York County. One of these, John Stegmann, was a land surveyor who eventually settled at Pine Grove near Woodbridge. Frederic Baron de Hoen, from whom Peter Reesor acquired 600 acres of land for a horse and a saddle, owned land in Whitchurch and in York Townships. Michael Quantz, an early settler in Markham Township, was also Hessian, as were doubtless other settlers born in Germany, who fought on the side of the English during the Revolutionary War.

Isaac Lundy emigrated from Lycoming County, Pennsylvania, in 1805 and settled on Lot 102, Concession 1, East Gwillimbury Township.

David Willson came from New York State in 1801 and settled at Sharon. At first he was a school teacher and, although brought up by Presbyterian parents, he joined the Friends shortly after his arrival in Canada and remained a member in good standing until the beginning of the War of 1812, when he formed a sect of his own known as "The Children of Peace" or "Davidites." Naturally he was dropped from membership in the Friends' Society. Some thirty families around Sharon following him, they constructed a unique temple at Sharon which is now a museum for the York Pioneer and Historical Society. No metal was used in the construction of this building; wooden pegs were used instead of nails.

Of The Children of Peace, Dorland says that they "must

have stimulated the imaginative and musical life of the community, and added to the gaiety of the nation, even if failing to make a deep impression on its religious life." [111] The society ceased to exist shortly after the death of its founder in 1866.

Waterloo County

Waterloo, the last area to receive settlers from Pennsylvania, is interestingly enough now the only locality in Ontario to retain the ethnic characteristics of its early settlers. Originally known as Block 2 and owned by Richard Beasley, James Wilson, and Jean Baptiste Rousseau, it had as its initial settlers John Bean and George Bechtel who bought land in 1800. Bean possessed 3600 acres on the west bank of the Grand River, known as "Bean's Tract," where we now find the villages of Doon and New Aberdeen, and Bechtel had some 3150 acres adjoining Bean's land to the north.

It is interesting to conjecture reasons for the Pennsylvania Germans settling in Waterloo County, in view of the fact that it was far inland and difficult to reach. Two possible motives can be advanced: the first, an inherent desire, like Ulysses, "to follow knowledge like a sinking star, beyond the utmost bound of human thought"—knowledge to them being new lands; the second motive might have been one of security. To withdraw from society was part of their religion, hence to seclude themselves inland was one way of obtaining security. Rev. A. B. Sherk, in his story of the coming of the earliest settlers, describes the way it came about if not the exact reasons: "In the fall of 1799, Samuel Betzner and Joseph Sherk crossed the Niagara River at Black Rock. . . . J. Sherk and his family found winter quarters in the vacant house of another Pennsylvanian, who had preceded them and taken up land on the Niagara River, a few miles from the International Bridge. S. Betzner pushed on to Ancaster and wintered there. The site of the city of Hamilton was at that time a dismal swamp, covered with heavy timber; Dundas had a small mill and one dwelling; Ancaster had a few houses, and was considered to be on the outermost limits of civilization. These two simple-minded Pennsylvanians came to this new country with their wives and little ones on a venture; apparently they had no definite idea when they would find a suitable place to locate. But the report had gone abroad that there was a fine tract of land about thirty miles beyond Ancaster, in the valley of the Grand River. There was, however, an almost impenetrable wilderness to pass through to reach this land of promise. Early in the spring of 1800, Betzner and Sherk went in search of the far-off country. They found it, were greatly pleased with it, and selected lots for future homes. . . . The two pioneers returned to Ancaster, settled for their lots, and got their papers." [112]

Ezra E. Eby tells their story in this fashion: "In the fall of 1799, Joseph Schörg (Sherk) and Samuel Betzner came from Franklin County, Pennsylvania, to Canada. . . . They arrived safely on the Canadian side of the Niagara River. Schörg spent the winter at or near the Falls, while Betzner came to the neighborhood known as Ancaster, and remained there until spring. Being dissatisfied with these sections as permanent places of location, they pressed onward about thirty miles beyond the then limit of civilization, the particular cause being a desire to discover and locate upon the bank of a fine river of which they had heard as traversing the region. No white settlers had as yet penetrated the depths of these forests, but a few Traders in furs had established themselves in temporary quarters at intervals throughout that part of the wilderness bordering on civilization; and of these, three located temporarily on the banks of the Grand River, within the County of Waterloo. Their names were Dodge, Preston, and Woodward. The last two named left this locality upon the approach of the pioneers, but Dodge remained and became a permanent and prominent landmark of the community. In the years 1799 and 1800 two Englishmen named Ward and Smith were engaged in slashing the way for a road which the government contemplated building from Dundas towards this County. . . . Dundas consisted of a small mill and a smaller store owned by Mr. Hatt. Ancaster had a few small houses and a little mill. Some settlements on the mountain had been made. The Hornings, Hesses, Beasleys, Springers, and others settled there a few years previously. . . ." [113]

There was no settlement between Horning's and Waterloo. George Clemens, a Mennonite, in 1801 drove the first horse-team that ever came through the Beverley Swamp to settle near Speedsville. Originally Clemens' name was Clement of Toft, Lincolnshire, England. James Clement, a Puritan, was forced to leave England and went to Holland, where a son Gerhardt was born in 1680. The latter came to New York in 1709, later settling in Montgomery County, Pennsylvania.

In view of the fact that such a large number of settlers arrived within a year or so of the opening up of this county, one is led to believe that there had been a rather careful study made of the possibilities for settlement there.

The method of migrating followed one of two ways—one the extension of the other. Two men would make the journey, usually on foot or horseback. If they found satisfactory locations, they helped each other put up some kind of log cabin. When the cutting of the logs for these buildings had cleared some of the land of trees, they planted wheat seed in the fall of the year if they happened to have any. Then they returned to bring back their families in the following spring. Perhaps, too, their reports were sufficiently attractive that when they migrated several other families came with them. It must be remembered that few of these settlers were without funds, consequently they were not dependent on the government for their supplies. Not infrequently they brought horses, cows, and some farm equipment in their Conestoga farm wagons. Hospitality was the order of the day. Should a settler and his family arrive without having first put a shelter, they would be kept at a neighbor's until by a "bee" the newcomer would have a cabin erected.

In the original York Registry we find a list of the properties in Waterloo County sold in the year 1800:

1. Mr. Horning bought 1000 acres from R. Beasley, situated on the east bank of the Grand River at Bridgeport, known as Horning's Tract. (Mr. Horning was a prominent merchant at Dundas and probably took the land as payment for Beasley's debts.)
2. John Bean bought 3600 acres.
3. George Bechtel bought 3150 acres—lived adjoining Blair.
4. John Smith bought 4018 acres—probably for debts.
5. Nathaniel Dodge, a squatter, bought 114 acres on the west bank of the Grand River below Blair.
6. Benham Preston—114 acres—sold to Dodge.
7. George Bechtel bought 409 acres.
8. Abraham Bechtel bought 200 acres.
9. Samuel Betzner Jr. bought 200 acres.

10. Samuel Betzner Sr. bought 200 acres.
11. Samuel Betzner Sr. bought 150 acres.
12. Joseph Sherk bought 261 acres opposite Doon.
13. Jacob Bechtel bought 100 acres.
14. Joseph Wismer bought 221 acres.
15. Ben. Rosenberger bought 260 acres.
16. James Wilson (partner of Beasley) bought 200 acres.

In 1801 the following purchased property in the county: Daniel Cornell, Jacob Meyers, Abraham Gingrich, Delman Kinsey, John Bean Jr., Sam Bricker, and Henry Lamb. In the following year George Clemens, Joseph Bechtel, John Bricker, Christian Richert, Rinear Van Sickel, Ben. Cornell, and John Cornell were registered as having bought land.

The development of this settlement almost came to an abrupt end, and in fact did so for a couple of years because Richard Beasley, who had sold the land to these settlers, was in financial difficulties and could not give clear deeds. The Mennonite settlers, however, were unaware of the situation until Sam Bricker, when in York to register the purchase of a farm from George Bechtel in December of 1802, overheard a conversation which led him to believe that there was a mortgage on their farms. He went to Beasley and the latter admitted that there *was* a mortgage. Now debt to a Pennsylvania German was anathema, and when this information was carried to the settlers there was consternation. They were faced with two alternatives—to return to Pennsylvania, or find enough money to cover the mortgage (some $20,000 for 60,000 acres).

Sam Bricker and Joseph Sherk went to Cumberland County, Pennsylvania, to try to obtain financial aid from their relatives. However, Sam's father was too ill to be consulted, and they were almost in despair. Joseph returned to Canada, but Sam went to his wife's people in Lancaster County and succeeded in interesting John Eby, who in turn gained the coöperation of other relatives so that Bricker was able to return with half of the mortgage money. Accompanying him were John and Jacob Erb, brothers of John Bricker's wife, Annie.

The money was loaned and a joint stock company formed under the name of the German Company. Benjamin Eby, the son of old Christian Eby and who contributed $2,500, was appointed secretary-treasurer of the Company. He later was made a bishop of the Mennonite Church and founded Berlin (Kitchener). John Erb built a mill at the junction of the Speed and Grand Rivers and became the founder of the town of Preston. A brother, Abraham, arrived in 1816 with a party of forty-eight relatives, built a second mill, and founded the town of Waterloo.

The first installment of the money was brought into the county on horseback; the second was placed in a keg and fastened to a light wagon, *leicht plaisir weggli*, and after being carefully guarded, reached the county safely. This time the settlers took no chances. Engaging William Dickson (a reputable lawyer of Niagara) to search the title and do the necessary legal work, they managed to obtain full possession of the 60,000 acres on June 29, 1805.

The next step was to have the property surveyed, and for this purpose Augustus Jones was engaged. He divided the 60,000 acres into 128 farms of 440 acres each (two for each share) and the balance was arranged into 32 smaller properties of various sizes. The survey was then sent to Pennsylvania, where the shareholders cast lots for their holdings.

Because of their difficulties in obtaining a clear deed from Beasley, a number of families had taken up grants in Whitchurch Township, York County. The following acquired 200 acres of land each on the 7th, 8th, and 9th Concessions of Whitchurch Township: Jacob Bechtel, William Bechtel, Sam Betzner, Sam Bricker, John Bricker, George Clemens, John Cornell, Benham Preston, Philip Salzberger, and Gilbert Vanderbarrow. The last named was the only one of the group to settle in the township as the others gave up their grants in 1806.

By July 1, 1805, some thirty-five families or single men had settled on land of their own within the County of Waterloo, and by 1808, some 26,000 acres had been taken up in units of 350 acres to 1400 acres. The first pioneers (practically all Mennonites) settled in Woolwich Township. Some of these were: John, Daniel, Joseph, Christian, and Abraham Bowman; John Jr., John Sr., and Jacob Brubacher; Peter, Christian, and Abraham Martin; John and Adam Reist; Samuel and Joseph Weaver; John Moyer; Martin Oberholzer; Christion Stauffer; Peter Sherck; Martin and Christian Shenk; Benjamin, Dan, Abraham, John, Joseph, and Christian Eby;

John and Daniel Erb; Christian Stolzfusz; David Hurst; Christian Kolnig; Joseph Wenger; John Schaeffer and John Gresman.

Dunkards came into Waterloo County with the Mennonites. George Shupe and David Gingrich migrated in 1801 from Lancaster County, Pennsylvania. Abraham Witmer was the first minister and with him were George Shupe, Peter Holm, David Witmer, Niel P. Holm, David Gingrich, Ben Shupe, and Wendell Hallman. Of these, Niel P. Holm was an interesting personality. Born in Denmark in 1774, he became a sailor and at one time sailed on a pirate ship. Escaping to an American port, he finally came to Waterloo County and settled at Hespeler. He married Susannah Cober, the daughter of Nicholas Cober of Vaughan Township.

Lincoln County

"Samuel Meyer (Moyer), born in Montgomery County, Pa., 1767, married Anna Bechtel in 1789 and lived at Blooming Glen. He was a leading promoter of, and actor in, the pilgrimage to Canada in 1786. . . . Two four-horse teams carried his family four hundred miles to the settlement at the 'Twenty,' in Lincoln County, where he at once purchased from William Wiers, a U.E. Loyalist, 200 acres of good land, paying $400 cash for same. There was a rude log cabin in the clearing and four acres of wheat ready for the sickle, and other vegetables growing for the year's need. Near the cabin stood a large oak stump burned out at the top in the shape of a mortar in which the Wiers family cracked their wheat and pounded their hominy. Later this was filled in with earth and used as a hot bed to start early plants for the garden. . . . Samuel Meyer taught for many years the first school in the settlement in a log building." [114]

In 1799 Amos Albright, Abraham Meyer, and Jacob Meyer came up from Hilltown, Pennsylvania, on foot, on a prospecting tour. They were so well pleased with the country that before returning they purchased 1100 acres, some at $2.50 an acre, some at $1.50 an acre. Depositing $40, they returned on foot to bring back their belongings the same autumn. [115]

The Fretz family emigrated from Bucks County, Moses Fretz coming in 1799 and John by horses and wagon in 1800. In 1801 the first Mennonite Church in Canada was established, known as Moyer's Church, with John Fretz the first Mennonite Deacon in Canada.

About this time nineteen families of German background in Pennsylvania migrated and settled at the "Twenty" (Jordan). They were: Culp, Albright, Fretz, Overholt, Hoch (High), Moyer, Wismer, Nash, Kratz, Althouse, Hunsberger, Housser, Grobb, Rittenhouse, Hahn, Hipple, Martin, Swartz, Gehman, and Sievenpipher.

Welland County (formerly a part of Lincoln County)

In 1796 eight townships, lying west and north of Fort Erie, were opened to settlers. Much of this area had been given to Loyalist soldiers as grants, but as many of these were not interested in owning or holding land, they were glad to sell it to these German immigrants who paid for their land in cash. The family names indicate that these settlers were Quaker and Mennonite. To quote Burkholder: "Abraham Neaf obtained a grant of land in 1794 and Benjamin Hersche from Lancaster came in 1795. The Mennonite families spread into Bertie and Humberstone townships along Lake Erie, and Willoughby Township, to the north along the Niagara River. The settlement was also known as 'Black Creek' because of the stream by that name which flows through Bertie and empties into the Niagara. . . . The following are some of the family names of these pioneers: Sailer (Saylor), Morningstar (Morgenstern), Beam, Waggoner, Shoup, Boyer, Barnhart, Flag, Neigh, Rickhart, Werner, Baker, Lapp, Miller, Danner, Whisler, Sherk, Herscherg, Zavitz (Tewits, Sevits, etc.), Storme, Zimmerman, Winger, Bearss, Fretz, Learn, Knisley, Neff, and Weaver."[116]

Dorland gives a list of settlers in this district as early as 1797: Asa Schooley, Joseph and Ann Marsh, Daniel and Patience Pound, John and Mary Herrit, John Cutler, Adam and Sarah Burril (Burwell), Joseph and Ann Stevens, Abraham Webster, Joseph Haven, Obadiah Dennis, William Lundy, Jeremy Moore, John Moore, Thomas Mercer, John Taylor, John Hill, Benjamin Hill.[117]

Willoughby Township

The earliest families who settled in the township were: Warren, Gilmore, Wintermutte, Ashbaugh, Hesky, Riseby,

Gilman, Wilson, Maybee, House, Morningstar, Beam, and Gonder.

Saltfleet Township

In 1786 Levi Lewis, John Pettit, Gershom Carpenter, Augustine Jones, John Biggar, and John Wilson settled here.

Gainsborough Township

In 1782 John Dochstader settled in the south of Welland Township. In the north part of the township the Snyders, Deans, Felkers, Roys, and Rozells (from New York or Pennsylvania) settled at the Jordan River from 1793 to 1794.

Clinton Township

In 1780 William Walker, a Loyalist from Virginia, settled in the township with his six sons and four daughters. Seven years later Francis Albright (Albrecht) came from Pennsylvania and settled on Lots 19 and 20, Concession 1. He brought his wife and one son.

Haldimand County

Other German Mennonite families who came into this district in this period were: Shank (a minister), Swartz, Strickler, Byers, Miller, Hess, Hare, Ball (Bahl), and Althouse.

Elgin County

Thomas Talbot was an Irish gentleman of good birth, station, and prospects who joined a regiment at Quebec in 1790. When Simcoe came to Upper Canada as Lieutenant-Governor, Talbot came with him in the capacity of private secretary. During Simcoe's regime he became enamored of the country, and in 1802 decided to settle in Canada after his retirement from the army.

"In 1803 he was granted a field officer's quota of 5000 acres in the Townships of Dunwich and Alborough, bordering on Lake Erie, and for every family he settled on 50 acres he was entitled to receive 150 acres for himself in lands reserved in the neighborhood for that purpose." [118]

His settlement was very successful, and for thirty-five years he carried on, placing permanently on the land over 30,000 settlers, receiving on their account some 302,330 acres of land.[119] Talbot saw to it that every settler performed his settlement duties before he was given his certificate, which the government exchanged for patent upon application.

"James Fleming, who is said to have accompanied Governor Simcoe, Talbot, and others, in the capacity of boatman, had settled in 1796 on Lot 6 on the river front of Aldboro, not far from the settlement of the Moravian missionaries who came in 1792. Fleming was thus the earliest known white settler within the confines of what is now the county of Elgin. Below, along the River Thames, as we have seen, there were, besides the Moravian mission, other settlers at rare intervals —Carpenter, a sailor, the Dolsens, and others—who had come in before the advent of Governor Simcoe, access from the older settlements about Detroit being comparatively easy and the route for traders and others who passed overland between Detroit and Niagara being usually along the river.

"Between the years 1808 and 1812 a number of families were 'located.' John Barber and James Watson came from Pennsylvania and settled in the north-east of Port Talbot, in Southwold. The Pearces, Storeys, and Pattersons skirted the shores of the lake by boat, from the same state, and landed at Port Talbot in 1809—thirteen souls in all, with looms and wheels for the manufacture of woolen and linen goods, and cattle, driven along the shore. Stephen Backus followed in 1810. These were settlers after the Colonel's own heart, and soon formed a settlement in Dunwich to the west of Port Talbot, known as 'Little Ireland.' [Perhaps these were Irish Palatinates.] Daniel Rapelje, of Huguenot descent, and Daniel Mandeville came from Long Point and built on the site of St. Thomas [then only known as Kettle Creek] their log-houses, the former at the top of the hill on the first lot in Yarmouth, the latter just below, in the valley on the Southwold side of the town line. David Secord, Garrett Oakes, Benjamin Wilson, and Moses Rice were among those who settled about this time on the Talbot Road. In Delaware, Bird, Brigham, Springer, Westbrook, and Sherick had established themselves." [120]

The majority of the earliest settlers just mentioned were from Pennsylvania with a German background, even if the name has been anglicized.

Oxford County, Norwich Township

The first Quaker pioneers in Norwich Township came from Dutchess County, New York State, in 1808. Peter Lossing joined his brother-in-law, Peter DeLong, and bought 1500 acres.

According to Robert Gourley in his *Statistical Account of Upper Canada*, eleven farmers with their wives and families, comprising eighty-nine persons, arrived in 1811. They were all Quakers and the names of the husbands were: Peter Lossing, Michael Stover, Fred Stover, Adam Stover, Sears Mold, Sam Cornwell, Sol. Sackrider, Peter DeLong, and Peter M'Lees—all from Dutchess County, N.Y. Elias Moore came from Nova Scotia, and John Syple from Albany, N.Y.[121]

Peel County

In 1792 the County of York was divided into two ridings—East and West. The east riding extended from the County of Durham to the eastern boundary of what is today the County of Peel. The townships of Trafalgar, Nelson, Beverley, and Flamborough and parts of the County of Wentworth were united and formed part of the west riding of York until the year 1816, when the Gore district was formed. The latter took in all the townships of the Home District west of Toronto Township. In 1865 the County of Peel was formed.

The first settlers came from New Brunswick, the United States, and parts of Upper Canada. They located in front of Toronto Township known as the "Old Survey" about the year 1808 or 1810. The greater part of the "New Survey" was settled by a colony of Irish from New York City who settled on their grants in 1819 under the superintendence of Messrs. Beatty and Graham. Chinguacousy was settled by farmers from the United States, their descendants, and other inhabitants of Upper Canada.

Toronto Township

The "Old Survey" of Toronto Township was laid out in 1806 by Mr. Wilmot, Deputy-Surveyor. One mile on each side of the River Credit was reserved for the Indians, with special privileges respecting their fishing rights. No white person was allowed to fish in the river without the consent of the Indians.

They subsequently sold out all their lands and privileges and removed to the Saugeen River.

The first settler in the township, and also in the county, was Colonel Thomas Ingersoll, who kept the Government House and Ferry at Port Credit previous to 1806. The population in 1808 consisted of seven families—those of John Silverthorn, Joseph Silverthorn, Philip Cody, Daniel Harris, Allen Robinett, William Barber, and Absalom Wilcox.

In 1819 twenty-six Irish families arrived from New York City.

Corporal John Schiller came to Peel County between 1811 and 1820 and discovered the suitability of the district for growing Clinton grapes.

Andrew Cook Sr. was born in England, went to Lancaster County, Pennsylvania, and from there to Ancaster in 1804. As a farmer settler he drew Lot No. 33 (consisting of 200 acres) in the 1st Concession north of Dundas Street, in the Township of Toronto, and received a deed for same dated January 11, 1808. He did not move there until 1816. In 1820 his son Jacob, born in Lancaster County, Pennsylvania, in 1796, purchased Lot No. 16 in the 1st Concession south of Dundas Street for $30. He bought and sold land, and in 1820 contracted to carry the mail between Ancaster and York, usually on horseback but occasionally on foot. The municipality of Cooksville is named after this family.

Halton County

Halton County, like Peel, was late in being settled because of the land still belonging to the Mississaugas. The occasional settler moved in making his own bargain with the Indians, but it was not until 1806 that the county was officially opened for settlement. From the County Atlas we learn that a number of the first settlers came from the Niagara Peninsula, having sold their property there and moving on to new fields in the Pennsylvania German tradition.

Trafalgar Township received its first settlers in 1806 and 1807. These were: the Sovereigns, Proudfoots (Stolzfusz), Kaittings, Freemans, Posts, Biggars, Mulhollands, Kenneys, Chalmers, Albertsons, Chisholms, Sproats, Browns, and Hagers.

Lawrence Hager, born in New Jersey in 1784, came from Pennsylvania in 1799 to Forty Mile Creek (Grimsby). In 1806 he settled in Trafalgar Township. He died in Palermo in 1870.

William Kaitting's father, John, was born near Utica, N.Y., and his mother in New Jersey. They settled on Lot 18, Dundas Street, Trafalgar.

The Springers were German in background. David's grandfather having been killed in 1775 in the Revolutionary War, his father, Richard, came to Canada at the close of the war and married Sarah Brice in Niagara in 1786. Moving to the head of the lakes in 1796, they took up 300 acres of land where Hamilton is now situated. Later they came to Trafalgar Township (about 1807).

William Albertson, born in New Jersey in 1793, came to the Township of Proudfoot in 1800 and to Trafalgar in 1811.

Isaac Van Norman, born in 1784, settled in Nelson Township.

George Ghent, the son of Thomas and Elizabeth Ghent, was born in North Carolina and with them came to Saltfleet, Wentworth County, in 1792. In 1805 he sold out and moved to Nelson.

Isaac Freeman, son of William, evidently of German background, married Miss Clawson from Holland. He fought in the Revolutionary War. In 1800 he migrated to Canada and settled first at Ancaster, then in Halton County.

Philip Sovereign, whose father had come from New York State in 1799 and settled at Waterford, Norfolk County, had owned a farm, a grist mill, a saw mill, a tavern, and a distillery at Waterford. In 1812 he moved to Trafalgar Township.

James Molyneaux was born in the South of France in 1797 and as a persecuted Huguenot moved to Ireland. From there he emigrated to Halton County.

Two other immigrants of German background who came to Halton later were Harvey Morris Switzer, who was born in Ireland and came with his parents to Canada in 1832, and John Read Bessey, born in Lincoln County in 1802. The latter's grandparents, having both fought in the Revolutionary War, had been given grants of land in the Township of Grantham. When John came to the county in 1819 he settled in Esquesing Township in 1822.

Wellington County

The first settlers in Erin Township were Pennsylvania Germans. They were: Awrey, Roszel, Morris, and Root.

They were granted tracts of land by the Crown in recognition of their loyalty. Roszel was the first white child born in Erin Township.

AFTER 1812

In March of 1814 a provincial statute declared that all persons holding land in Upper Canada who had come originally from the United States and who voluntarily had returned thither without license after July 1 of 1812, should forfeit their lands.[122] This remained in effect, with minor changes, for fifteen years. In 1815, as a result of the instructions from Bathurst, the commissioners for administering the oaths to United States settlers were forbidden to do so save by a special license from the government.

This decree soon worked a hardship, since land in Upper Canada was the only source of wealth. Agitation on the part of land speculators forced the authorities to allow United States citizens to take the oath and hold land only after a residence of seven years.

One important result of this ruling was an influx of immigrants from Britain, assisted to some extent directly by the British Government. "The reasons for this movement were complex. The war had brought Canada more directly to the notice of those in Britain. At the close of the Napoleonic Wars social and economic stress led many to emigrate to the colonies on the chance of bettering their condition. The government favored such emigrations as a means of relieving discontent and also, in the case of Canada, as a means of defense against further aggressions on the part of the United States. There was also a minor consideration, though one of practical consideration. The restoration of peace rendered it necessary to send to Canada a number of ships to remove the British troops which had been serving there. If free passage were given in these vessels, a considerable amount of emigration would be diverted from the United States to Canada." [123]

To implement this action, a grant of 100 acres was given together with free passage, provisions for a limited time, and tools. These grants of land provided no end of trouble. The settlements were to be on the Rideau River. Unfortunately, financial difficulties arose and there was confusion and trouble both for the settlers and the government until 1819 when a Board might deal with persons arriving from the United States provided these bore certificates of British birth. Two settlements were successful—Perth and Lanark—where the British Government located Scottish immigrants.

Land available for purchase became very scarce. There was none at all in the Niagara district, so that in 1823 about 19,500 acres of Crown land were advertised for sale in order to create an endowment fund for provincial schools. These Crown lands (having been set aside in 1798) had been a handicap in the development of the province, and as time went on and such lands were sold, this drawback was reduced considerably.

With this background of land settlement problems, let us now turn to the Plain Folk. The War of 1812 put a temporary stop to the immigration from the United States. Because they were pacifists, the Quakers, Mennonites, and Dunkards were again under suspicion as to their loyalty, but the government kept its word and they were not molested. In fact, they managed to keep contact with their American relatives and the migration, although theoretically stopped, continued into Waterloo County even during the period of the war.

Following the close of the war, immigration from the United States picked up again in spite of adverse land regulations. There seemed to be ways and means of circumventing them, probably because these immigrants brought cash with them and ready money was at a premium in Upper Canada, particularly among the land speculators. By this time the Niagara Peninsula no longer had much appeal for the incoming American settler. This was also true of Eastern Ontario where the original settlement had largely been arranged by the government and where there was little spontaneous immigration. Here, persons from the British Isles (many of them Scottish) took over the settlement problem and immigration from south of the border was negligible.

York County

York County received a fair number of settlers from Pennsylvania, but the majority of those who came were largely of British stock. As the latter moved into a settlement which was partly opened up, they soon learned and practised the methods used by their German and Quaker English predecessors.

Immigration into this county was most important during the 1820s. However, to understand this importance one must refer to William Dickson, the lawyer who searched the titles of deeds for the Mennonites. Becoming a man of wealth, he built the first brick house in Upper Canada at Niagara Falls. Because he was a leading patriot and lived so near to the American border, his house was demolished during the war in May, 1813, and he himself made prisoner and taken to Albany. However, he was released after some three months. His importance increased after the war and he finally bought land in Waterloo County (now known as Dumfries Township) for £24,000 cash. He engaged a young German, Absalom Shade from Pennsylvania, to develop this region. This Shade did, building mills which soon became the center of the village later to be named Galt. There had already been a sprinkling of German settlers in the county before the outbreak of hostilities, but it was not until after the war that Scottish settlers began to migrate from Genesee County in New York State.

When the Mennonites in Waterloo Township bought their lands from William Wallace in 1807, their agent, Benjamin Eby, had assured them that the titles were valid. These settlers developed their farms and then, to their dismay, some fifty years later a certain John Washington Wallace of New York City laid claim to their lands. As consternation arose among the Mennonites, the government, considering all sides to the matter, decided against Wallace, leaving the Mennonites to enjoy the properties they had created.

Up to this point all Germans who had settled in Upper Canada had come by way of the United States. Besides, they had all originated in the southern provinces of Germany and in Switzerland. But one more group of these south Germans was to come to Canada, this time directly from Germany. Christian Naffziger of Munich, Bavaria, belonged to the Amish group of Mennonites who, being pacifists during the eighteenth and early nineteenth centuries, had not been too happy because of the wars in Europe. Naffziger, having learned that people of his faith had lived happily for many years in America, determined to find out for himself. Taking ship from Le Havre, he crossed to America and landed at New Orleans. From there he trudged north to Pennsylvania only to learn that if his people wanted free land they would have to go to Canada.

Finally, with the help of the Mennonites he reached Waterloo, where he appealed to the Waterloo County brethren. When, upon their advice, he took up the matter of emigration with the government, he was offered fifty acres for each family from the German Company lands in the valley of the Nith River. More land could be purchased on easy terms.

Returning to Europe, he approached the British Government and had the arrangement ratified. In 1824 the first group of Amish people arrived, eventually to take up over 60,000 acres of land now known as the Township of Wilmot. These settlers, considered Germans because they were Mennonite farmers and spoke German dialect, were basically French from Alsace Lorraine. They had the French build, coloring, and spoke the French language. Naffziger returned in 1827.

About 1825 a mass migration began from Germany which continued as far as Upper Canada and which lasted for some twenty-five years. Those who composed this group were Lutherans and Roman Catholics. As many came to avoid war service, they were able to leave their native land only by stealth. Though most of them came to New York by various routes and remained in the United States, many of them preferred to move on to Canada where the land was cheap. From New York they came by boat and on foot to Buffalo where they crossed by the ferry at Black Rock. Often transported to Waterloo by incoming Mennonites, they usually worked for Mennonites until they became established. Nevertheless, as most of them were more interested in industry than in agriculture, they eventually drifted to the towns and villages where they established businesses of many kinds. Ebytown, the settlement founded by Benjamin Eby, the Mennonite bishop, developed very rapidly with his encouragement and was later renamed Berlin, and still later, during World War I, Kitchener.

Jacob Hespeler came to Preston in 1835. Born in Elmingen, Württemburg, in 1809, he was educated in Nancy, France. As a young man he set out for the United States, later coming to Preston, where he opened a store, then a mill, a distillery, and a vinegar factory. In 1845 he developed a business at New Hope, the name of which was changed in 1857 to Hespeler.

Another important family was called Bauman, later often spelled Bowman. Wendel Bauman, born in Switzerland in 1681, emigrated to Pennsylvania in 1700. His son Christian was born in Berks County in 1724, his grandson Wendel in 1758, and his great grandson Benjamin in 1787. The latter married Susannah Bechtel of Montgomery County, and they came in 1818 to Waterloo Township. His grandson, the late Dr. Isaiah Bowman, born in Waterloo Township, became President of Johns Hopkins University.

Jacob Wissler and his wife emigrated from Switzerland, settling in Pennsylvania in 1720. Their son Jacob and his wife Anna came to Waterloo Township between 1802 and 1805 and bought over 7000 acres, but Jacob Sr. did not migrate himself. Subsequently selling all but two farms at a considerable profit, he gave these to his son John, a tanner, in 1834, who built the Eagle Tannery, a store, saddleshop, and shoe shop two miles north of Bridgeport. Three years later he was joined by his brother Levi, and five years later by his youngest brother Sam. Sam married Jane Robertson in 1841, and three years later moved to the township of Nichol to the place now called Salem, where he built a large tannery and saw mill, developing a very large and successful business until his sudden death in 1865.

Simcoe County

The Sixth Line German Settlement, Simcoe County, is located at Nottawasaga. In the year 1834 a small group of families, including those of Swalm, Mattz, Kinder, Bulmer (Boomer), Knuff, Klippert, Moyer, and Stoutenberg, left their homes in Hesse-Cassel, Germany, to find new homes in Canada. After thirteen weeks on the ocean, enduring cholera (from which a number died), they arrived at Quebec. Coming on to Barrie, they had to wait until the government road had been opened out from Sunnidale Corners to Duntroon where the free five-acre lots were awaiting them. A certain amount of provisions were provided in exchange for chopping or other labor. After spending two years on the five-acre lots, some of this group were the first to form the settlement on the Sixth Line near the batteau.[124]

These settlers were originally Lutherans. Conrad Swalm's wife, while reading the Bible one day, had a vision that she and her husband should seek spiritual help from the Brethren

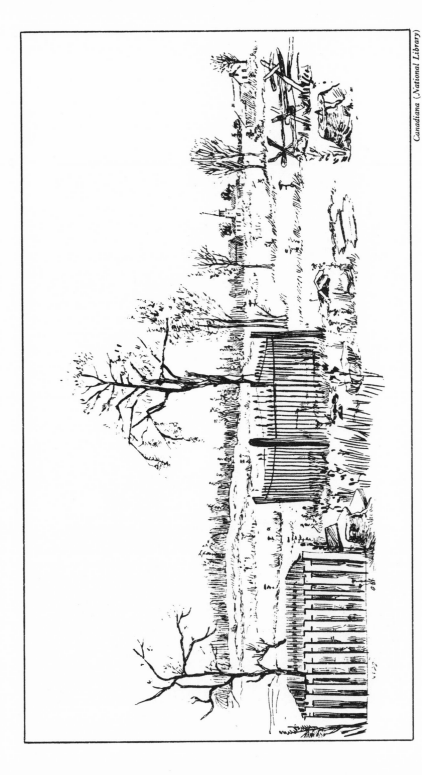

Butler burying-ground near Niagara

Oldest house in Markham Township; erected by Phillip Eckhardt,
who settled on the farm in 1794

Bank barn on the farm of Amos Baker, Concord, York County—
built in 1822 and still in use

David L. Hunsberger, St. Jacobs, Ontario

who lived in Markham Township, York County, some eighty miles away. Impelled by this vision, she and her husband walked to Markham, making it in two days. Upon their arrival they were kindly received and their interpretation of the vision was given much consideration. Some time later, after they had returned home, Markham Brethren came to Nottawasaga and baptized Conrad Swalm and his wife, thus making them the first members of the Brethren in Christ in that district. After a time, John and Christine Long, Charles and Elizabeth Dilson, and John and Barbara Baker moved into that area from Markham. John Baker was the first minister in the Duntroon settlement, where there is still a thriving congregation under the direction of Bishop E. J. Swalm.

IV

CONTRIBUTIONS TO CANADIAN AGRICULTURE

AGRICULTURE in Upper Canada began with the Indians. Contrary to statements made by many historical writers, the Indians did not live by hunting and fishing alone. Carrier, in his *Beginnings of Agriculture in America*, says: ". . . there were a few wandering tribes of Indians who had no more significance than have the tramps and scallawags in our own society. The historical evidence beyond question proves that the great majority of the Indians lived in fixed habitations, tilled the soil, and subsisted fully, as much if not more on their agricultural products than they did on those of the chase. The more the matter is studied from an unprejudiced point of view, the more remarkable appear their achievements in farming. No people anywhere in the world ever made greater strides in plant breeding than did the American Indians.

". . . From the Indians we have maize and the method of its culture, potatoes both sweet and Irish and their culture, tobacco and its culture, peanuts, some varieties of cotton, all the edible beans except horsebeans and soybeans, all varieties of squash, field pumpkins, sunflowers, Jerusalem artichokes, tomatoes, garden peppers, pineapples, watermelons, cassava, bananas; also many native plants have since been more or less domesticated as strawberries, American grapes, raspberries, gooseberries, pecans, and other nuts. . . .

"A comparison in the United States shows quite clearly that our agriculture is at least one-third native American.

"The one crop which stands pre-eminently at the head of the list of American farm products—maize or corn—is of Indian origin. The Indians had achieved marvelous progress in its culture. . . . They originated the dent corns of the Middle West. They had corn which would mature in less than 90 days in southern Canada and which grew but four or five feet in height...." [1]

To substantiate some of the above statements we have a record of a party going into camp at the outlet of Lynn Valley (Norfolk County) about the middle of October, 1769. A Catholic priest, Father Gallinee, describes the grapes as being as large and as sweet as the finest in France, and the wine made from them as being equal to *vin de grave*. He also admired the walnuts, chestnuts, wild apples, and plums.

Ralph H. Brown, in *Mirror for Americans*, writes of western New York State: "Numerous trails threaded the forest, leading to hunting grounds or connecting village with village. The beaten path from the Genesee to Niagara Falls was clearly marked and useful to white travellers. The members of the Six Nations, at least the Mohawks, Senecas, and Oneidas, were not a wandering or roving people in their unmodified state but occupied villages of some size and importance. Their villages were shifted from time to time. . . . The evidence for this lies in Indian old fields and orchards to which travellers frequently refer; these observers also suggest that large tracts of land now treeless or nearly so resulted from the practice of the Indians of firing the original forest beyond their villages." The writer goes on to say, "The Indians, it would seem, had been industrious farmers from whom the whites could have taken lessons in patient husbandry." [2]

Agriculture is dependent to a great extent upon the character of the soil and upon climate. "The types of crops and classes of livestock found in the various type-of-farming areas are determined climatically by their adaptability to the variable length of growing season, by the intensity of heat and cold during the summer and winter seasons, by the amount and distribution of precipitation and the evaporation of moisture efficiency. . . . There is very close association between climate and topography.

"The vast area of the province of Ontario results in a wide variation in climate. Topographical and geological features limit the agricultural areas largely to the southern part of the province.

"The climate of the more southerly part of Ontario is tempered to a large extent by the proximity of the Great Lakes. . . . average length of the frost-free season is 216 days at Leamington, 203 days in counties along Lake Erie, and 197 days on shores of Lake Ontario and the Bay of Quinté." [3]

As for soil, the "Grey-Brown Podsolic soil occurs in southern and southeastern Ontario and also southern Quebec. These soils were formed mostly by glacial drift and by lake sediments in the southeastern section of Ontario. These soils were developed under deciduous forest conditions and usually have a thin dark surface soil over a greyish-brown leached layer which rests upon a darker brown layer or horizon. The soils of southwestern Ontario are more deeply weathered and are considered to be more mature than those of Eastern Ontario and the Eastern Townships of Quebec. Here also the reaction of the soil varies from alkaline to moderately acid as compared to slightly alkaline to moderately acid for clay soils and moderately to strongly acid for sandy soils. . . .

"There are also several relatively large tracts of sandy soil which have been formed as deltas and outwash deposits near the mouths of large streams which existed during the recession of the last great ice sheet. These are the counties of Norfolk, East Elgin, South Oxford, and West Brant and are now used extensively for tobacco production." [4]

Having given some attention to the soil and climate of Ontario, let us turn to Pennsylvania to see if there was a situation there which was comparable. If such were the case, we have one reason why Upper Canada made such a strong appeal to the German farmer.

Henry F. James points out the natural resources of southeastern Pennsylvania, resources which were typical, with some additions and subtractions, of all of Pennsylvania. There was stone from quarries; deer and buffalo meat; hides for leather; wild fruit, small game, wild fowl to eat; sugar from maple trees; ample supply of wood for fences, houses, sheds, bridges, wagons, and fuel; numerous springs for fresh water; streams to be dammed up for water power; and iron for implements. [5]

In speaking of climate, Levi B. Huber asserts that there is fairly abundant and well-distributed precipitation; a long growing season (approaching 170 days per year); lack of frequent and extensive dry spells; hot summers and not too severe winters. [6]

Now let us consider the soil. To quote Ralph H. Brown:

"The greater part of eight hundred thousand Pennsylvanians live in the southeastern part of the state, between the Susquehanna and the Delaware. . . . The agriculture of southeastern Pennsylvania is naturally one of great variety. The face of the country between Philadelphia and Lancaster, for example, contains nearly every variety of soil, from sandy and light to a rich black mould. *Here, limestone underlies much of the arable land.* [Italics mine.] This rock is often quarried and spread upon the top soil for its fertilization." [7] Thus, in considering the over-all conditions of soil and climate, one can see quite a similarity between Upper Canada and Pennsylvania.

Finally, let us consider the European homeland of these people. The country they came from centers mainly around the fertile valleys and plains of the Rhine and Vosges Rivers. The slopes of these valleys were excellent for raising fruits, especially grapes.

Ernst H. Correll, in his discussion of the Swiss Mennonites, points out that these Anabaptists had the reputation of being the best farmers wherever they voluntarily located or were forced to settle. They made great use of manure, also gypsum and lime, and a three fallow system. Clover was one of their main crops and they irrigated whenever possible. They also gave great care to their domestic animals. Their motto in the latter part of the eighteenth century was: Kein Futter— Kein Vieh; Kein Veih—Kein Dung; Kein Dung—Kein Ertrag. (No food—no cow; no cow—no manure; no manure —no profit). In addition, they had an outstanding knowledge of livestock breeding and milk production.[8]

Some consideration should also be given to the farming background of the English who came as Quakers to Pennsylvania, if for no other reason than to point out the differences between the two countries in this particular aspect. The industrial revolution of the eighteenth century in England had as its counterpart the agrarian revolution. The basis of the whole movement was the enclosure of the common fields and the common lands. The common fields were the arable holdings of the villagers and the object of the enclosure was to encourage enterprise by consolidating holdings. The enclosing of common lands usually called commons was an effort to bring waste lands under cultivation.

The force behind the enclosing movement was the advance

of agricultural method and practice. Efforts were made to improve animals as well as increase production. Deep ploughing, rotation of crops, winter food for cattle, and cultivation of root crops were recommended.[9] Good as these methods might be from an agricultural point of view, they had far-reaching effects in a social way since they made for the extinction of the century-old yeoman—a working farmer who owned his own land. Large landowners took over and the yeoman became a laborer. Following the Napoleonic Wars, the agricultural depression finally terminated the prospects and the career of the small owner.

"Barns varied in size," writes Seebohm, "according to the method of threshing and dressing the corn prevalent in the country. In the north where the corn was threshed, fanned, and winnowed with a machine fan, a barn with a threshing floor 15 feet by 10 feet was considered large enough for two men. In Norfolk where corn was threshed loose and cleaned by casting right across the floor from one porch to the other, 24 feet by 18 feet was considered a good-sized threshing floor, and it was in this county where the largest barns were found." [10]

"The general principle of rotating crops was to insert a crop of roots, pulse, or grass between every two crops of corn. The best of the new rotations was the famous 'Norfolk course' of wheat, turnips, barley, clover (or clover and rye grass), and back to wheat again, without any interval of fallow, the turnip crop, if well hoed, answering that purpose. In many places the old rotation continued regardless of roots and grasses. It was common to grow wheat, barley, and oats after each other with some years of pasture or sometimes clover and rye grass before returning to wheat." [11]

"The favorite dressing for all kinds of crops during the eighteenth century was lime, and almost as popular was the method of paring the surface of the ground, burning the sods and sprinkling the ashes. . . . Ordinary farmyard manure was comparatively little used except on pasture lands. . . ." [12]

Montague Fordham, in *A Short History of English Rural Life*, asserts: "In the latter part of the eighteenth and first part of the nineteenth century the villages contained, therefore, a mass of poverty-stricken laborers, who had been depressed, in part through the dying out of village industries, but in the main by the loss of their land or common rights. . . .

"The laborers were poor, many miserably so, and a large section were constantly sinking into the position of paupers." [13]

From the foregoing certain conclusions might be drawn. The conditions in England and the methods of farming were vastly different from those possible or existent in Pennsylvania and Upper Canada, whereas those found in the Palatinate and Switzerland closely resembled those in America. It is quite reasonable to assume that the Germans and German-Swiss found themselves much more at home in Pennsylvania than did the immigrants from the British Isles.

In the first place we find a different type of settler. The English, and later the Scotch-Irish immigrant, had usually been reared in different surroundings. They had been tenant farmers or tenant farmers who had been forced into the ranks of laborers. Besides, their farming practices were quite different from those they found possible in America. Climatic conditions, too, were far from being the same.

The Palatinates, on the other hand, having lived in small holdings in the homeland, had learned to preserve the best soils, to tend and improve livestock, and to vary and cultivate their crops. What is more, they were accustomed to and expected the hardest kind of labor. They came to America to find a new way of life—perhaps semi-feudal—rather than to make quick profits.

Shryock says: "The whole German pattern of settlement was different [from the English] from the start. While English pioneers seem to have headed for the loose dirt, which meant bottoms and somewhat sandy uplands, the Germans waded into 'the more permanently fertile, heavy-textured wooded lands among which the clay loams of limestone origin are conspicuous.' This was not due to any peculiar genius on their part, but simply to the fact that the virtues of such soils had long been known to them at home. The Scotch-Irish, who often settled in close proximity to the Germans, likewise sought out the soils with which they were familiar; but unfortunately for them, these were the inferior ones often found in hilly terrain. . . .

"While the English settlers were girdling the trees or at best leaving the stumps in the fields, the Germans pulled everything out by the roots. While the English scratched their loose soils lightly, the Germans ploughed their heavy lands deeply and held them intact. While the tidewater Virginians let their livestock roam at will and actually claimed that to house cattle would ruin them, the Germans built their barns even before their houses were up—occasionally combining the two in the old Teutonic manner." [14]

This mention of barns brings up an interesting characteristic of these Germans because it persisted even in the migration to Upper Canada. The type of barns they built contributed to three phases of farming: the storing of crops, the winter care of animals, and the preservation of fruits and vegetables. Emil Meynen describes them as follows: "They go under the name of 'Swiss barn,' sometimes also 'Mennonite barn.' They are massive two-story buildings, 40 m. long by 15–18 wide (often 40 ft. by 60, 80, or 100 ft.), topped by a rafter roof once with shingle and straw, now covered with roofing felt. The ground floor contains the stables. Frequently the gable walls were built of stone or brick. The rest of the barn is built of wood. The forebay extends some 10 ft. which enlarges the granary space and protects the eve-sided stable entrances. A broad ramp on the rear side makes possible a level entrance to the threshing floor, the hay granary, and fruit storage. . . . With the erecting of a barn the farmers see to it that it faces almost exclusively southwards in order to get the morning sun and heat entering the stable doors. In the valleys of the Alleghanies an angle barn has been developed by a side projection; the protected yard looks toward the southeast." [15]

These barns became distinctive in the colonies of the German countryside, not only because of their size—which was extraordinary—but on account of their being painted a red brown and decorated with the so-called hex signs such as six-pointed stars or wheels. Much has been written about these hex signs to prove how superstitious these Germans were; that they were painted on the barns to drive away bad luck and evil. Such might have been the case in Europe, but the symbolism has been lost in America, for now they express only adornment—perhaps a means of release for repressed color expression.

Not infrequently the barn far outshone the house both in size and finish, such apparent disparity pointing out the importance of the barn in the farming set-up. The house at first was made of logs but differed from the log cabins built by the Quakers in that the latter had fireplaces at each end, whereas the German's cabin had the fireplace in the center. These Germans were familiar with the log cabin, since it was common in the Black Forest and the Swiss Alps. The Swedes also built log cabins, but the Germans preferred to square the logs and fit them together at the corners with exact notchings.

The arrangement of the central fireplace, which later developed into a stove, is novel. A five-plate stove was made as early as 1726 in Pennsylvania. The back plate was missing and was placed against a hole that led into the back of the fireplace. By this means two rooms could be heated, because the more heat you desired in the second room, the more embers you pushed into that section. Later, a back plate and a stove pipe were added and the stove could then be moved away from the fireplace to any part of the house.

The American Germans, unlike their ancestors in Europe, separated the house and barn but built numerous small buildings in close proximity to the house, such as a summer kitchen (often topped by a dinner bell), smoke house, wash house, tool shed, bake oven, and spring house. When the original house gave place to a larger one, it was usually built of stone or brick. To quote Emil Meynen once more: "Today the prevailing farm house has two stories, covered by a rafter roof, a two-room-deep, four or five-windowed house with covered house door in the middle. While door and hall especially in the five-windowed house divide the house into two halves, the four-windowed house is often built with two entrances, one of which is in the kitchen, the other leading to the best rooms." [16]

The "two-door" house had its origin in Europe where because of taxes on houses several generations lived under the same roof. In America the two-door house was often known as the *Grossdawdy* or Grandfather house. It was an extra apartment built on to or even separate from the main house.

Let us now consider the farm practices in Pennsylvania in contrast to those we have noted in England. Arthur D. Graeff, in an article entitled *The Influence of the Pennsylvania Germans*, declares: "They have no peers as farmers. In this form of husbandry their leadership has never been challenged. Today there are 3000 counties in the United States. Of the 25 most productive counties in the nation, nine are peopled chiefly by persons of this lineage. They were first to develop the system of rotating crops and contour ploughing; the first to devise guards against soil erosion and the first to practise conservation of our forests. . . .

"Horticulture, as applied to garden produce, was unknown in England at the time William Penn invited the distressed and persecuted Germans of the Rhine Valley to share his province in the New World. England did not grow vegetables in gardens until William of Orange brought with him some Dutch gardeners at the time of his accession to the English throne in 1688." [17]

"The Pennsylvania German farmer," states Walter M. Kollmorgen, "showed a strong predilection for family-sized holdings (100 to 300 acres) and relatively intensive forms of agriculture. He looked upon his calling as a preferred way of life and not primarily as a commercial occupation. He sought an acreage sufficient to feed and clothe himself well and to yield the necessary means with which to secure farms for his children. In his work program, self-sufficiency was his ideal. Plantation agriculture and slavery in particular were anathema to him. . . .

"The English, Welsh, and Scotch-Irish, on the other hand, showed a strong predilection for commercial farming and large holdings." [18]

Two practices generally observed by the Pennsylvania German were the preservation of the woodlot and acreage for fallowing. His method, as previously stated, of clearing the soil of trees was to cut them down—not girdle them and leave them to rot—clear out the stumps, burning the wood and using the potash as fertilizer.

Once the land was cleared, wheat was usually a first crop, following with a variation of grains such as corn, oats, buckwheat, barley, and rye. Grasses early assumed considerable importance. Penn's Woods—Pennsylvania—were not completely covered with trees, since the settlers found clearings of various sizes covered with native grasses, mostly along streams and in low lands. It is believed that some of them had been used by the Indians as places to grow corn and beans. Such spaces were not extensive, since the Indians had no grass-eating domestic animals and therefore had no use for grasslands.

However, it was different with the colonists. They had been used to dairy animals in Europe, although as far as we know they brought none of them to America. The Dutch and Swedes had brought cattle from Europe long before the English settlers arrived, and it was from this stock that the German settlers acquired their first animals.

Raymond E. Hollenbach writes in this connection: "Before long every family had two or three cows which during the summer were allowed to range day and night on the native grasses that grew in the forest. The grasses on the uplands were mostly annuals and this foraging soon exhausted their growth. This left the meadows, where the perennial grasses grew, as the only source of fodder, and the early farmers valued their land according to the amount of meadowland that was included. All lands along streams were turned into grasslands as far as possible, and to promote the growth of grass and to make it possible to harvest two and sometimes three crops a season, the early Pennsylvania Germans resorted to meadowland irrigation." [19]

E. E. Edwards, writing on *The Settlement of Grasslands*, states: "Some time before 1750 the German farmers of Pennsylvania began to irrigate natural meadows. The streams flowing through meadows were diverted along the hillsides and the water distributed by lateral ditches over the lowlands. The procedure often took much labor but the increased hay crops apparently justified the expense. Farms with a large acreage capable of irrigation were highly valued." [20]

The cultivation of red clover is mentioned in England as early as 1633. William Penn, in 1685, speaks of an experiment of sowing English grass and "great and small clover." [21] Peter Kalm, the Swedish scientist, saw fields of red clover near New York in 1749.[22] It was not, however, until after 1768 that a discovery became known that made the growing of clover a success and revolutionized, so to speak, the whole farming industry of Pennsylvania. This discovery was the use of gypsum, or plaster of Paris, in the raising of clover.[23]

It happened in this fashion: About 1770 a Pennsylvanian went to Germany for redemptioners and while there heard of a discovery by a laborer employed in mixing stucco mortar at a large building. This man noticed that the path used, or made by him, threw up a luxuriant crop of clover in the following year, when all other parts of the field showed the opposite. On the assumption that this extraordinary growth was due to the dust from his clothes, he tried out some gypsum on some clover near his cottage and was amazed at the result.

The visiting Pennsylvanian brought back some samples and after much hesitation some farmers were persuaded to try it. At first it was feared that it would attract lightning, hence was always taken out of the buildings during an electric storm. In time, this fear abating, the wonderful effects of using it soon became apparent.[24]

The gypsum or plaster of Paris was imported in rock form from France (it was first obtained from the Hill of Montmartre, near Paris) and later from Nova Scotia. It was then crushed in an ordinary flour mill. Although the use of gypsum as a fertilizer has been entirely abandoned, the Pennsylvania German farmers used lime and barnyard manure on their crops for a long time.

Timothy was cultivated in Pennsylvania about the same time as clover.[25] Although a native of Europe, it was first cultivated in America, when, some seeds being dropped accidentally (probably from an English ship), it began growing near Portsmouth, New Hampshire. About 1705 a man by the name of John Herd saw it and for a time it was called Herd's Grass. Because Timothy Hanson introduced it into Maryland a few years later it was named timothy, so called in a letter by Benjamin Franklin to Jared Elliott in 1747. The use of this grass increased rapidly, until by 1880, it was in general use. The Lehigh County farmers adopted the custom of raising mixed clover and timothy.

Interestingly enough, it was a Pennsylvania Quaker who made himself renowned in another branch of agriculture—botany. "John Bartram, a Quaker of Pennsylvania, started a botanical garden in 1730 on the banks of the Schuylkill River about three miles north of Philadelphia. Bartram was an incessant collector, an accurate observer although comparatively uneducated, a great traveller, and he detected and collected more different species of American plants than has any other man of his time. A thrifty business man, he financed through sale of seeds and plants his travels and the increase of his garden. He afterwards received an appropriation of fifty pounds a year as Royal Botanist in America and has been credited with having started the first botanical garden in America." [26]

So far, although attention has been called only to the qualities of the Pennsylvania German as a farmer, it must be recognized that many of those who came from Europe were artisans, not farmers. As Graeff puts it: "The Pennsylvania German brought with him many skills which were known to some continental Europeans but unknown to immigrants from the British Isles. . . . The objects designed and wrought by the early cabinet makers, iron-workers, weavers, needleworkers, and fraktur artists are among the most highly prized antiques and Americana. . . . The three vital partners in the conquest of the West were the rifle, the covered wagon and the chimney cabin." [27]

Discussion of the Pennsylvania Germans would be incomplete without some information about Conestoga wagons, horses, drivers, and legends about them, since they played such an important part in opening up the western parts of the United States; also (and in this fact this study is most interested) in transporting emigrants to Canada.

The following information is taken from *Conestoga Six-Horse Bell Teams, 1750–1850:*

"The probability is that the first Pennsylvania wagons were modified English covered wagons, suggested by those of the English settlers in Chester and Delaware Counties, the carters' or farm wagons of England, rather short and wide, dumpy—but strong and serviceable. It was not what our farmers wanted, but it had the makings of a good wagon, and our wagon makers kept on improving on it, largely at the suggestion of the purchaser, until a ponderous four-wheeled vehicle rumbled behind half a dozen strong draught horses.

"The excellence of the wagons made in the Conestoga Valley of Lancaster County caused the name to become famous throughout the country, and the wagons were known as Conestogas. They were designed and built by local wheelwrights out of swamp oak, white oak, hickory, locust, gum, and poplar, from the neighboring woodlands, and were ironed by the village blacksmiths. All the work was, of course, done by hand.

"They differed from their English prototype in that the Conestoga wagon bed was long and deep and was given considerable sag in the middle, both lengthwise and crosswise, so that should the load shift, it would settle toward the center, and not press against the end gates; while the bed of the English wagon was flat and straight at the ends, and its bows, holding the white cover, were vertical. The bows of the American wagon, however, followed the line of the ends of the body, slanting outward and giving the distinctive and unmistakable silhouette of the Conestoga. Infinite variations occur, but always these characteristics remain.

". . . The top of the front hoop was eleven feet from the ground. The white homespun cover was two dozen feet long. The top ends of the wagon bed were sixteen feet apart and the rear wheels five or six feet high.

"The driver, instead of having a seat inside, rode on the lazy board, a sliding board of strong white oak that was pulled out on the left-hand side of the wagon body, when he was not walking beside his team or astride his saddle horse. From the lazy board he could operate the brake and call to his horses. The saddle horse was the wheel horse on the left-hand side. The wagoner was the first driver to drive from the left side. Coaches and all other vehicles of his day were driven from the right side; but the wagoner, for whom all other traffic had to make room, sat on the left and inaugurated the American custom of passing approaching traffic to the right instead of following the English rule of driving to the left." [28] The wagon boxes were made water-tight in order to be used as boats when they came to rivers such as the Niagara.

Two types of tires were used in the construction of the Conestoga wagon: a narrow one about two inches wide, an inch thick and perhaps six feet in diameter for the rear wheel of the road wagon of the professional wagoner or regular; and a broad tire, four or five inches wide, three-quarters of an inch thick and five feet in diameter for the farm wagons. Broad tires persisted because of the soft roads.[29]

The Conestoga wagon gave its name to the "Stogie" cigar, a long thin coarse cigar, supposed to have been originally a foot long and made to last from one tavern to the next. Also, heavy boots are still sometimes referred to as "stogies."

The Conestoga horse, like the wagon, grew out of the needs of the situation. The early settlers' horses were small riding horses, sure-footed, with great endurance, that could go any place. With the clearing of the land and the necessity of hauling heavy loads long distances, a new type of horse became necessary.

The origin of the Conestoga horse is a bit obscure. One explanation is that William Penn had three Flemish stallions of the draught-horse type that were sent into the Conestoga Valley and bred with Virginia mares. Certainly the Conestoga horse had the characteristics of the Belgian draught horses—short arched necks, full manes, good legs, and a weight of fourteen hundred pounds or more.

"Another possibility is that they were bred away from the English draught horses belonging to Penn's countrymen who had settled at Philadelphia and Chester, just as the coach or stage horse was bred away from the English race horse. At all events, in the leafy Conestoga Valley of Lancaster County, there was bred a race of large, patient, burden-bearing animals with sleek round bodies. They were well fed and never over-worked, and so they arrived at a degree of perfection far surpassing the original stock." [30]

Another indispensable item to the Pennsylvania German farmer was a set of Conestoga wagon bells. "Whenever one wagoner helped another in distress on those rough or slippery roads, he received as a reward the hame bells of the hapless one. . . . These were usually little open bells suspended from flat iron hoops, the round ends of which pointed downwards and passed through eyes in the hames. The number and size varied, generally four to an arch, but sometimes three or five or even six; and each great horse plodded along to the leisurely lilt of the chime above his shoulders. Perhaps at first the bells were a necessity on the narrow wooded roads, just as horse bells were in narrow English lanes, to warn other travellers of an approaching team.

"Many a wagoner did not use bells on his saddle horse because they interfered with his jerk line and whip and jangled beneath his very nose. For the wagoner rode a horse not a wagon. The rear pair of horses were called the wheel horses, the one on the right being the off horse and the one on the left the saddle horse. The saddle was low but ample after the English type, having a rounded pommel and brass-bound cantle with rings to fasten packages. The skirt was quite long and square cornered, while the stirrups were of brass or iron, although later they sometimes had wooden ones with leather guards. There was no useless ornamentation, but the leather was of the best. The team was guided by a jerk line to the forward or lead horse." [31]

In a letter of August 9, 1929, Mr. William H. Breithaupt of the Historical Society of Kitchener, Ontario, writes: "You asked me in a letter of April 25 about bells on teams drawing settlers' wagons. Curiously enough, we have just received what may be called a chime of bells, which came on the back of a horse, one of a four-horse team, driven by Samuel Bricker, who came to this locality from Pennsylvania in 1802.

"There are eight bells mounted on a broad double strap or thong, the bells spherical, varying from three inches in diameter to two inches, and giving a pleasing composite sound together. They are quite loud and could I think be heard a quarter of a mile away in the woods."

As for the harness, the jerk line to the forward or lead horse was stronger on the road wagons than those used by the farmers. It was made of heavy leather, with a slit in the after end, by which it was hung over the near hame, and the slack was looped about once or twice. The wagoner held the line, giving short jerks to turn the lead horse to the right and long pull to turn him to the left. This was helped by having the outside rein a little over an inch shorter than the inside one. The lead rein was fastened to a ring into which a jerk line was buckled. The wagoner also talked to his horses, and "haw" and "gee" meant "left" and "right" to Conestoga horses, as they have to horses all over the country since those days.

The whip was of leather sewed to form a cylinder-like handle, which was filled solidly. The end tapered and was finished with a plaited leather cracker, and this was tipped with a plaited waxed thread.[32]

W. J. Kennedy, of Iowa Agricultural College, writing on "Selecting and Judging Horses" in the *Year Book of the United States Department of Agriculture, 1902,* states: "The Conestoga horse had no growth of long hair or feather between the knee and the fetlock, as this would have been an unending source of trouble to the driver on muddy roads; a long tail was also a nuisance. The feet were moderately large but not flat, the top of the neck or crest well arched, body and legs rather short than long, stride rather long than short, temperament rather docile than nervous, movement forward steady, and not wabbling, height to withers sixteen to seventeen hands, and weight 1800 pounds or over in normal condition. The horse must be well muscled, less so than a brewery wagon horse; and the best colors in order are found

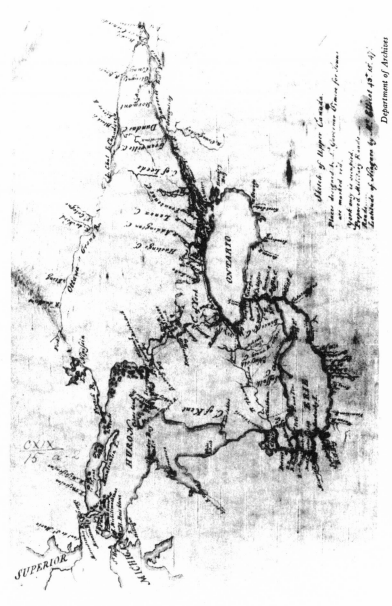

Sketch of Upper Canada during Lieutenant-Governor Simcoe's regime

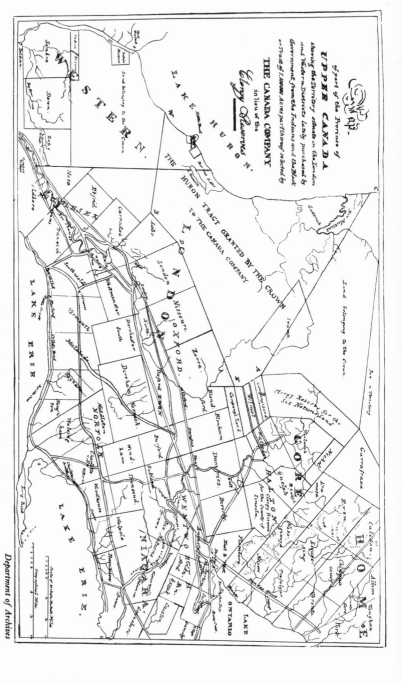

The Huron Tract granted by the Crown to the Canada Company in lieu of the clergy reserves

Department of Archives

to be bay, black, gray, brown, chestnut, sorrel roan, without too much marking." [33]

The Pennsylvania German is also known for his care of animals. Because he grew much grain he needed cattle to consume it and provide the manure so essential in keeping up the fertility of the land. From his livestock he obtained milk for his butter and cheese, meat for his table and for market. All of these either saved him money or made it for him. Since he had a horror of debt in any form, particularly in the form of mortgages, he lived very frugally, keeping all his money as hard cash until such time as he required it to purchase land for his growing sons. Although he held tightly to his money he never hesitated to lend money to a brother in need and always without interest. This was according to his interpretation of the Biblical reference in regard to usury. Each member of the Plain Sects felt duty bound to help in every way possible the activities and requirements of other members of his sect in his community. For this reason the borrowing of money from banks or the use of insurance were for a long time resisted by these people. Nevertheless, as a group they were always solvent and law abiding, both of these characteristics being ingrained in the life of their children from their earliest years. The whole family worked on a patriarchal pattern. The father controlled all the money until the sons were set up for themselves. The wife and daughters looked after the house and did as much work outside as time and necessity permitted. The flower and vegetable gardens, the poultry, the milking of cows, care and processing of milk fell largely to their lot. Occasionally the women helped out during haying or harvest. When the daughter married she was given a dower often in the form of a cow.

As a farmer the Pennsylvania German might be conservative—even ultra-conservative—in his attitude to the outside world, but in one essential particular he was most progressive. He was most eager to learn new ways of being a better farmer and he never stinted himself in the use of machinery if it would help him get better returns.

One last feature should be mentioned: he lived by traditions and many of these were closely associated with superstition. Next to his Bible, he lived by the Almanac. He was a great believer in the effects of the changes of the moon on such operations as planting grain, killing hogs, picking apples, setting hens, shingling houses, and such like. Numerous omens were carefully observed, such as the neighing of a horse or the barking of a dog at certain times; the effect to be expected from the breaking of a looking-glass or the kind of weather to be looked for under certain conditions. The Pennsylvania German had an endless number of proverbs by which to guide his actions, many of them as binding as sayings in the Bible.

The question arises: Were the Quakers (English) and the Scotch-Irish influenced in any way by the Pennsylvania Germans, and if so, to what extent? The geographer, Lewis Evans, visiting the "Dutch" settlements of Pennsylvania in 1753, commented on their superiority to those found in Virginia. "It is pretty to behold," he wrote, "our back Settlements [in Pennsylvania] where the barns are large as pallaces, while the owners live in log hutts; a sign tho of thriving farmers." He concluded by declaring "how much we are indebted to the Germans for the Oeconomy they have introduced and how serviceable they are in an infant colony." [34]

Shryock states: "It may or may not have been a coincidence that even the English-speaking counties which showed the greatest agricultural improvement in Virginia after 1800 were usually those adjacent to counties of large German population. At the present time, there are still definite areas in the South, such as Cullman County, Alabama, in which superior farming is ascribed to the presence of German elements." [35]

Robert Russell bears out our contention on the difference in agricultural practices between the British Isles and Canada when he says: "Some days after this, I met a farmer from Fifeshire nine years ago, and whom I formerly knew. He had 100 acres of cleared land, most of which was a light loam, resting upon gravel. Upon this extent he had 50 acres in wheat, his usual crop being 1000 bushels. He informed me that all his ideas respecting the nature of soils best suited for wheat were completely changed since he came to Canada." [36]

Considerable details have been given as to the farming conditions found first in Europe and later in America and to the methods adopted by the settlers to meet these conditions. We have tried to show that the climate, soil, and vegetation in Upper Canada closely resembled those found in Pennsylvania and other Colonial states and were not dissimilar from those found in the Rhineland. The great difference in the pattern of agriculture found in England and in the point of view of the emigrants from the British Isles has also been pointed out.

In view of these facts it is not unreasonable to assume that the immigrants who came to Upper Canada from the United States would feel very much at home and would practise the same forms of agriculture that they had had in their native states. Also, it should be noted that the British settlers who belonged to this group had in most cases already adopted the German methods in the United States before they emigrated to Canada.

John Murray, in his *Sketches of Canada by a Backwoodsman*, gave an interesting description of the method used in choosing the best soils for farming. He wrote: "The timber is such as in this country indicates the best land: and it is necessary that you should, in the choice of land, be aware of what kind of timbered land is the best. A mixture of maple, basswood (a kind of lime), elm, and cherry indicates the very best soils; an intermixture of beech is no objection; and black walnut is found on first-class soils. But if beech be the only wood or the prevalent one, you may be sure that the soil is light. Pine grows on sandy soil, as often does oak, and always chestnut." [37]

It has been said that the Germans in selecting their land in Upper Canada followed the trail of the black walnut. Because this type of tree grows best on limestone soil and because this was the kind of soil the Germans preferred, the black walnut tree made the selection easy. But the method of selection had also to do with all trees: the land that grew the tallest trees must be the best land. Of course, choosing land covered with heavy timber meant that the settler was selecting a location which would require much physical labor. No matter how excellent the land, it could not be of much value until it was cleared of trees. There were two ways of doing this: the settler could girdle the trees and they would die in a couple of years, or they could be chopped down. The Plain Folk settler preferred the latter. Furthermore, as soon as possible he took out the stumps, thereby giving himself a piece of ground which could be readily cultivated and planted. This procedure was in accordance with the colonist pattern in Pennsylvania.

143

The chopping down of the forest was no job for an amateur. The only tool used was what is known as the American chopping axe, an article differing considerably in shape from the axe of Europe, and generally weighing from four to five pounds, according to the strength and skill of the person handling it. An average chopper would cut down an acre of trees in a fortnight.[38]

Chopping required experience, since the trees had to be felled in "windrows" or "jam piles." A skilled chopper could fell his trees just where he wanted to. When the trees were cut down, the limbs and branches were cut off so that the trunk lay flat on the ground. Then the tree was cross-cut into lengths which could be conveniently handled.

If there were many logs to burn, a "logging bee" was held to which all the neighbors were invited with their oxen. On the day chosen the men assembled early and the fallow (ground from which the trees had been cut) was apportioned and staked out into equal divisions. Leaders were then appointed, each of whom selected the men to form his own particular group, and at a given signal the work commenced. A fierce struggle then ensued to see which group finished its work first, the winners always enjoying a proud satisfaction.

After the logs had been piled, a day was chosen with little wind so that they could be burned with safety. Usually a second logging or "branding" was necessary for the unburned pieces. These were hauled into a pile and again set alight. Of course, the stumps were still left, but by means of a hoe potatoes or wheat could be planted among the stumps, the latter cut by sickle, scythe, or cradle. The pioneer seeded down to grass as soon as he could and let it remain as hay or pasture for five or six years, at the end of which time the stumps were sufficiently rotted to either break out or burn out. A harrow of primitive make was used among the stumps, usually made of thick round poles shaped like the letter "A," the iron teeth being placed along the two long legs and slanted backward at an angle sufficient to help the harrow over roots and other obstacles. Where the timber was pine or hemlock the stumps didn't decay but had to be either dug out or pulled out by a stumping machine. Often instead of burning these stumps they were hauled to the side of the field where they were put side by side, thus making a very strong and serviceable fence.

As the spirit of coöperation was very much to the fore in pioneer days, it expressed itself in all kinds of "bees" which were both a physical and an emotional necessity. Many of the tasks were exceedingly difficult, if not impossible, for the average settler to accomplish by himself. Mr. Alex D. Bruce tells a story told him by his grandmother, Mrs. John Dickson, of Dickson's Hill, Markham Township, York County:

"When a girl in her teens, Mrs. Dickson made the acquaintance of Mrs. Miller [wife of the above-mentioned Nicholas Miller, the first settler on Lot 34, Yonge Street]. Mrs. Miller claimed to have been the first white woman to live on Yonge Street, and related how she, and her husband, began life on their land in the spring of 1793; how they commenced housekeeping in a wigwam; how they planted potatoes, this being their first venture in the cultivation of their farm. Then commenced the work of literally hewing a farm out of the wilderness. As the work of felling trees progressed, they began to make preparations for building a house. As they had no neighbors they expected to raise the house without assistance; consequently, selected timbers that the husband and wife, unassisted, would be able to handle. The clearing expanded; the potatoes grew; and the summer had turned to fall when one day unexpected visitors arrived.

"The visitors were Governor Simcoe and his company, who were on their return journey from Penetanguishene and Lake Simcoe: an exploratory journey, preparatory to making the survey of Yonge Street. Simcoe and his men were hungry, having been on short rations. Mrs. Miller had not much with which to feed so large a company, but she had an abundance of potatoes. . . .

"The Governor made particular enquiries concerning the progress that the Millers were making. Upon learning that they had logs prepared, Simcoe ordered his men to 'raise' them; and this was completed in quick time. Mrs. Miller's one regret was that had they known that they were to have such a strong force at their house raising, they would have selected heavier timbers and would have had a better house." [39] This story is substantially the same as Mrs. Simcoe relates in her diary of September 25, 1793. [40]

Probably loneliness was one of the greatest hardships experienced by the pioneers. The "bees" gave a reason for the settlers to come together and express their social instincts.

To give an authentic picture of agriculture as it applied to the Plain Folk in Upper Canada, we have been obliged to work from two ends towards the middle. In other words, one must understand how these people farmed and lived in the United States and then consider how they had progressed by the middle of the nineteenth century in Upper Canada. By this method it should not be unfair to get some sort of accurate idea of how they operated in pioneer days in Canada. Professor Jones, in his *History of Agriculture in Ontario, 1613–1880*, has given a well-documented statement of farming conditions in Ontario during Loyalist times.[41] And yet one questions the validity of some of the statements quoted, for, as Professor Jones states, many of the visitors, during the era 1785 to 1812, often travelled by boat whenever possible and when they did touch on land they kept to the main roads.[42] Their "Cook's Tour" usually began at Montreal, touched at Kingston, perhaps Toronto, and finally Niagara Falls as they entered the United States. Usually, too, since these travellers belonged to the military class in Europe they came armed with introductions to military personages in Upper Canada. Duc de La Rochefoucault-Liancourt is an example of the latter. Arriving with letters from the Duke of Portland and others, he enjoyed the hospitality of Governor and Mrs. Simcoe but evidently was unable to report favorably or fairly of the latter, hence when he comes to record his impressions of the country one is inclined to accept his statement with reservations.[43]

Howison is another writer some thirty years later who returned to England a disgruntled man because he was not allowed to practise medicine in Canada.[44] He had many caustic remarks to make of the settlers and conditions in Upper Canada, which may or may not be true.

Robert Gourlay, writing about the same time, speaks very favorably of the livestock situation in Upper Canada, noting particularly the good size and quality of hogs.[45] This is quite contrary to the statements of some writers who claimed that the hogs were a very poor type—razor-backed—and that they were allowed to run wild. Because Gourlay attempted an accurate survey in his report, it might be wiser to accept his findings rather than those of observers who were making a hurried trip.

Apparently, as far as the Plain Folk are concerned, there

is a still more important factor in the deliberate desire on their part to pass unnoticed. Visitors to the province would seldom get a close-up view of them because in many cases, having gone into the hinterland, they preferred to keep out of the limelight. Only when they got unfair treatment did they call the attention of the ruling authorities to their existence. Two instances might be recalled: firstly, when they approached Prince Edward for having been unjustly charged for certain supplies, and secondly, when Beasley had given the Waterloo Mennonites fraudulent deeds. These Plain Folk, because of their experiences in Europe and later in the Colonies, had a dislike for having to do anything connected with the government, hence they came in contact with government officials as little as possible.

Three things cannot be overemphasized in considering these people: they were physically equipped both in knowledge of what to do in the wilderness and the strength to do it; they came with money and equipment; and they aided one another, whether Quaker, Huguenot, Lutheran, or Mennonite. Religious or racial differences meant little in a community.

It would have been impossible for the Plain Folk to neglect the care of animals, or to girdle trees, or to continue to plant around stumps rather than to take them out; or to have no flowers, gardens, or fruit trees.[46] Any reputable Pennsylvania German or Quaker who offended in any or all of the foregoing ways would have been ostracized by the community in which he lived. This does not imply that there were no scallawags or careless and lazy folk among them, but it does mean that there were so few of these that any outsider who took the trouble to look into their ways of farming would have discovered (as did Croil) that they were the best farmers in Eastern Ontario.

In describing one "Dutch" farm, Croil says: "His farm embraces 500 acres, whereof 300 acres are cleared, and 200 in woods. The whole is enclosed with cedar fences, proof against all intruders, by which means his cattle have the exclusive, and unrestricted privilege of roaming through the woods, with all the benefits thereto appertaining.

"Of his cleared farm, 120 acres are devoted to pasture, 100 to meadow, and 80 to tillage. His stock consists of 20 milch cows, 6 working horses, 2 brood mares, and 60 sheep. He makes from 10 to 12 acres of summer fallow each year, to which he applies all the manure made upon the farm, and as much more as he can procure from the neighboring village of Morrisburgh; say from 50 to 60 two-horse wagon loads of farmyard manure to the imperial acre. The proportion of different grains is regulated entirely by the adaptation of the different fields entering into his rotation. He sows each year a certain portion of fall wheat and rye, the former he does not consider a reliable crop, the latter seldom fails to yield a large return. He avoids carefully running to extremes in any particular branch, and ascribes his success mainly to the diversity of his productions, together with general economy in management...." [47]

Such a description would be true of farm conditions in Pennsylvania before 1800. However, not all settlers in Canada were as successful. Croil remarks that "the extensive operations in lumber consequent upon the clearing up of a new and well-timbered country [Dundas County], resulted in a state of matters unfavorable to agricultural improvement. Having spent the winter in the woods, the farmer had to spend a great part of the summer in conveying his timber to Quebec. The farm was neglected, and, as a consequence, he rarely raised provision enough for his own use." [48] This man would then be compelled to get loans from the store-keeper, who often in the end had to take over the property to pay for the store accounts.

The foregoing situation would seldom happen to a member of the Plain Folk, since they never believed in putting all their eggs in one basket. It is difficult to conceive of them not putting the growing of food first. Besides, as previously mentioned, they had such a horror of debt that if they did have to be in debt, it would be to someone of their own faith who would loan money without interest.

As the Pennsylvania German farmer was unique in his care of animals, he put up a barn as soon as he was able to. This was possible because he lived in a community which believed in and practised co-operation. A barn of this kind was "raised" in 1822 on Lot 11, Concession 2, Vaughan Township, York County, near Concord Post Office, and is still in use today. This Baker homestead was set up on property bought in 1816 and resembles the Pennsylvania pattern in that the house is large enough for two families—the son and the *gross-*

148

daddy—and includes a number of smaller buildings, such as summer kitchen, smoke house for curing meat, wash house, implement shed, leach house for the making of soap, and maple syrup shanty.

Probably one of the most exciting events in the community was the barn raising. Coming into being when the first log-house or barn was erected, it developed until upwards of a hundred men would be engaged in putting up a barn. For several days ahead of the raising the housewife and her neighbors were busy preparing food, since a good meal and a social time were all the payment the helpers looked for.

A master carpenter looked after the layout of the barn, selected the necessary timbers, and cut and fitted them ahead of time, so that all the helpers had to do on the day of the raising was to fit the parts together and set up the framework of the barn. The frame consisted of "bents," one at each end, with two or more in between, according to the length of the building. These "bents" consisted of two upright timbers or posts and one or two cross-beams, according to the height required. Framed and laid together on the foundation timbers, they were raised in rotation.

After all the "bents" had been raised by men using pike poles (poles ten to fifteen feet long with iron spikes in the ends), two "plates"—one on each side of the barn, for receiving the rafters—were placed on top of the posts, which stood on the cross-beams. After that, the "purline" plates, for giving support to the roof, were placed on the top of short posts, which stood on the cross-beams. Last of all, the rafters made of poles hewed on one side were run up and put in position. The frame was now ready for the siding and the sheeting. No iron was used in the framing, the timbers being fastened with wooden pins driven in by big wooden "commanders" or mallets.

Usually the excitement ran high because the men would be divided into two sides with experienced captains, each side taking one end of the building. The side finishing first always raised a lusty cheer and rushed to the tables where they were served first. Usually two to three hours were all that were required to raise the barn, but this period of time was crowded with excitement for both men and women.

Bank barns in Ontario are almost exact replicas of those found in Pennsylvania. They may be 40 feet by 100 feet with a 10-foot fore bay, built entirely of lumber on a stone foundation. Usually the barn is set beside a bank with the ramp level. Barns in Ontario are seldom painted and bear no hex signs or decorations of any kind. The countryside in Ontario has many barns of this kind still in use.

The large barn in Ontario, as in Pennsylvania, served several purposes. It firstly provided storage for a considerable amount of hay and grain, the latter being threshed during the winter at the convenience of the farmer. Also, animals such as cows, horses, pigs, and sheep could be wintered successfully. Because of these animals much manure was made available for fertilizer. With this organic fertilizer these Germans used firstly, gypsum and later lime, both of which were available in Western Ontario.

In the early days, potash was one of the best means of obtaining ready cash. During the winter the farmer and his sons cut down the trees and stacked them in piles. These they set on fire during the summer, burning most of them at night when they seemed to burn better. When the ashes from these burnings were carefully collected, they were put into barrels and sold. From 1800 to 1840 they brought $40 a barrel. "Wood ashes were an absolutely vital source of cash revenue to new settlers before their crops were reaped. Loyalists who fled Vermont and New Hampshire in the 1780s, after the American War of Independence, one writer says that 'great hardship was experienced and the only cash crop for a time was the potash salts by burning the beeches and maples. . . .' " [49]

"Most of this Canadian potash found its way to the export trade. Not only was it required in the peaceful arts such as glass and soap making, but it probably influenced the balance of power in Europe, since potassium nitrate was then a vital ingredient in military explosives." [50]

Gray, in his *Letters from Canada*, describes the method of making potash: "The best ashes are made from beech, maple, elm, or some other hardwood. None of the pine genus, nor any of the soft woods, answer the purpose.

"The process of making potash is very simple: the wood ashes are collected free from extraneous matter as possible; they are put into wooden pots of considerable size, with small apertures in the bottom; the ashes are saturated with water, which filters these apertures, carrying with it the salts of the ashes. More water is added until the ashes are entirely deprived of their salts. The water now holds in solution a very strong vegetable alkali; by boiling it in large kettles, the water is evaporated and the salts remain. They now receive the appellation of potash. The potash is sometimes calcined (by lime) to deprive it of all extraneous coloring matter; it becomes extremely white and is denominated pearl ash." [51]

Lye for soap was made in much the same way. A leach was made of boards, perhaps six feet at the top and diminishing in size until it looked like a large hopper. The ashes from fires and stoves during winter were put in this leach and rainwater poured on them. As the liquid drained out at the bottom, it was known as lye and put into an iron kettle. When all scraps of grease such as fat, pork, and rinds had been thrown into this lye, a brisk fire was built underneath the kettle, thus making two kinds of soap—hard and soft. If hard soap was to be made, it required more boiling than for the soft, besides the addition of a little salt and resin. Among the early soap makers it was held that soap should be made in the right time of the moon, otherwise the soap would shrink and not be so bulky.

The above statements apply not only to Central and Southern Ontario, but particularly to Eastern Ontario, where the settlers were frequently destitute when they arrived. According to Croil they were given, in addition to their land, food and clothes for three years, besides seed to sow on their new clearances. Implements such as an axe, hoe, spade, and plough (along with one cow) were allotted to two families, and a whip and cross-cut saw to every fourth family. Quite often boats were also included in the list, and portable corn mills were supposed to be distributed. [52] However, as so often happens when the government is supposed to make certain contributions, the articles promised were not forthcoming. Occasionally, too, the tools were inadequate, such as the short-handled axe which was really a hatchet. The fact that settlers in Eastern Ontario migrated in large numbers at the same time, locating in contiguous areas, tended to give them a solidarity and also a hold on the government not possessed by settlers who had come in as individuals. In many cases, however, they had not had very much experience in pioneering, consequently they were not quite as successful as the German farmers from

Pennsylvania. They built their log cabins differently, for instead of putting the fireplace in the center of the building they put it at one end. Nor did they build large barns, partly because of the lack of saw mills. Canniff states: "Sawing mills were introduced originally into America by the Dutch (Germans) and it was their descendants who introduced them into Canada. But it was slowly done. It required no little capital to procure even the small amount of machinery which was then used and to have it brought so long a distance. Indeed, millwrights were not plentiful. . . . In the meantime a whip-saw enabled them to construct something like a door for a house and log barn and rough sort of furniture was made for the house. . . . The first frame house was built about 1800 and the oldest brick house, the Myers House, near Belleville, was erected in 1794." [53]

Practically every Pennsylvania German was very handy with tools although he might not be a skilled craftsman. Many a home in Ontario today possesses chairs—rocking, Windsor, or straight-back with rush seats—made by some ancestor. The manufacture of furniture in Ontario has during the past century centered largely in Pennsylvania German areas.

Because many of the settlers had had experience with iron before migrating, they became efficient blacksmiths and were able to make their own wagons and many of their implements. The harness used for the horses was made from skins of animals, tanned and made fit for use. Articles such as forks, sickles, scythes, and cradles were often made of wood, iron being added where necessary.

These transplants also brought with them the love and culture of flowers and vegetables. Every farm soon had its kitchen garden, tended usually by the wife assisted by her daughters and female "help" if she had one. As they expressed a human innate love of color not in their dress or living surroundings but in flowers, flower beds were common in the summer and their windows were filled with bloom during the winter. Herbs and spices were much cultivated both for flavoring foods and for medicinal purposes.

Enough has been said to point out that the pattern of life followed by these thousands of transplants resembled very closely the one they experienced in the United States. Soil, climate, and other physical conditions were so similar that they knew exactly what they had to do and proceeded to do it. Let us now go into more detail in regard to agriculture, noting any similarities and differences. Firstly, let us consider animals.

Livestock was brought into Upper Canada from two sources: purchases by the government for gifts to the settlers, and animals brought in by the German settlers. As has been noted, these Germans or their parents were in most cases prosperous farmers in Pennsylvania. Hence, when he decided to emigrate, each settler brought at least one team of horses and in many instances two or more pairs, and one or more cows. There is an occasional reference to sheep, fowl, or hogs. Ezra E. Eby relates: "In 1801, David Gingerich with his wife, his father Abraham Gingerich and wife and eight children left for Canada. They brought one wagon with five horses attached to it, two horses to ride, twelve head of cattle and as many sheep. It took them five weeks to come as far as Binkley's, below Dundas, and one week from there through the Beverley Swamp to Waterloo." [54]

"Jacob Schneider brought nine horses (two four-horse teams and one saddle horse), Christian Schneider had one four-horse team and one two-horse team. As this company brought a number of cattle with them they had an abundant supply of milk and butter on the way. The bread and eatables were prepared as required." [55]

"In the same year (1801) seven families more together with some single persons came to Waterloo from Montgomery County in one company. . . . There were nine teams in this train, two of them having four horses. . . . They also brought a number of cows with them." [56]

In 1793 the Sovereign and Culver families originally from New England, later New Jersey and New York, settled in the townships of Windham and Townsend in Norfolk County, bringing with them 20 wagons, 40 yoke of oxen, 300 sheep, and a large number of horses, cows, etc.[57]

Doubtless these horses belonged to the Conestoga breed, a strain which was most popular until about 1845. Jones quotes from a letter of Eli Irwin in 1846: "Not many years since this section of Home District [York County] was noted from one end of Canada to the other for its valuable race of horses; and by the introduction of the small race of English blood horses from England, to cross upon our large Pennsylvania mares (to produce a farm horse quicker in action than the Conestoga), the whole race is considerably run down and reduced in value." [58]

The Clydesdales and Shires were imported as early as 1836, but the Shires were too slow. However, the crossing of the Clydesdales with the Conestogas produced a heavy-draught horse quite satisfactory to the farmer.

In the eastern part of the province, French-Canadian horses were the favorite breed. One authority, William Evans, was enthusiastic about their suitability in Upper Canada farming, but they, like the Conestoga, were bred down by being crossed with importations from the United States.[59]

One other breed should be mentioned—the "Indian Ponies," animals belonging to the Mohawk Indians on the Grand River, near Brantford. Not more than thirteen hands high, they were wiry, surefooted, docile, and made excellent horses for the poor roads which then existed.

Gourlay in 1822 stated that "the horses in Upper Canada are of the American, the English, and Canadian French stocks. . . . There are few full-blooded English horses; but considerable portions of English as well as French blood are intermixed with the American breed." [60]

Some years later Robert Russell wrote in his diary: "27th September—This was the chief day of the show [at London], and about 40,000 persons were on the grounds. I was quite surprised to see so many fine specimens of cattle, sheep, horses, and pigs. Of the first class I admired the Shorthorned cattle, and their crosses with the common breeds. The Leicester sheep, too, were remarkably good, and numbers changed owners at high prices, as much as from ten to twenty pounds sterling being given for lambs of the best stocks. The rearing of sheep and cattle seems to be occupying fully more attention in Canada West than in the northwestern parts of the State of New York." [61]

For a consideration of cows, again we must keep in mind the fact that in Eastern Ontario they were bought rather indiscriminately by the government for the settlers, while the majority of cattle to be found in Central and Western Ontario were brought in by the settlers from herds in Pennsylvania.

Probably the French-Canadian breed predominated in Eastern Ontario. This animal was usually black or brown in color and a near relative of the Jersey. Ayrshire cows may have been sold to the settlers, although the better type did not come into Quebec until about 1820. Cattle brought in from the New England States or New York State were either Holsteins from Holland or Devons from England. However, no attempt was made to keep the breeds pure and many of the animals were of a nondescript type.

Because the Pennsylvania Germans made a practice of breeding good livestock, it is not unreasonable to assume that the cows they brought with them would be of a fairly good quality. "The occasional birth of black and white calves among the common cows of Ontario long before the importation of Holstein-Friesians suggests that the animals these settlers brought with them had strains from the breeds of Holland. Such cattle were probably brought over by Dutch colonists of Manhattan before 1664." [62]

Robert Gourlay gives some interesting statements about pioneer cows. He says: "A cow will give (including summer and winter) in the course of one week 21 quarts of milk, which will make three lbs. and a half of butter, or four lbs. of cheese." [63] Compare these quantities with the modern cow which will give approximately 85 quarts a week on an average.

S. W. Fletcher says that the early pioneer cow was a triple purpose animal—for meat, milk, and motive power.[64] Devon cattle were the first English breed to be imported. They were a "triple purpose breed," well suited to the plow, giving beef of good quality, and milk, although only about six quarts a day, of high butter fat content.

Swine were profitable animals to keep because they multiplied rapidly, requiring little care, for they lived on nuts, such as acorns, beechnuts, chestnuts, and various roots. Because they had to fend for themselves, they tended to revert to the wild boar hog from which they had sprung in Europe —lean, swift, fierce. In build they were narrow in body, with long snout, arched back, large bones, which gave them the name of "razor backs." As soon as the settler was able to house his pigs he fed them grain, thereby providing a much more palatable kind of pork for himself.

Sheep raising was much more difficult, for sheep could not fend for themselves as did swine. They were easy prey for wild animals or dogs. Besides, they could not live on nuts or roots but required grass. In most instances they were kept mainly to clothe the family. In shape they were small, slow to mature, producing two or three pounds of coarse wool at a clipping.[65]

The Pennsylvania German farmer always sought to be more or less self-contained—that is, he wanted to have control of his animals at all times. To that end he fenced his property as soon as he was able, since letting his livestock run wild never appealed to him. Probably his first fences were stump fences, for that was a quick way of getting rid of pine stumps. The split rail fence, known as the "worm" or "snake" fence, could be quickly put up as soon as the rails were split. Red cedar was preferred for this purpose as it would last the longest. The rails were about eleven or twelve feet in length.

It cannot be over-emphasized that it was the custom of the Pennsylvania Germans to house all their livestock. This custom was bred in them as we have seen, first in Europe, later in the United States, and is still a feature of Ontario agriculture, as distinguished from the practice in Quebec. When Adam Fergusson on his tour of Canada reported that "the cattle and pigs are but very indifferent," he was obviously not referring to the animals of the Germans. In a later note he states: "We passed through the township of Waterloo settled mostly by the Dutch. The soil appeared to be good, useful, sandy loam, well-watered by streams and springs. I was delighted with the cultivation, especially upon the farms of Schneider and Warner. Each farm might be from 200 to 300 acres laid out into regular fields and *not a stump to be seen.* The ploughing was capital, the crops most luxuriant, and the *cattle, horses, etc., of a superior stamp,* with handsome houses, barns, etc., and orchards promising a rich return. Waterloo satisfied me above all that I had seen of the capability of Canada to become a fruitful and fine country.

"The forest around consists of heavy timber, and the township does not enjoy the advantage of direct water-carriage; yet these Dutchmen, within a period of twenty years, produced farms, which in general respect very nearly resemble well-cultivated land in Britain. The farmers are primitive and simple-minded, attending to little beyond their own affairs, and so indifferent in regard to politics, that Mr. Dickson doubted much if some of them were yet aware of the death of George III. A great deal of capital flowed into this settlement during the large expenditure at Guelph by the

Sharon Temple, near Newmarket—built in 1825

Conestoga wagon

Hunsberger Photos, St. Jacobs, Ontario

Canada Company, the Dutchmen supplying teams, provisions, etc." [67]

In another instance he states: "A little farther we pass an older farm, the mansion and offices commodious and neat, rich orchards loaded with blossom, fine wheat and pasture or meadow land, healthy looking children at every door, *with pigs and poultry in abundance.*" [68] (Italics mine.)

Jones, quoting from such writers as Talbot, Strickland, and Trail, paints a very unfavorable picture of the treatment of cattle by the early settlers, but it is inconceivable that this could be true of the Pennsylvania Germans since it was against their whole tradition. [69]

In considering farm practices we must keep in mind the responsibility which these Plain Folk had towards their lands. They never forgot that they were custodians of it and that what the land brought forth should be returned in some form or another. This meant that in farm practice they were not dependent on outside markets. Each farmer or group of farmers were more or less self-contained, and they were more interested in increasing their herds and acquiring more land for their families than in obtaining cash for their products. Since money was scarce in their day, most of their business transactions were carried on by trade. What the farmer had to buy he got by bartering something he had grown, for to him to waste anything was a major sin.

As soon as the trees had been cut down, the stumps uprooted, and the barn built, the settler was ready to undertake his farming activities in an adequate fashion. The Palatinate was a great believer in the value of manure—either organic, green, or artificial. Because he fed most of his grain to his animals he usually had plenty of manure. He also grew plenty of clover and this he could plough down when necessary. He also used lime and gypsum quite extensively as both were readily available in Upper Canada.

As time passed he grew a variety of crops, but wheat was by far his most important crop, even in the present time. Other crops have been and still are: oats, barley, peas, corn, rye, buckwheat, potatoes, and turnips. In spite of government encouragement, flax and hemp were never grown in large quantities. The little that was grown was usually used to provide the cloth that was required in the family. Tobacco too found favor as a crop in Southern Ontario.

Again, true to their traditions, these farmers practised crop rotation. One year fall wheat, clover, and timothy seed would be sown. The following year or two would see a hay crop, oats, or barley succeeded by a corn or root crop. Summer fallowing was also rigorously followed in the belief that the land needed not only a rest to build up the necessary nutrients, but also to kill weeds.

Once again following precedent, the German farmer in Ontario practised improved methods of stock breeding both for dairy and beef purposes. Conservative though he would be in most things, he always had an open mind in regard to new ideas in farming practices, hence when the first Holstein-Friesian cows were introduced into Canada in 1883, farmers with a Pennsylvania German background were among the first to experiment with this breed.

Poultry was always considered to be the work and the property of the wife, and so she decided as to the type and number, but it was the duty of the husband to provide the feed. Guinea fowl were usually to be found in every Pennsylvania German poultry yard, not only because they were supposed to foretell the coming of rain but because by their shrill cries they frightened away hawks, crows, and other birds which were likely to carry off small chickens.

The fruit and vegetable garden was also the province of the wife, though the husband was supposed to plough the ground, to work in the manure, and to do any pruning when it was necessary. From that point the women took over and planted, hoed, and picked the crops, whether fruit or vegetable. Every self-respecting farm had a good apple orchard aside from pear, cherry, or other fruit trees. After the required jams had been made, the surplus of the harvest was usually dried or made into apple or pear butter.

Sweetening was obtained from honey and from maple sugar. The credit of bringing the first bees into Ontario must go to a Delaware Indian, Peter, who was directed by the Moravians and who brought his hive of bees from Pott-quotting.

The Indians had also taught the pioneer settlers in the United States how to make maple sugar. The pioneers in this country made it during the latter part of February or in the first week of March when the sap in the hard maple trees commenced to flow from roots to branches. Holes were bored into the trees with augers and into these were inserted wooden spouts or "spiles" for running off the sap. Wooden troughs were then set at the foot of each tree, the sap being collected by the farmer each day in wooden pails which he attached to a wooden yoke placed over his shoulders in order to carry them to the big iron kettles. Three or four of these kettles were used for each boiling, since after boiling down to a syrupy substance it was placed in a second kettle. After the water had been evaporated, only the sugar was left. A healthy tree would produce a gallon of syrup in a season, and if this were boiled down it would make seven pounds of sugar.

As soon as markets developed in towns or cities, the Pennsylvania German was quick to take advantage of an opportunity to make some ready cash; consequently, there has never been nor is there now any reputable market where they are not seen, often in the dress of the Plain Folk, their stalls usually displaying the most appetizing food.

Elmira in Waterloo County has held a Pig Fair for many years. This is in the heart of the Amish and Mennonite settlements where horses and buggies may still be seen in large numbers. Originally held for the purpose of buying or exchanging pigs, it has now developed into a place where one can buy almost anything. This fair is held once a month.

Farm implements in the last century and a half have changed from hand power to practically all machine power—from the sickle to the combine. Originally the farmer from Pennsylvania was skilled enough to make his own tools, first from wood and later from iron when it became readily available. In the early days the women and children worked alongside the men. Jonathan Baker describes the division of labor in reaping on a typical farm thusly: "In 1840 there was on said farm again 11 acres in three fields, about 35 bushels to the acre; the same was cut with cradle (and that was the first year the owner of said farm cut with his own cradle; although he was on said farm already ten years sickles were the only implements he, before 1840, owned for cutting grain, they at that time had to live very economical), Joseph Johnston being the cradler, Michael Baker and his wife being the binders; the same was threshed with horses." [70] In the same account he states that 1844 was the first year that a threshing machine with cleaner was used in that district (Vaughan Township, York County).

Before the threshing machine was invented, the grain was either threshed by a flail (a round stick about four or five feet long fastened by a leather thong to a pole about six feet long) or by horses or oxen treading out the grain. It was then thrown into the air by a fork, the wind carrying away the chaff, the straw remaining on the fork.

The next machine was a beater which took the place of the flail or the treading by animals. Finally came the threshing machine with cleaner, which removed both the chaff and the straw. This machine was used for three-quarters of a century with little change. It usually took about sixteen men to do a threshing—three or four in mow, six on stack, two tending boxes, one cutting bands, one feeding, with one driving the horse power (later an engine), and another looking after the machinery and alternating with the band cutter. As building a stack was the job for a specialist, usually in each community there was someone who was looked upon as an expert stack builder. The trick was to build a stack which was symmetrical yet one that would turn the water.

The mowing machine and horse-drawn rake replaced the scythe and the hand rake for grass, while for grain the reaper was the first advance on the cradle. The reaper would cut the grain as a man walked behind and raked the grain off the table, the sheaves having to be bound by a band made of straw. Finally a reaper was invented which would arrange the grain in bundles and tie a cord around them. This was called a binder. According to local history, the knotter on the Massey-Harris binder was invented by a descendant of a Pennsylvania German family—Abram Reaman of Ringwood, Markham Township.

In pioneer days, the first plough was made of wood (usually a piece of bent oak) and covered with iron. Some very rude ones were made out of a natural crook, as the root of the tree; others had wooden mould boards and iron points.[71] For the eastern settlers George III donated the old English plough. "It consisted of a small piece of iron fixed to the colter, having the shape of the letter L, the shank of which went through the wooden beam, the foot forming the point, which was sharpened for use. One handle and a plank split from a curved piece of timber, which did the duty of a mould-board, completed the rude implement. At that time the bark of the elm or basswood was manufactured by the early settlers into a strong rope. About the year 1808 the 'hog-plough' was imported from the United States and in 1815 a plough with a cast-iron share and mould-board, all in one piece, was one of the first implements requiring more than the ordinary degree of mechanical skill, which was manufactured in the province." [72]

The early farm wagons had wooden axles with a strip of iron above and below to prevent the wood from wearing away. They were greased with tar, made from the pitch obtained from pine trees and mixed with lard to prevent it from becoming too thick. This wagon had no springs and the wheels were fastened on by linch-pins which were dropped through a hole in the end of the axle. As these did not secure the wheel very tightly when the wagon was in motion, they made a rattling noise which could be heard a long distance off. The driver sat perched on two poles, the ends of which were fastened in the wagon box.

Early methods of curing hay consisted of cutting it with the scythe, after which it was raked up by wooden rakes and set up in heaps known as cocks. Later, when the mowing machines came in and the horse rake replaced the hand rake, the hay was still set up in these cocks. The trick in setting up hay in this fashion was to have the base as small as possible and the cock sufficiently high and proportionately built so that the rain would run off rather than penetrate the heap.

Before the days of the hay loader and the basket rack, the building of a load of hay was an art not acquired in a short time. It was customary to have a flat rack with a V-shaped ladder at the front and a square one at the rear. The person pitching the hay on the rack was expected to place the forkful in the area in which it was to be left, since this eliminated moving the forkful and disturbing its form.

The bottom of the rack was first filled, starting from the back. Care had to be taken so that it was not made too full, else the hay when put at the sides would slide off. The center being filled, forkfuls were placed on each of the two front corners, followed by forkfuls alternately placed on each side, until the rear was about reached (sometimes the loader started at one corner and went around the rack). When the back corners had been placed, they were bound on by a forkful on each side for which a space had been left.

When the sides had been covered with a uniform layer, they were bound by filling in the middle. Again care had to be taken to see that the middle was not filled too much, otherwise the next layer would not stay on. When the front had been reached by filling in the middle, the corners of the second course were placed and the second course laid in the same manner as the first. This procedure was followed until the tops of the ladders had been reached. For the last course the middle was filled in as high as possible. A well-built load, rectangular in shape, was capable of being driven over rough ground without any portion of it slipping off. When unloading, the exact opposite procedure was followed, each forkful being removed in reverse order from that in which it had been loaded. In the mow the forkfuls of hay were placed in rows starting from either front or back. The front row was always placed and bound in by a second row, and well tramped to prevent the front row from slipping out.

The reason for following such a system either on the load or in the mow was for the ease in which the hay could be removed. The novice either unloading or taking hay from the mow would stick his fork in anywhere and pull and tug, usually ending up with only his tines full of hay and a red face.

When the binders were used it was customary to set the sheaves into shocks, each shock containing from six to eight sheaves set on the butt ends with heads together. Good shocking meant that the sheaves were set as straight as possible. Sometimes if the grain was wheat and was to be left out for some time to harden, round shocks would be used. Two sheaves would be set against two other sheaves, then one sheaf on each side of these four, making a round shock. The sheaves would then be capped by placing a spread-out sheaf over the top and another on top at right angles. This latter arrangement prevented the water from penetrating the sheaves.

Again, loading grain was a specialized piece of work. Using the rack with the V-shaped front ladder and a square rear ladder, the person pitching the sheaves was expected to turn them according to instructions from the loader—"tops" or "butts" meaning tops or butts away from him. Usually the pitcher could see just how to turn the sheaf and where to put it.

The loader began with about two rows of sheaves in the middle of the rack at the back with the butts up. The rest of the middle was then filled with sheaves with the heads up. Having reached the front, a sheaf was then placed at right angles to the rack with the butts out and at the extreme end of the rack next to the front ladder. The loader would probably place another alongside of it, then the third sheaf would be placed next to the ladder facing length-wise of the rack, thus binding the two sheaves and preventing them from slipping. The sheaves would be arranged in the same way on the opposite corner. After placing sheaves first on one side and then on the other, the loader would then proceed to the rear ladder. Following this the center would be filled in, the first row with butts up and the balance with heads up, care being taken not to fill the center too fully, else the next row would slide off. When the front had been reached, the second and succeeding rows would be placed in a similar fashion to the first row. The last center would be filled as full as possible. A good pitcher would place the sheaves in the locations directed by the loader. As in haying, the unloading process was simply the reverse of the loading procedure.

Grain was unloaded into the mow by starting the first course at the front of the mow and by laying two layers of sheaves with butts out. The rest of the course consisted of sheaves placed in rows with tops up. When the back of the mow had been reached, some two or three rows of sheaves were placed against the boards with butts up. The second and succeeding courses always began at the back by placing sheaves tops up and by not laying them too flat. Hence it was the back row which determined the angle the rest of the sheaves would take. When the front of the mow was reached, two layers of sheaves were placed with butts out at the very edge of the mow and these were bound in by a couple of rows of sheaves running at right angles across the mow. This method of laying sheaves permitted a maximum number of sheaves in the mow. Also the men in the mow knew exactly where to start and how to proceed to remove the sheaves at threshing time.

As one looks over the agricultural field in Ontario today,

it is clear that the pattern followed during the nineteenth century closely resembled the one set in Pennsylvania during the preceding century, which, in turn, had its genesis in the eighteenth. This is understandable when one considers the similarity of physical conditions such as soils, forests, and climate. Such conditions were not found in the British Isles, hence settlers from these areas, finding themselves in unfamiliar surroundings first in Pennsylvania and later in Upper Canada, were quite willing to adopt the ways of living and the farm practices of the Germans.

The pattern of agriculture called for selection of land by the height of trees, with a preference for the black walnut since that particular tree grew on limestone soil which these pioneers sought. After the selection of land, the next task was the clearing of trees and the building of a log-house together with a large barn. (It is an accepted fact that only settlers from the continent of Europe knew how to build log structures.) The barns were large because the Palatinates gave great care to their animals and the barns provided not only shelter but also storage for fodder. These animals made available the organic fertilizer so highly valued by these people.

Conservation of the soil was never any problem for these Germans, since they felt themselves the custodians of it for future generations. Furthermore, to this day conservation to them has not only been a mere farm practice but also an attitude of mind. Being custodians of the soil, they have religiously and rigorously kept soil erosion to a minimum. The generous application of manure and the use of clover as hay and pasture have materially aided in preventing erosion. Another factor is the retention of timber and wood lots. In Vaughan Township there are several farms where there would be forty acres of virgin timber and in these districts conservation has never been a problem. From this timbered land (which is excellent farm land), dead trees are taken out each year for winter fuel but the owners prefer to leave their investment in trees. Contour ploughing and strip cropping are gradually being adopted by those who are buying farms where severe erosion has taken place, but generally speaking, the average person of Pennsylvania German background has been brought up to use farm practices which are currently being promoted under the title of conservation.

Because farming to this ethnic group is not only a way of making a living but a way of life, the farms, no matter in what part of Ontario they settled, are still family farms of from 100 to 200 acres. The following is a fairly accurate picture of a farm in Waterloo County in 1944: "The average farm includes approximately 100 acres . . . with a high proportion of productive land and the diversifications of crops. Crop yields are high, with a list of farm products excluding livestock, which average 160 to the square mile, include wheat, barley, rye, oats, corn, buckwheat, hay, potatoes, turnips, mangels, peas, soybeans, tobacco, vegetables, small fruits, and others. . . . There is also a domination of forage crops—oats, mixed grains (largely of oats and barley), and hay make up 78 per cent. of the entire area under crops. Woodland and wasteland includes 13 per cent." [73]

V

CONTRIBUTIONS TO CANADIAN CULTURAL LIFE

RELIGION

As to which of the terms "melting pot" or "mosaic" fits the situation that now exists in Ontario, no definite conclusion can be reached. Some parts of the province are said to be predominantly English, Scottish, Irish, French, or German. Where such is the case the term "mosaic" is perhaps more accurate. However, there are many portions of the province where these races have so intermarried and where their original church affiliation has so changed that the term "melting pot" gives a more accurate picture.

Thomas Cuming Hall, in *The Religious Background of American Culture*, makes the following statement which is quite relevant to our study: "History deals with ruling classes and with State documents. It can hardly do otherwise, because these constitute almost the entire material at hand. At the same time it must ever be borne in mind that ruling classes never in any land or at any time represent more than a small percentage of the actual population, and that great forces are ever at work unseen and unrecorded." [1]

As stated previously, until very recently little attention has been given by historians to the so-called Pennsylvania Dutch or the Pennsylvania Germans, as they are designated in this study, or to the Plain Folk generally. True, most of them have been written about from the religious angle, but in so doing little attention has been paid to the innate characteristics of these groups, or to the contribution each has made to the body politic of the province. In fact, few persons have been willing to admit that they were descended from such stock. What is more, fewer persons have had much knowledge of their background unless they could call themselves United Empire Loyalists. In this appraisal of these Pennsylvania Germans and Plain Folk no effort has been made to prove that they were or were not of this group, since anyone who has given study to these early settlers will have discovered that in the past the term United Empire Loyalist has been applied very loosely. As interest has been directed rather to the time of arrival in the province of this group of settlers, it has been left to the reader to decide whether they qualify or not.

What would seem to be of more importance is an assessment of their contribution to the cultural life of the province. Is it not significant that so many persons have either no knowledge, or at best only a vague appreciation, of the fact that they are descendants of the Plain Folk? No longer do they think of themselves as descendants of Quakers, Pennsylvania Dutch, or Huguenots. They regard themselves as Canadians. From a sociological point of view the ability to be assimilated into the *milieu* in which the group decides to live is a definite asset, provided, of course, that certain worthwhile characteristics of their racial background are retained in some form or other. In view of the fact that most of the many thousand immigrants from the American Colonies during the years 1776 to 1850 have been practically if not wholly absorbed, our task is to discover if possible what particular contribution they have made in this assimilation process, in addition to what has been discussed as their contribution to the pattern of agriculture.*

There is one locality where the assimilation process has proceeded more or less along ethnic lines only, and that is in the County of Waterloo. Here the term "mosaic" is more accurate, since in many districts German mores still exist—in some instances alongside those of British origin. An attempt will now be made to explain the persistence of these early patterns.

Geographically, Waterloo County is situated inland, and therefore removed from the impingement of metropolitan influences such as were operative in York County, or American influences which exercised considerable effect on the Niagara, Essex, and Eastern Ontario districts. Historically,

* Dr. Arthur D. Graeff, visiting Ontario in 1946, made a very trenchant, understanding, and objective study of what he prefers to call the Pennsylvania "Transplants" in Ontario. His approach was both historical and sociological and reflects the judgment of an experienced American historian. The results of his appraisal were published in the 1946 *Annual Report of the Pennsylvania German Folklore Society.*

too, this was the last important district to be opened up, while those who came in were pretty much from one section of Pennsylvania and of one branch of the Plain Folk—the Mennonites. Practically no English Quakers settled in Waterloo County, and only a few Dunkards.

But perhaps more important still in the maintenance of ethnic solidarity was the migration of the Amish in 1824 directly from Germany and the somewhat later influx of European German Lutherans and Roman Catholics. None of these latter groups had had any association with Anglo-Saxons such as had the Mennonites in Pennsylvania, consequently they tended to live much to themselves, spoke their own language and made no gestures of coöperation. The Amish, too, were a very conservative group who were completely self-contained, hence there was no encouragement for any assimilative process to take place. High German remained the language of their church services.

Because of certain language and religious similarities between the Mennonites and the newcomers, the former were given encouragement in maintaining any special characteristics which they had brought with them from Pennsylvania, such as language, dress, religious observances, farm practices, and the like. The conservatism of the immigrants from Germany formed a background for a continuance of their own way of life. Besides, the economy of the country was all of one piece, or should we say two pieces—agricultural and industrial. The Mennonites from Pennsylvania and the Amish from Germany were agriculturists in the main, particularly the latter, while the Lutherans and Roman Catholics from Germany were industrially inclined. Thus we see that self-contained both agriculturally and industrially as these Germans were, and lacking strong outside influences, it is not hard to understand why of all the groups which came either from Pennsylvania or Europe, the Waterloo group is the only one where there is any definite racial or religious consciousness which ties in with their backgrounds.

Attitude to higher education has been an important factor. The Amish and some of the more conservative Mennonites have not encouraged their children to continue beyond grade VIII, for they have found that those proceeding to High School frequently become dissatisfied with the conservative way of living of their parents, and leave the farm to become "worldly."

Let us now see what possible explanations there are for the fact that the majority of the early settlers in such localities as Niagara, York, and Eastern Ontario have lost their racial characteristics and changed their religious affiliations. From a racial point of view no one group was preponderant in numbers. Wherever there were Germans, there were English Quakers and French Huguenots. Take Eastern Ontario as an example. These three groups were forced to leave New York State together—the Germans and French because they fought, and the English because they wouldn't. The Moravians might also be included in this latter group. Moreover, even before they emigrated, many of the Germans and French had Anglicized their names. There were two possible reasons for this: often the assessor was English and knew no foreign language, hence when the German or Frenchman pronounced his name, the assessor spelled it phonetically (Young for Jung, Chrysler for Griesler, Ball for Bahl, Youss for Jauss, Cole for Kohl, Ryder for Reuter, Rife for Reif, Gold for Gould); and too, it frequently proved advantageous to have an English-appearing name. Thus Zimmerman became Carpenter and Jaeger, Hunter. MacCausland has an interesting derivation: a family leaving Germany was considered Ausland, but going to Scotland it took up a Scottish plaid and became known as Mac-Ausland or MacCausland.

In the Colonies there was considerable intermarriage among members of these three races, hence, when they came to Upper Canada (all at the same time and for the same reasons), they to a certain extent pooled their customs and adopted the English language in its entirety. Their native language being forgotten and foreign names no longer existing, it was not long before the next generation ignored any particular characteristics of their ancestry and thought of themselves as Canadians.

But it is possible that there was a deeper reason why these three foreign groups assimilated with one another and it goes back to their religious backgrounds in Europe. It will be recalled that Pietism and Quietism originated in Europe about the same time and for the same reasons and that they had much in common. Pietism, developing among Lutherans and Moravians, was basic to the beliefs of the Methodists.

169

Because the Lutheran Church and the Church of England were both state churches, they had much in common. Calvin, being a Huguenot, had organized the Reformed Church in Switzerland and Holland, out of which grew the Presbyterian Church, hence it was not difficult for the Huguenots, the Holland Dutch, and the Scottish Presbyterians to join hands religiously.

Many settlers from the New England States had a Puritan background.* These found themselves quite at home among the sects in Upper Canada, since Puritanism, according to Hall, originated with the Lollards, hence was closely allied with the movements out of which grew the Plain Sects." [2] To quote Hall in this connection: ". . . the Calvinistic type of Protestantism, which has come to America (was) almost wholly in the form of English Puritanism or Scotch or Scotch-Irish Presbyterianism. The influence of English Puritanism was confined to the clergy and a few of the leaders of Massachusetts, and soon was quite swallowed up in Congregational dissent. At the same time it stressed again the old Wyclif-Lollard teaching on the authority of the Bible, on the subject of predestination, and the pulpit as a substitute for the altar. It was overcome by the emotional individualistic message of conventicle Protestantism, but at the same time compelled the sectarian movement to seek in its own way organization as a means of self-preservation." [3]

Mention should be made of settlers whose background was definitely Puritan. Let us take two families to illustrate—the Conants and the Aylesworths. Roger Conant may have been a Quaker, for he refused to join the patriot army, although two of his brothers did.[4] Disposing of his land, he set out from the vicinity of Boston in 1777, with $5000 in gold, in a covered wagon drawn by two horses and followed by an ox-team drawing a cart laden with household goods and farm implements.

"Leaving his family at Geneva, Roger Conant came on to Canada arriving at the locality afterwards called Darlington,

*W. A. Raleigh, ed., *Shakespeare's England*, Clarendon Press, Oxford, 1917 (pp. 56–57): "The English exiles who during the reign of Mary went to Geneva and other cities where the Genevan spirit of Calvin was dominant accepted a far more clear and logical realization of evangelical aspirations than they had been acquainted with in England. When they returned to England it was to their private congregations that the word Puritan was first applied about the year 1569." Thus we see the relationship between the Puritans in America and the Reformed Church.

County Durham, Ontario, in October, 1778. The first Crown grant of land to Roger Conant was made December 31st, 1778. It consisted of Lots 28, 29, 30, and 31, 1st Concession, Darlington, County Durham—in all about 1200 acres. After building a house on his land and probably clearing some portion of it, he returned to Geneva." [5] He brought his family over in 1794. John Burk and John W. Trull with their families accompanied him.

From the *Aylesworth Family History* we learn that Arthur Aylesworth emigrated to America about 1670 and settled in Rhode Island.[6] The family home was at Naunton in Gloucestershire. The head of the family dying in 1725, his two sons, Job and Philip, came to Canada about 1788, Job choosing a farm lot in Ernestown near the village of Bath and Philip going to the township of Hallowell in Prince Edward County. The original settler, Arthur, was a Puritan and a member of the small group that came from the New England States. In the same history it is stated that Robert Perry settled with his wife in Vermont and became an officer in the Revolutionary War. He must have come to Canada early, since a child was born to them at Michichi, Lower Canada, in 1781. Both Robert Perry and Arthur Aylesworth were ancestors of the late Sir Allen Aylesworth.

Considerable credit should be given to the Methodist Circuit Rider for what he accomplished in bringing all these groups together. It is interesting to note that Methodism was introduced into the United States by an Irish Palatinate woman, Barbara Heck, and the Emburys, and that she and they introduced it into Canada. "There has been a class formed in Augusta (Township) as early as 1778 made up of Paul and Barbara Heck, their three sons, some of the Emburys, John Lawrence, and perhaps other Methodists who, influenced by feelings of loyalty to the British Crown, had left New York and come that year to reside in British Territory. The Irish Palatines who bore the 'precious seed' across the sea and became the founders of Methodism in New York, were thus the founders in Canada." [7] The photograph of Barbara Heck always shows her wearing the bonnet and shawl of the Plain Folk.

To return to the Circuit Rider. The direction of the various church denominations was an important—in fact, often a determining—factor in their promotion in a new country like Upper Canada. From some points of view the Church of England was in a preferred position because, being recognized as the state church, it had almost a monopoly when it came to performing the marriage and burial ceremonies. Also, approximately one-seventh of all the land was set aside to finance it. The Presbyterian Church, known as Calvinist (Reformed in the Colonies), was also recognized as having the right to marry persons.

The Lutheran Church in Colonial America had a close connection with the Church of England. For this, Prince George of Denmark (the consort of Queen Anne) was responsible; he endowed the German court chapel at St. James's which became the Royal Chapel after the death of Anne. Here the Lutheran pastors were in control, and after due consideration it was decided that the doctrines of the Lutheran Church and those of the Church of England differed only in the matter of episcopacy, hence clergymen could serve in either church if and when necessary. This would seem to explain why in Upper Canada the Lutheran Church later shared with the Presbyterian Church and the Church of England the right to perform the marriage ceremony; also, why there were two recorded instances, one in Dundas County and one in Markham Township, York County, of Lutheran clergymen "selling out" to the Church of England.

Because the Church of England, the Lutheran Church, and the Reformed Church all insisted on an educated ministry, only those who had qualified either in England or in Philadelphia could represent their respective churches in Upper Canada. For this reason it was difficult to find preachers who would go into the wilderness where there were no churches and few parishioners. This situation was found also among the Quakers.

Compare this with what obtained with the Dunkards and Mennonites. As the adherents of these sects tended to settle in groups and since their method of selecting a minister was either by election (Dunkards) or by lot (Mennonites), it meant that they always had a preacher in the group. Thus, the Dunkards and Mennonites were always able to look after the spiritual needs of their own people, but very little effort was made to reach those persons with other or no church affiliation. The Church of England, the Presbyterian, and the

Hunsberger Photos, St. Jacobs, Ontario

Covered Bridge (also known as Kissing Bridge), West Montrose, Waterloo County

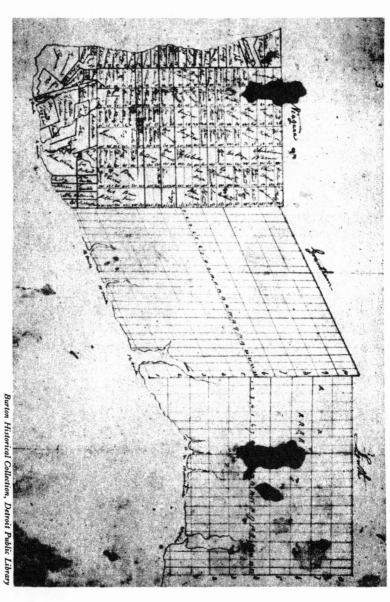

Part of the original map showing the settlement of Niagara Township, Niagara County

Lutheran members had only a few ministers sent to them from outside the country and these, in many cases, were little interested in doing much for anyone outside of their own denominations.

Into this situation came the Methodist Circuit Rider, who put into practice as far as Upper Canada was concerned John Wesley's dictum: "The World is my Parish." Some day, perhaps, the great socializing influence of the Circuit Rider will be properly appraised, because it was he who went the length and breadth of the province bringing the comfort of religion to those who were entirely cut off from any religious ministration. He travelled on horseback or on foot; he held meetings in the homes of the settlers; he organized camp meetings, and his fervent yet sincere emotionalism provided the spiritual sustenance that many of the settlers needed. The Methodist system of lay preachers (class leaders) fitted in admirably with pioneer requirements for, as the preacher passed on to another area, his converts and their religious needs were looked after by these lay leaders. This arrangement, distinctly democratic, was especially suited to pioneer conditions.

The results were remarkable. Because ministers of the Anglican, Lutheran, and Presbyterian Churches were so few, many adherents of these faiths turned to the Methodists for want of ministry from their own churches. Persons intellectually inclined and young people for whom the conservative services of the Plain Folk (Quaker, Mennonite, or Dunkard), made little appeal, turned eagerly to the Methodists' camp meetings, later to become members of that faith. This is what happened to the writer's family. In Pennsylvania they were Lutherans but they came to Canada with Dunkard neighbors. On their arrival in York County there was no Lutheran church, and since the Dunkards were always organized to hold regular services, they attended the Dunkard church, in whose burying ground at Concord all of the family who lived in that vicinity have been buried. Tradition has it that the writer's father and uncle as young men attended a Methodist camp meeting and were converted, the former to be an official of the Methodist Church in that community for fifty years, and the latter to be ordained a minister of that denomination.

As stated at the beginning of this chapter, because of the interlocking backgrounds of Moravians, Quakers, Huguenots, Lutherans, and Reformed (not omitting the Mennonites and Dunkards), it was not difficult for persons of any of these denominations to join the Methodists. At that time, it should be noted the Methodists were very conservative in their dress and beliefs, and dancing, card playing, attending the theater or even a circus, swearing, the use of tobacco or liquor in any form, were strictly forbidden.

To quote S. D. Clark, in *Church and Sect in Canada*: "Many Lutherans, Congregationalists, and Quakers found their way into the Methodist camp. . . . Even the smaller exclusive sects, lacking the evangelical aggressiveness of the Methodists and Baptists, experienced heavy losses of membership to those areas where geographical isolation could not be obtained.

"Failure of the traditional institutions of religion to adapt to new social conditions accounted for the weakening of their influence within the Canadian community. . . . Within the new backwoods settlements the traditional attachments of the Old World—ties of folk and class—broke down in face of powerful forces of individualization, and new attachments had to be established in terms of a new social purpose. It was the failure of the traditional churches that they offered no effective support of forces of social reorganization in the Canadian backwoods society." [8]

Methodism had its first preacher in the person of Major George Neal, who was born in Pennsylvania, February 28, 1751, but who resided at different periods in North Carolina. In 1786 he crossed the Niagara River at Queenston to locate on the grant of land which he received by virtue of having been a major in the British Army during the Revolutionary War. "Soon after his arrival he was forbidden by the officer commanding at Queenston to hold religious meetings, on the grounds that none but clergy of the Established Church of England should preach in the colonies. Neal, feeling that he had certain rights as a British subject, determined not to yield to this dictation, so the officer commanded him to leave the province within a certain number of days. But before the time had expired, his prosecutor died, and Neal suffered no further molestation. In 1788 he gathered his first converts together and formed the first Methodist class in the Niagara district at the home of Christian Warner, who was their leader for forty-five years, until his death in 1833." [9]

Christian Warner was a sergeant in the Rangers for seven years. His ancestors were Swiss (their name was spelled Wanner) who came to New York State in the early part of the eighteenth century. Christian came to Niagara with his wife and two children in 1783. He was given land and settled west of St. Davids, where his home, following his conversion by Neal, was a rallying place for all Methodists of that area, and where Nathan Bangs, a teacher and land surveyor, was converted. Bangs became an indefatigable Circuit Rider who covered on horseback a wide territory from York County to Elgin County.

William Losee, a Loyalist, was the pioneer Circuit Rider in Eastern Ontario, "crossing in 1790 probably at St. Regis, passing up the northwestern branch of the St. Lawrence, preaching in Mathilda—cheering, mayhap, by the way the little coterie of German-Irish Methodists, the Hecks, the Lawrences, and Emburys, in the township of Augusta. . . ." [10] Losee remained in Canada for two years, when, his health breaking, he returned to New York, but in that short time he had established Methodism in Eastern Ontario.

Samuel Coate presided over nine parishes in Upper Canada. He was a native of Burlington, New Jersey, of respectable Quaker parentage, who embraced Methodism. He entered Canada in 1796.[11]

Carroll mentions another German who suggests an Amish background—Peter Vannest, born in New Jersey in 1759, who came to Canada in 1802. He "must have been a primitive looking man. . . . He wore no buttons on his coat, but fastened it with hooks and eyes." [12]

Canniff refers to the very great influence of these early Methodist Circuit Riders. He says: "Although the Lutheran, Presbyterian, and English churchmen had preceded the Methodists into Canada, none seemed to obtain that hold upon the hearts of the plain U.E. Loyalists that the Methodists did." [13] These preachers were looked upon by the government as being Yankees, and therefore disloyal. Yet in spite of all these handicaps, their revival services, their camp meetings (the first in Hay Bay in 1805), and their lay preachers seemed to meet the needs of the scattered settlers, and besides bringing them religious inspiration, carried on a socializing influence which helped to knit these people of varied backgrounds into a unity which was evidenced during the War of 1812–1815.

The facts about the early Circuit Riders have been given rather fully, not for the purpose of pointing out their religious success, but rather to suggest one reason for the early assimilation of these different groups. In *Sketches of Canada by a Backwoodsman* (written in 1833), one finds substantiation of the foregoing statement. The author comments: "There is no sect in this province in its earlier stages, owed more than to the Methodists. They were the pioneers of religion, kept the spirit of it alive, and prepared the way for other sects." [14]

In contrast, according to Clark, the Quakers "without a strong central body, had no means of professionalizing its ministry or of developing, even, a ministry which was itinerant in character. . . . It became increasingly an ethical and educational society, commanding the respect of the more enlightened sections of the population, but at the price of exerting any powerful religious influence within the society of the backwoods." [15] Then too, because the English Quaker attended the same church gatherings as the Lutherans, Huguenots or Germans, it was not long before there were intermarriages, thereby hastening the assimilative process.

Clark further states that "in contrast with the Quakers, however, the isolation of the Moravians and the Mennonites was supported by ethnic as well as sectarian differences. Language was employed as an effective means of segregation from the outside world. Thus the process of sectarian disintegration operated much more slowly. Efforts of the evangelical churches to break into the following of these sects were almost completely unsuccessful. Secular influences, in the end, rather than evangelical religious influences were to lead to a weakening of their close group controls." [16]

The Reformed Church (known in Ontario as the Dutch Reformed Church) was largely responsible for the establishment of Presbyterianism in Canada. In about 1820 the Presbyterian Church absorbed the Dutch Reformed Church and also the Huguenots who had come into Canada. As far as can be discovered the Huguenots never functioned as a group but allowed themselves to be absorbed into other denominations. Doubtless many of them found it natural to join with the

Presbyterians because of their Calvinistic background. There was one distinction, however, between the Continental Calvinists and the Scottish. The latter followed John Knox in his dislike of musical instruments in the church, whereas the Dutch Reformed Church held no such objection.

The second Presbyterian congregation in Upper Canada was established at Montreal. In 1786 the Reverend John Bethune (a member of the Church of Scotland), who had served as a military chaplain in the American Revolutionary War and who had been released after being imprisoned, came to Montreal and settled there as minister of a congregation which he himself organized. His pastorate lasted but a year, after which he left for the upper Ottawa country and settled among the United Empire Loyalists of Glengarry County, where, for twenty-eight years, he ministered with great acceptance.[17]

In 1793, at the request of Governor Simcoe, the Reverend Jabez Collver came from New Jersey to settle in Norfolk County on a tract of one thousand acres granted by the government. Here he formed a congregation along Presbyterian lines.[18] Rev. John Dunn, a resident of New York State, arrived at Niagara in 1794 and preached to congregations at Niagara and Stamford.

In 1795 the Dutch Reformed Church sent the Reverend John Ludwig Broeffle (or Breffle) to eastern Upper Canada. From 1784 to 1795 he had preached at Canajoharie and Schoharie in New York State. In Canada he preached from 1795 to 1815 in Osnabruck, Williamsburg, and Matilda, in the counties of Stormont and Dundas, as well as in Glengarry. Since many of his congregations were German, he used that language when preaching.

In 1798 the Reverend Robert McDowell was sent to Canada and his parish extended along Lake Ontario from Elizabethtown (Brockville) to York (Toronto). In this area he preached, taught, organized congregations, and celebrated the sacraments for forty years. In a report to the Albany Synod in 1806 he states: "The Country is settled about thirty-five miles towards the north from York, through which he has travelled several times and preached to the inhabitants, who were very desirous to hear the gospel. They were anxious to have a minister settled among them and able to give him a decent support."[19] This is an interesting statement, for presumably most of these people had Presbyterian leanings, and yet the majority of the settlers we have record of in that area at that time were supposed to be Mennonites, Dunkards, or Quakers, none of whom would be attracted to Presbyterian services. Could it be that there were settlers in that area of of whom we have no record? *

As the war of 1812 tended to cut off the Upper Canada congregations from the Dutch Reformed Church, we find only the occasional minister from the United States after the war. (This was also true of the Methodist connection.) Cornelius Bogardus, who came in 1818–1819, reported that Mr. McDowell had eleven missions and needed more help. However, in a few years he withdrew from the Dutch Reformed Church and joined the Church of Scotland. Gregg, in his *History of the Presbyterian Church*, also states that the Canadian churches were "quickly abandoned" by the Dutch Reformed Church at the time.[20]

Gregg further states that in 1800 there were three Episcopal ministers in Upper Canada—Stuart at Kingston, Langhorn at Ernestown, and Addison at Niagara.[21] There were also six Methodists, four Baptists, and four Presbyterians (Bethune, Broeffle, McDowell, and Collver).

Among the Loyalists who came to Upper Canada at the close of the American War, only a few were Baptists, but they must have been made of good stuff, for the denomination grew and increased rapidly. Tradition asserts that a congregation was organized at Beamsville, Lincoln County, as early as 1786. (This seems unlikely as Jacob Beam did not settle in Beamsville until 1790.) That a church edifice was erected there in 1796 with the Reverend William Holmes for its pastor is well authenticated. This church flourished during the first half of the nineteenth century (with Jacob Beam as its leading member) and became the mother church of many others in the Niagara district.

The oldest Baptist congregation in Eastern Ontario originated in 1785 through the preaching of Reuban Crandall, a young evangelist from the United States. The society was formally organized in 1798 when a little log church (twelve by sixteen feet) was raised in Haldimand Township.

* Mr. Alex Bruce of Unionville answered this question in the affirmative. He stated that many settlers never bothered to obtain deeds for their properties until they were well up in years.

Its first recorded pastor was Rev. Peleg Card in 1818. A church was also founded in Harlem, County of Leeds, by Abel Stevens, a United Empire Loyalist, who was ordained its first pastor in 1804.

Mention of the Baptists has been made for two reasons: first, this denomination was active at an early date (1785) in Upper Canada; secondly, according to Frank S. Mead there is a very close relationship between the Baptists and the Mennonites.[22] The first Baptist congregation had been formed in Holland in 1608 of persecuted Anabaptists. Many of them crossed the Channel and established another church in London, England. In Ontario many settlers of Mennonite background joined the Baptist Church.

ARTS AND CRAFTS

Not the least of these peoples' contributions to the cultural life of Ontario is the arts and crafts they fostered and which have been adopted by its residents. Again, the origin of many of the designs used is never understood. Fortunately, man, having a creative instinct which will not be denied, reacts against machine-made and designed articles from time to time.

In pioneer times waste of any material was a sin, hence, when clothes reached the stage when they were no longer wearable, they were torn into strips, sewn end to end, rolled into a ball and eventually made into rugs or carpets. These rugs usually followed conventional patterns which had been brought in most instances from Pennsylvania, and consisted of scenes of different kinds or sometimes mottoes. Rugs were of two kinds: hooked on a buckram base, or plaited or braided with the braids sewn together.

Associated with rugs was the piecing and quilting of bedspreads. By these two mediums the housewife added color to her drab rooms. Quilting provided much more scope than the making of rugs, as the designs were much more intricate; besides, patterns were inserted by the stitching. To discover whether quilting is still popular, the author interviewed Mrs. Menno Brubacher, who lives a short distance out of the city of Waterloo and who in her lifetime has pieced some seven hundred quilts. When shown the designs illustrated in Marie Knorr Graeff's booklet, *Pennsylvania German Quilts*, she was sure she had used all but one, and, in addition, many more not mentioned by Mrs. Graeff.[23] Her list consisted of such patterns as Tangled Garter, Diamond Twinkling Star, Fish, Blocks and Stars, Diamond Stars, Sad Iron, and Stars and Cross.

For these quilts and for other materials, dyes used by the early settlers were obtained from the following plants: yellow from golden rod; green from leaves of knott grass or smart-weed; brown from husks of the walnut or butternut; yellowish-brown from onion skins; and red ink from the fruit of the strawberry blight.

Like all well-to-do parents in Pennsylvania who supplied the bride-to-be with certain customary pieces of decorative furniture, the Canadian farmer might give an order to a cabinet-maker in the village for a walnut chest, a great wardrobe, a corner cupboard, or a kitchen dresser for the dowry of his daughter. The Pennsylvania German cabinet-maker was a skilled workman who could not be hurried, but once the job was done, it never had to be done over again.

One of the favorite gifts was the dower chests, which might be made of soft wood and painted, or of walnut finished with a high polish. Such a piece of furniture often served in place of non-existent drawers and chests. Being portable, it could be used as a trunk, lifted by iron handles, and hauled to the new home. It could be made by anyone who knew how to make a dovetailed box, and the blacksmith could be relied on to furnish the strap hinges, handles, and locks.

Tables were made with tops of broad boards and turned legs, usually with two drawers. Practically all chairs (straight-backed and rocker) were hand made. Bedsteads might have square or turned posts, according to the fancy of the maker. But whatever was made, it showed good craftsmanship and was built for utility rather than show.

Examples of "Fraktur," or pen-and-brush illumination of Gothic letters, are to be found in birth and marriage certificates, but it is difficult to know whether they were made in Upper Canada or in Pennsylvania. One is inclined to think that in most cases they were made in the latter country. Some of the "Fraktur" was religious, and some was secular, where the owner's name was surrounded by borders composed of overhanging tulips or birds and trumpet-blowing angels.

Sandstone and limestone, sometimes slate, were used for tombstones, and the motifs carved on them were usually the tulip, the lily, and the tree of life, with leaves used as bands. Lettering was often shaped with excellent delicacy and proportion.

Decorative metal work was to be found in metal hinges (usually of wrought iron), and consisted of four types—straps, angle, T, and H. Knobs, latches, latch grasps, and handles followed a few well-defined patterns and were frequently the created design of the craftsman. Locks and keys were usually more massive than decorative.

Examples of small articles of domestic use made of wood can be found in butter moulds, handles for pie markers, wooden spoons, small buckets, and the like. Often the farmer was handy with a knife and whittled many an object both useful and ornamental.

Cookie cutters might be of wood, but were usually made of tin. These cut cookies in various patterns, many of them resembling animals if these people had had contact with Moravians.

Unfortunately, little if any study has been made in Canada of the early Pennsylvania German arts and crafts, with the result that there is little appreciation of it. Many very interesting articles have been lost to Canadians, but have on the other hand been discovered by Americans and taken to the United States, where they are much valued.

Food

Few persons, as they put their teeth into a particularly juicy apple or raisin pie, are acquainted with the fact that when they are eating a fruit pie of any kind made with a double crust, they are indebted to the Pennsylvania Germans for it. True, the English of Shakespeare's time knew how to make an apple tart, but this was a deep pie with a crust on the top only.

There were many varieties of fruit pies made in the summer, according to the ripening of the different fruits. Rhubarb, strawberries, raspberries, elderberries, mulberries, gooseberries, and cherries provided variety until the early apples ripened in August. Other fruits such as plums (sometimes wild), peach, and grape followed in rapid succession. Of course, berries and fruits, both wild and cultivated, were generally made into rich preserves. The housewife who valued her reputation not only had pie on the table at each meal, but preserved fruit as well.

About the only fruits which were bought were prunes and raisins, both of these being used at the time of funerals, doubtless because of their sombre color. Two other types of pies should be mentioned here because they were enjoyed during the fall and winter—pumpkin and lemon sponge. Because the Pennsylvania German housewife never spared good ingredients, her pies made with plenty of eggs and milk were most appetizing. The "shoofly" pie never gained in Canada the popularity outside the German home that it has in Pennsylvania, perhaps because it is more cake than pie. Steamed apple dumplings were also a favorite dessert dish and one much used by the Plain Folk.

Of course, apples were a staple fruit with this group because they could be served in so many different ways. They were equally acceptable when raw, as apple sauce, in pies, as steamed apple dumplings, as apple butter, or as dried apples. Following the proverb, "Waste not, want not," these settlers saw to it that no fruit was wasted, and because apples were usually a staple crop, they could be preserved by cutting them into pieces and drying them (snitz), or by making them into apple butter.

The making of apple butter was a social event as well, as friends and relatives gathered for an evening to both work and have fun while the apples were being cut. Sometimes pears were substituted for apples, sometimes pumpkins, the latter making "Punkin' Sauce." As the fruit had first to be peeled, this was done by a mechanical parer. Then the apples were quartered and cored until several wash tubs had been filled. The following day the large copper kettle was hung over a wood fire in the yard, boiled cider was poured into it and the cut apples dumped in, together with some flavoring such as cinnamon, allspice, or cloves. It is just there where the work began, because if this mixture was not kept continually stirred, it would stick to the bottom of the kettle and burn. To prevent this, the large wooden paddle set in the kettle had a long handle which made it revolve, yet kept the person stirring some distance from the fire. This was a job which lasted from early morning until night without any let up, but the brown, flavorsome sauce amply repaid the efforts required in making it. When the apple butter had cooled it was put into crocks and set away for winter use.

There are three dishes which are frequently recognized as of "Dutch" origin. They are: sauerkraut, coleslaw, and smearkase. Sauerkraut is made by shredding the cabbage, placing alternate layers of cut cabbage and salt in a large tub, then pounding it until the liquid covers the cabbage. When the vessel is filled, it is then placed in a warm place where it ferments. In a month or so it is ready for use. Coleslaw is made in much the same manner only it is not allowed to ferment.

Smearkase or soft cheese is made of cottage cheese. First the curd is mixed with sweet cream, then salt is added, and all are mixed until smooth. Eaten with apple butter this dish is most delicious, although sometimes a taste for it has to be acquired. In the United States smearkase is called "Cottage Cheese," sometimes "Koch Kase" or "Crock Cheese."

Chicken pot-pie of a certain type can also be attributed to this group. Into a dish of partially cooked chicken, dumpling dough cut into layers of $\frac{1}{4}$ inch thickness and about 3 inches square was put and covered with potatoes cut into slices. When these layers had been alternated, a cover was placed on the dish and the pie boiled until cooked.

The Pennsylvania Germans preferred their lettuce trimmed with a dressing of cream and vinegar. They were also aware of the medicinal value of early greens such as dandelion, horsedock, burdock, and lamb's quarters. These were eagerly sought out in the early spring and cooked as greens. And, too, no one before them had discovered how delicious raw potatoes could be when cut into thin strips and fried over a slow fire.

Most people are fond of cinnamon buns, waffles, and fat cakes (doughnuts), also animal cookies, but they know little of their Pennsylvania German origin. It was customary for the housewife when making bread to use some of the dough for buns. Studded with raisins, spicy with cinnamon, and topped with a light coating of sugar, they were very appetizing. Doughnuts were called fat cakes and were made of cake dough. After being fried in deep fat they were rolled in sugar; in shape they might be twisted or round, like the doughnut of today. Mention of doughnuts would be incomplete if attention were not called to "dunking." This is the German word for dip, and so those who like to "dunk" their doughnuts or their tea cakes are following a custom established by Pennsylvania Germans. The waffle is also said to be half Holland Dutch in origin; however, it was the Pennsylvania Germans who popularized it. Cookies (especially those cut to resemble animals) originated with the Moravians who were also noted for the emphasis they put on baking during Christmas festivities.

The Pennsylvania Germans originated in a part of Europe where grapes were plentiful and where wine was a common drink. As grapes never grew very satisfactorily in Pennsylvania, other drinks took their place. It was not until about 1830 that Rhenish grapes were introduced into the Niagara district. Because of the abundance of apples, cider was a popular drink, and the housewife made less potent but nonetheless palatable drinks out of blackberries, wild cherries, currants, raspberries, elderberries, or plums. Even the lowly dandelion contributed a very refreshing drink.

Any mention of food of the Pennsylvania Germans would be incomplete without calling attention to the wonderful way in which they could cure their pork, make their sausage, head cheese, and liverwurst. In the first place they saw to it that their hogs were not too fat (200 lbs. being an acceptable weight) and that they had been fattened on grain.

Butchering was a major event in the farmer's life because it came in the category of a "bee." Neighbors and relatives assisting one another had their efforts recognized by being given backbones, spare ribs, and sausage to take home with them after their day's work. The hams and shoulders were rubbed with salt in order to preserve them until they were given a careful curing by rubbing them with saltpetre and brown sugar; then they were packed in a large barrel. If a smoke house existed—and it usually did—this meat was cured by smoke from green maple wood. After the curing, the meat was hung up in a dry place, sometimes in the granary. Anyone who has sampled meat cured in this fashion will agree that no finer tasting meat can be found anywhere.

If any criticism can be made of the meals of the Plain Folk, it would be that their food was very rich, much of it being fried, and the quantity and quality encouraged overeating. Breakfast, dinner, and supper saw the tables laden with meat, potatoes, vegetables, pies, cakes, bread, buns, together with some of the traditional seven sweets and seven sours. But these people worked hard physically; not infrequently the day began at four in the morning and ended at nine in the evening. Women worked equally as hard as men and each child from his earliest years was given tasks commensurate with his age and strength. Hence we see that although their food was rich in quality and plentiful in quantity, it suited their way of life and helps to explain why so many of them lived long lives and enjoyed such good health.

LANGUAGE

Immigrants from New York and Pennsylvania, who were in the majority among the Plain Folk, have had a determining influence on the meanings of words and expressions now used in Ontario. The following synonyms have been taken from Kurath's *A Word Geography of the Eastern United States* and are but a few selected at random.[24] The italicized word is the one introduced by these people into Ontario: *pail*, bucket; *whiffle tree, whipple tree*, swingle tree; *creek*, brook; *Johnny cake*, corn bread; *darning needle*, dragon fly; sick *at* the stomach, sick to the stomach, sick on the stomach; *coal oil*, kerosene; a *piece*, a *bite*, a snack; *nigh horse*, near horse; *picket* fence, paling or paled fence; *eaves troughs*, eaves spouts, gutters; *frying pan*, spider, skillet; *at* home, to home; *shafts* (pronounced shav or shaffs), shafts; stone *boat*, stone sled; *stoop*, piazza, verandah; *fat-cake*, doughnut; *smear case, smearkase*, Dutch cheese; *bull*, male of the cow; *lowery*, gloomy; *pig pen*, pig sty; *sitting room* (settin' room), living room; scaffold pronounced *scaffle*; *tongue*, pole; *coal scuttle*, coal hod, coal bucket, coal pail; whinny, *whinner*, nicker; *co-bossie, come bossie*, coaf, co-wench; *sook, sookie*; co-calfie; *woa, hoa*, whoa, waw; *wheel the baby*, roll the baby, ride the baby; *I want off*, I want to get off.

PROVERBS

"The Proverb plays a surprisingly prominent role in the speech of the Pennsylvania Germans; it is the very bone and sinew of the dialect, the spontaneous expression of one's own experience, a judgment or dictum which has gained vogue or taken on a definite form as a result of years of observation." [25]

In the above words Edwin Miller Fogel introduced his monumental study of Pennsylvania German proverbs, a work which contains some two thousand proverbs. He stated that of this number he found approximately one-half are German in origin, one-tenth British, one-tenth both British and German, and the remainder seemed to have no parallels in either language.[26]

The following have been selected as commonly used by persons who have associated with the Pennsylvania Germans; furthermore, they are not listed in Fogel's collection as having a British origin. This does not mean that they may not be current in the British Isles, but, even so, they may have originated in Germany. It is a well-known fact that the English people adopt words, phrases, and expressions from other languages quite freely, later coming to look upon them as an integral part of their own language.

The following are some proverbs and sayings of the Pennsylvania Germans which have been introduced into Canada:

It costs nothing to take a look.

Better break an arm than the neck .

Every one must look out for himself; God helps those who help themselves.

Ask me no questions and I'll tell you no lies.

A poor excuse is better than none.

As the tree falls so it lies.

If it does no good it will do no harm.

Beef to the hoof.

It costs nothing to say "thank you."

Don't bite off more than you can chew.

As you make your bed, so you must lie in it.

He must have gotten out of bed left leg first; he is as crabbed as a wet hen.

To stink like a polecat.

Every little helps.

A place for everything and everything in its place.

As plain as the ABC.

He swells like a bullfrog.

That shows which way the wind blows.

He blows hot and cold.

You can't get blood out of a stone.

To bellow like a bull.

Half a loaf is better than none.

If you turn up your nose at food, you aren't hungry.

I can read him like a book.

When you get down to brass tacks.

What is not worth thanking for is not worth having.
The better the day, the better the deed.
The shorter the days, the longer the nights.
It is not Sunday every day.
The paper wants rain.
Wonderful sick.
Who do you go with?
Ain't it his birthday today?
Wonders them.
Slip up town.
The candy is all.
Leave them be.
Here's your money back.
I got that down my Sunday throat.
Now help yourself.
To get shut of.
I never woke up until I heard Mom making breakfast.
A long time back.
Sloppy, slurpy.
Dunking.
Apple-pie order.
Get her dander up.
Get brushed off.
Het up.
To hatch.
Splutter.
Elbow grease.
Come clean from Montreal.
Sprinkle down the clothes.
Washerwoman who always wrenched the clothes.
Come out the small end of the horn.
Today was a week long. It seemed as though the hours had
    leaden feet.
So lean that his bones rattle.
One must keep on good terms with the devil.
Speak of the devil and you'll hear the flop of his wings.
Stretch your legs according to your covers, and your feet
    won't get cold.
There's a lid for every pot.
The dearest is always the cheapest.
As "dutch" as sauerkraut.
He doesn't think further than his nose is long.

You think more of your daddy than your mammy; your skirt hangs out.

Best to keep one's feet under one's own table.

He shows him the door.

He looks more like a corpse than a living being.

One man's loss is another's gain.

I won't trust him any further than I can see him.

One good turn deserves another.

He's not dry behind the ears; he is still in his teens.

Do as I say and not as I do.

Everybody's business is nobody's business.

If you want a thing well done, do it yourself.

Too stupid to get in out of the wet.

He acts as though he were born yesterday.

Bully for strong; not pretty for nice.

Too many irons in the fire.

Strike while the iron is hot.

He has one too many.

There are many two-legged donkeys.

He's afraid of his own shadow.

It takes two to make a quarrel.

They fight like cats and dogs.

That's a feather in his cap.

To laugh up one's sleeve.

As fat as a pig.

There are just as good fish in the sea as ever were caught.

Yield a finger and they will want the whole hand.

He drinks like a fish.

As quick as a cat.

We must not forget on which side our bread is buttered.

Old enough to know better.

The wife wears the pants.

It all went down his throat, i.e. he is a drunkard.

You can lead a horse to water but you can't make him drink.

If it won't, it won't.

Don't let the first little thing scare you off; don't make a mountain out of a molehill.

Money makes the mare go; money makes the world go round.

You can get used to anything, even hanging—if you hang long enough.
Clothes make a man.
They stick together like burrs.
Not all is gold that glitters.
Don't crow too soon.
Don't cry before you are hurt; don't "holler" till you're hurt.
You are as green as grass. Just take care that the cows won't eat you.
It's coming—yes, so is Christmas.
As crooked as the hind leg of a dog.
You are too smart, you won't live long.
A cold hand and a warm heart.
He has soon shot his bolt.
To stir up a hornet's nest.
His skull is empty; nobody home.
He is chicken-hearted.
Nothing but skin and bones.
Laugh before breakfast, you'll cry before supper.
He's off his nut.
He is weak in his upper story.
As handy as a pocket in a shirt.
To go to bed with the chickens.
To stand on one's hind legs.
Make hay while the sun shines.
He's going to the bowwows.
As sick as a dog.
Cold as Greenland.
You can't get honey from a vinegar barrel.
Give a calf rope enough and it will hang itself.
He got the mitten.
He won't leave till the last man is hanged; he wouldn't miss a trick for all the world.
The burned child is afraid of fire.
Two heads are better than one even though cabbage heads.
Many men, many minds.
Not right in the head.
What you haven't in your head, you have in your heels.
The cow that bellows most forgets her calf quickest.
One must learn to walk before one can run.
Slow but sure.

As long as it is broad; six of one and half a dozen of the other.

To laugh till the tears run down one's cheeks.

Never too old to learn.

Eavesdroppers never hear good of themselves.

Half a loaf is better than nothing.

While there's life there's hope.

To read someone a curtain lecture.

Don't tell all you know.

It takes all kinds of people to make the world.

It is a long lane that has no turning, and sometimes it turns pretty quick.

The last shall be first.

The same old song and dance.

Liars should have good memories.

He lied a blue streak.

It makes my mouth water.

Shut your fly trap.

He speaks from the shoulder.

Stay on your own dunghill.

I rubbed it under his nose.

What goes in will come out.

Silence gives consent.

What goes up comes down.

To put a spoke in a person's wheel.

It's a poor rule that doesn't work both ways.

There's a black sheep in every family.

As clean as a pin.

Put up or shut up.

There's a screw loose somewhere.

She is as thin as a bean pole.

As strong as a bull.

Never throw a stone so far away that you can't fetch it; you never know what you may need.

If the shoe fits, wear it.

Accidents will happen—in the best regulated families.

To watch a person as a cat does a mouse.

When the wind blows over the oats stubble, fall is coming on.

Nothing ventured, nothing gained.

Time to take tarts is when they's a-passin'.

A dog that will bring a bone will carry a bone.

To haul one over the coals.
To pull the wool over one's eyes.
It goes in one ear and out the other.
Enough to make a pig sick.
Strong enough to carry an egg.
To suck the thumbs, i.e. to be idle.
He burnt his fingers.
One might as well talk to a stone.
This I can put in my eye.
Throw in your hat.
Knows no more about it than the man in the moon.
Land hungry.
He got the short end of the stick, i.e. the worst of the bargain.
He has it well salted, i.e. money in the bank.

SIMILES

Round as an apple.
Flat as a pancake.
Thin as a fence rail.
Legs like a broomstick.
Wet as a dish rag.
Thick as hair on a dog's back.
Straight as a bean pole.
Bleed like a stuck pig.
As dead as a mouse.
Dirt cheap.
To work like a dog.
Proud as a peacock.
Face like a full moon.
To look like a sick hen.
To look like a drowned rat.
Lie faster than a horse can trot.

BELIEFS, SUPERSTITIONS, CUSTOMS

As the Pennsylvania Germans (like all Germans) have a touch of the mystic in them, it is not difficult to understand why superstitions played such an important part in their lives. Much has been written about the so-called "hex signs" found on the barns in Pennsylvania. These signs were not to be found in Ontario as the barns were seldom painted. As one travels through the countryside today one will see the occasional painted barn but the only decoration on it will be the name of the farm with the owner's name below it. Occasionally one will find a painted figure of a horse or a cow but never any of the wheels or stars found in Pennsylvania.

Pow-wow doctors still exist to "charm" certain diseases. The methods of these conjure doctors are varied. Whereas some use mystic words, others repeat certain passages of scripture, but the majority use the following form of invocation: "In Namen des Vaters, des Sohnes, und des Heiligen Geistes" (In the name of the Father, the Son, and the Holy Ghost).

Some of these "charmers" do not attempt to cure a disease until the moon is on the wane, and never after sunrise or before sunset, and often not in the presence of their patients. Before a "charmer" can undertake to cure a person, he must know the patient's age. Another peculiarity in connection with the practice is the belief that a woman cannot impart the knowledge of "charming" to any members of her sex; it must always be communicated to her opposite.[27]

Cures for diseases are legion and unusual. The following are but a few that are practised by the "charmers" today:

A tea brewed of flowers of the mayweed, catnip, and bark or twigs of the spice bush or flowers from the common mullein is a cure for the common cold.

To remedy a sore throat, a sock should be taken off the left foot, turned inside out and worn around the neck. (A red sock is best.)

For bee stings, mud applied on the spot will ease the pain. Also, if the bee is killed, the sting will not last.

A horse chestnut carried in the pocket is a remedy for rheumatism.

Dew rubbed on the face before sunrise during the month of May will remove freckles and give one a beautiful complexion.

The Pennsylvania Germans are also great believers in "good luck" charms. It is good luck, for example, to find a four-leaved clover or a horseshoe. It is bad luck to sing while eating at the table, open an umbrella in the house, kill a spider that is crawling over you, spill salt, or start on a journey on a Friday. They also believe that it is not a good idea to borrow either needles or salt from a neighbor as this will lead to a quarrel; nor should one present a friend with anything pointed such as a knife, brooch, or pin.

They also have a strong belief in the influence of the moon. Garden vegetables such as potatoes and peas should always be planted at full moon. Beans especially should be planted at this time and at eleven o'clock in the morning. Also, if meat of hogs killed during a new moon is placed in a pan, it will shrivel away.

The signs of the Zodiac are important to these people. For example, peas planted under the influence of the Twins will be double-podded. If cucumber seeds are planted under Virgo they will bear false blossoms; if planted under Pisces the crop will be plentiful.

There are practically no limits to the sayings about the weather:

It is a storm sign if the tea-kettle hums.

If it thunders before breakfast, it will thunder again before supper.

A bright red sun means fine weather for the following day.

It will rain: if a hen crows; if guinea fowl cry continually; if crows are unusually noisy; if there are many women out; if trains can be heard at a great distance.

If it rains on Whit Sunday, it will rain for seven Sundays in succession.

If the sun shines while it rains, it will rain for seven successive Sundays.

When a fowl seeks shelter on the approach of a shower the rain will not last long, but when it remains out in the rain there will be a continual downpour.

The weathervane is a common sight on Pennsylvania Dutch farm buildings—especially a weathervane in the form of a rooster. The following is the story of its origin:

The Dreadful Story of Hünchen and Händchen

Hünchen went to the forest and found some nuts for his wife, Händchen. She choked on the nut that he cracked for her. To bury her he chose six birds and hitched them to a hearse of rushes that he had made. Fox came along and got into the hearse; then wolf, lion, bear, giraffe, zebra, monkey, and flea. When flea sat down the hearse bogged down and disappeared in a mud hole. A cock flew up on the church steeple not far away, and so now he looks each day for fair weather so that the bog will clear and he can go to work to bury Händchen.

It seems very likely that some of our Christmas and Easter customs are also contributions of the Pennsylvania Germans to the American way of life—such as the Christmas tree, Santa Claus, and the Easter bunny. Easter like Christmas had its folklore with its Easter rabbit and the Easter egg, both of them being symbols of the regeneration of life in the spring.

The funeral customs of the Pennsylvania Germans are also of interest. Phebe Earle Gibbons, writing in 1882, described the procedure when a death occurred in a family thusly: ". . . When a death occurs, our 'Dutch' neighbors enter the house, and taking possession, relieve the family as far as possible from the labors and cares of a funeral. Some 'redd up' the house, making that which was neglected during the sad presence of a fatal disease again in order for the reception of company. Others visit the kitchen and help to bake great store of bread, pies, and rusks for the expected gathering. . . . An invitation is extended to the persons present to return to eat after the funeral, or the meal is partaken of before leaving for the graveyard; hospitality, in all rural districts, where the guests come from afar, seems to require this. The tables are set sometimes in a barn, or large wagon-house, and relays of guests succeed one another, until all are done. The neighbors wait upon the table. The entertainment generally consists of meat, frequently cold; bread and butter; pickles or sauces, such as apple butter; pies and rusks; sometimes stewed chicken, mashed potatoes, cheese, etc., and coffee invariably. All depart after the dish-washing, and the family is left to quiet again." [28] The writer attended a funeral a few years ago in Vaughan Township of an Old Order Dunkard where the above description is precisely applicable.

It will be found that most present-day families of Pennsylvania German background carry out in some modified form the procedure just mentioned. From a psychological point of view such ways of doing things are definitely sound.

VI

HUGUENOTS

RESEARCH concerning the Huguenots has revealed that French Huguenots were responsible for the discovery of Canada and for making Ontario a bi-cultural province, although that fact, if ever realized, has long been forgotten. It is not difficult to substantiate such a statement if we stop to consider the kind and number of French settlers of Huguenot ancestry who were among the first to locate in Ontario and the number of persons who have become prominent in public life, the professions, industry, and commerce, particularly in Ontario.

Such being the case, the question may very well be asked why historians have overlooked them and have made no reference to them in our textbooks. The answer can partially be learned when we explain who is a Huguenot.

In 1453 when the Turks took Constantinople (Istanbul), there was an exodus of the teachers of the classics, and many of these came to Italy. There arose a school of thought which came to be known as Humanism, and Petrarch has been recognized as its outstanding exponent. The term Humanism embraces a new ideal of culture that had come into being and a new view of life. For the first time in history the individual asserted the right to think for himself and the Humanistic movement of the Renaissance meant the entire liberation of thought from the confined teachings of the Mediaeval Church.

This movement entered France from Italy and received ready acceptance by many of the nobility and upper middle classes. But it had purely an intellectual appeal and lacked any association with religion. About this time, Lutheranism was being widely acknowledged and its principles were becoming acceptable in France when John Calvin, a lawyer from Picardy, for whom they made a strong appeal, began to advance them. His life threatened by the Jesuits and the

195

Sorbonne, he took refuge in Geneva where in 1536 he combined Humanism and Lutheranism into principles which came to be known as Calvinism. This form of Protestantism was so widely accepted in France that by 1559, when the followers were called Huguenots, one quarter of the population belonged to it.

These Huguenots were bitterly persecuted both by the Roman Catholic Church and the monarchy, largely because their creed emphasizing the individual's right to think for himself constituted a threat to both institutions. John Knox came over from Scotland in 1555 to Geneva and adopted Calvin's doctrines. He took them back to Scotland where they became known as Presbyterianism.

During the reign of Francis I, the French became increasingly jealous of the fact that the Pope had given Charles V of Spain complete control of the New World that Columbus had discovered in 1492. Consequently, when Pierre de Chabot, governor of Burgundy, urged Francis I to send an exploring expedition to America, there was a ready response. Jacques Cartier (of Protestant family) was selected to carry out an expedition in 1534. In 1542, Roberval, a Huguenot, was given command of the second expedition, along with Cartier. An effort was made to establish the first colony in New France at Port Royal but with little success.

For the next fifty years, New France was forgotten because of wars in Europe; however, Coligny, advisor to Charles IX of France and an ardent Huguenot, kept the possibility of exploration alive. But Coligny was killed in 1572 in the massacre of Huguenots on St. Bartholomew's Day. Henry IV of France, brought up a Protestant, abjured Protestantism in 1592 in order to hold his throne. He enacted in 1598 the Edict of Nantes which was designed to give Huguenots liberty to practise their religion without hindrance. However, persecution still continued and many French of the upper classes, family by family, left France, taking with them not only their skills but their financial resources. These were the fortunate Huguenots, for they did not emigrate to find themselves destitute upon their arrival in the new homeland, whether in contiguous countries or in the British Isles.

When Henry IV came to the throne, he responded to requests for the granting of the monopoly of the fur trade in America to Pontgravé and Chauvin, both Huguenots, and gave them his support. It was they who arranged for Champlain to make his first voyage to New France and it was de Monts, a personal friend of Henry IV and a strong Huguenot, who was given the fur-trade monopoly and who financed Champlain for his first three voyages of exploration in America. Consequently, it is fairly obvious that, had it not been for the enterprise of the Huguenots, there would have been no expeditions to New France. If this had not happened, it is doubtful if there would be many French in Canada today because the Dutch and English were already in New York and would have come north, attracted by the fur trade, and would have taken control of the country.

The Huguenots were active in the fur trade in New France until 1633, when Richelieu, after defeating the Huguenots in France, forbade them to have anything to do with New France. They were not allowed even to land. Garneau, the first and admittedly the best historian of early Canada and a Roman Catholic, has this to say about Richelieu's decision: "Richelieu committed a great mistake when he consented to excluding the Protestants from 'New France'; if it was necessary to expel one of the two religions, it would have been better, in the interest of the colony, to let the expulsion fall on the Catholics who emigrated in small numbers. He gave a mortal blow to Canada by establishing the Company of One Hundred Associates ...."[1]

Of the twelve governors of New France from 1534 to 1633, six were Huguenots, four were Huguenot-Catholics (those born in a Protestant area and/or willing to work with Huguenots towards the common end of exploration) and only two, who served for only a very short time, were Roman Catholics.

Who then is a Huguenot? He was a person with an enquiring mind, belonging to the nobility of France or the upper middle classes of artisans, who desired personal salvation which he could not obtain through humanism, though it sharpened his desire for it. For these principles, he was prepared to suffer persecution by the Roman Catholic Church, to die if necessary, or to escape from France as an individual to another country. There he could use his skills and organizing ability and might find it to his advantage to lose his identity as a Frenchman, even changing his name.

Intellectually, he was of a superior type with a shrewd business sense and a keen interest in exploration.

Two examples of the change of name, deliberately or from external reasons, are: Two brothers by the name of Tonnelier, which means "cooper," escaped in 1685 from Paris and went to Zweibrücken in South Germany where they had the name translated to Küfer. Eventually, this became Kieffer, Keefer, Keffer, and when this family emigrated to Pennsylvania, it was considered to be German. About the same time, a French family by the name of Le Quesnel fled from France to Dublin, Ireland, where it ultimately became Connell.

The Edict of Nantes, which had given Huguenots some measure of protection, was revoked by Louis XIV in 1685 and Huguenots were expected to abjure their religion at once and become Roman Catholics. The result was that about a half-million Huguenots escaped from France to contiguous countries, some 80,000 of them going to the British Isles, where they were welcomed because of their skills. They were responsible to a large degree for turning a pastoral country into an industrial nation. They established the textile, fine steel, glass, and paper industries. Many of them, having been highly trained officers in the army and navy of France, were able to give the British forces the benefit of their expert leadership.

However, the British Isles were for many families but a way station to North America. Queen Anne gave assistance in 1709 when ships were provided to take religious refugees to the English colonies. The Huguenot settlement at New Rochelle in New York State is well known and came into being at this time. Because of the warm climate many persons went to the Carolinas, although New England got her quota. Pennsylvania is said to have received the largest numbers, although many of them came directly from Germany and Switzerland. Because they had married German women, perhaps Germanized their names and spoke the German language, they were designated as Germans. Here we have the tendency on the part of these French Huguenots for complete assimilation. Nevertheless, no matter how enthusiastically they consider themselves Americans, they still have a deep pride in their ancestry. And well they might: five of their presidents and countless numbers of business and professional persons as well, have had Huguenot ancestry. Thirty-three states have Huguenot societies with a National Society as well.

The assimilation of French Huguenots in Canada, particularly in Ontario, has been almost complete, so much so that the name is almost unknown. Although they no longer speak the French language, their French culture has become part and parcel of Ontario's way of life.[2]

The migration of French Huguenots into Upper Canada began as early as 1776. William Canniff gives us the first record: "In 1776, there arrived at St. Fort George, in a starving state, Mrs. Nellis, Mrs. Secord, Mrs. Young, Mrs. Buck, and Mrs. Bonner, with thirty-one children, whom the circumstances had driven away."[3] Of these we know from records that Mrs. Nellis (de Nélis) and Mrs. Secord (de Sycar), probably Mrs. Bonner (Bonheur), and Mrs. Young (le Jeune) were Huguenots and even Mrs. Buck (le Bouc). When the American Revolutionary War ended, their husbands joined them, thus becoming the vanguard of a number of Huguenot families to settle in the Niagara Peninsula.

In 1784 the British government brought five boatloads of emigrés from New York City to Eastern Canada. Among them were a large number of French Huguenots who were settled along the Bay of Quinte and in the Edwardsburgh and Augusta townships. Essex and Kent counties also received some French settlers but these came up the Ohio River.

During the nineteenth century, there were many immigrants coming from the British Isles whose ancestors during the preceding century had escaped from France and had taken refuge in the British Isles. When they came to Canada, they came as Britishers for, in many cases, they had intermarried with them. It is interesting to note that French blood has a dominant characteristic. It may skip several generations and then will be evident because of the typical French build, features, and a keen, logical mind. In Ontario, there would appear to be two types: short and small of build with a narrow face, black hair, and dark eyes of a peculiar intensity—the Mediterranean type. Then there is the Teutonic, coming from the north of France. Such persons are tall but not fleshy, often with blue eyes, and a long, narrow face.

Now that persons in Ontario are becoming aware of the

outstanding characteristics of their Huguenot forebears, there is being uncovered a pride which, until a recent study, has been entirely latent. In all probability, it is only a matter of time until Huguenot societies come into being similar to those already organized in the United States.

VII

THE SIX NATIONS INDIANS

IN Canada, the Six Nations Indians, to whom the French gave the name of Iroquois, have had difficulty in getting full recognition, because of their stand against the French in the colonial wars. In general, the information that is found in our history texts originated from the French who were their enemies. And this is not all. Their reputation in the United States has become the black legend of the north as a result of their loyalty to the Crown in the American Revolution. Thus, on both sides of the border, they have been penalized for their loyalty to the English Crown.

Considerable archaeological and anthropological studies have been made of the Iroquois both in Canada and the United States, but no comprehensive history of them has ever been written from the British point of view. For many years it was thought that the Indian population would decrease and even disappear; however, the opposite is now the case, for the numbers of Indians are increasing and our governments are giving serious consideration as to how the Indians can again become active members of the community.

Probably the first thing for Canadians to do is to cease to look upon them as second-class citizens incapable of managing their own affairs or making a worthwhile contribution to Canadian society. One fundamental fact should be recognized; it is generally accepted that the Six Nations as a tribe were superior in intelligence to all other Indians in Canada. This is shown by their ability to work during some four hundred years with the whites and still maintain their independent characteristics. Hence, these Six Nations should be regarded as a people, without whose valiant loyalty there might be no English-speaking North America today. For it was the Indians who provided the protection behind which the feeble English coastal colonies developed strength, first for self-defense and then for victory over France. It was they who, when strategically settled in Upper Canada, provided a bulwark against invasion in the war of 1812–1814 from either Niagara or Detroit and who thereby played a major role in preventing Canada from becoming part of another country. History has yet to give them full credit for this contribution.

The Six Nations are unique among the Indians in Canada; they were never conquered by either the French or the English. Having lost their homes, at the invitation of the British government they came to Canada of their own free will and preference at the same time and for the same reasons as the British, Palatine German, and French Huguenot settlers with whom they had allied themselves during the war. Hence there is no logical reason for not considering them United Empire Loyalists; for, in these days of recognizing human rights, we cannot make any distinction of race or color. It should also be recorded that the Iroquois played a major role in the early settlement of Upper Canada, for they constituted the largest group of settlers to come to Canada at that period under one leader on one grant. They came to make their living by agriculture as they had in the English colonies.

The origin of the Indians is obscure. It is thought that they came in bands to America from Asia by crossing the Bering Strait and made their way southward from Alaska about the time of the last Ice Age on a route roughly corresponding with the present Alcan Highway from Fairbanks, Alaska, to Edmonton, Alberta. They spread out all over the two Americas, leaving a trail of spear points from Alaska to Tierra del Fuego. These Indians were of Mongolian extraction.

The North American Indians can be divided into seven cultural areas: Eastern Woodland, Southeastern, the Plains, the Southwestern, the Plateau, the California, and the North Pacific. There are about thirty language families spoken by these groups and some six hundred dialects. Hence, with all these numbers, when we say that the Iroquois were a superior tribe, it speaks volumes.

"Current archaeological research has added substantial support to Dr. R. S. MacNeish's hypotheses of an *In Situ* development of the Iroquois peoples in the northeast. The 'In Situ Hypothesis' proposes that the Iroquois evolved in place (Southern Ontario, southern Quebec, New York, western Vermont, northern Pennsylvania) from a common Middle Woodland culture base. . . . This development has been traced down in time from the historic tribes to approximately 900 A.D."[1]

Our interest lies in the Five Nations: Mohawk, Onondaga, Oneida, Seneca, and Cayuga. The term Six Nations could not be applied until about 1715 when the Tuscaroras came up from North Carolina and joined them. However, the Tuscaroras were never given a voice in the Long House Council, being considered "women." (Women could attend but not vote.)

Unfortunately the Iroquois, like all Indians, had no written language. Everything we know about them has come through archaeological research, oral tradition, or tribal memory. Early white writers were biased, and either friendly disposed, such as the Dutch and English, or bitterly critical, as the French, particularly in *The Jesuit Relations*.

They had certain outstanding characteristics, however, of which there is plenty of evidence: they were skilled agriculturists and second to none in political organization, statecraft, and military prowess. Richard Pilant, in an address to the Institute of Iroquoian Studies stated: "The Six Nations in Canada constitute the most complete survival we have today of one of the highest cultures of one of the races of mankind—the Indian. Unlike the Mayas and the Incas to the south, the Long House People developed a democratic form of self-government. They alone amongst the Indian Nations made a major political contribution in their form of government, which can be maintained to have furnished a prototype for the United States and the United Nations. Socially, the Six Nations met the sociologist's test of higher cultures by having given a preferred status to women."[2]

Politically, the Iroquois made their greatest contribution by setting up the Confederacy about 1560. Daganawida and Hiawatha, an Onondaga chief, were the legendary initiators of this pact which was built on three great doctrines or principles:

(1) Health of mind and body.
(2) (a) Peace among individuals and groups of individuals.
    (b) Righteousness in conduct; its advocacy in thought and speech.

(3) (a) Equity in the adjustment of rights and obligations.

(b) Orenda or magic power of people and institutions.

Based on this code a mighty political unit came into being for the purpose of maintaining peace and efforts were put forth to have all the Indian tribes join. It was a model social order where each tribe was autonomous and, regardless of size, had the same voting privileges. Its democratic form of government was accepted by Jefferson as a basis for the Constitution of the United States and it is easily recognized that the present United Nations has a similar structure with a similar purpose.

Contrary to accepted opinion, the Iroquois were a matrilineal society. Women held a very high place. They selected the chiefs and could depose them; furthermore, the chiefs must come from the mother's lineage. For instance, the son of a chief could not be eligible to become a chief, whereas the nephew could. Matrons attended the Long House meetings. They could speak but not vote. Women owned the crops and the land as much as Indians approved of ownership. (It was their belief that they were the custodians of the land for future generations, hence could never "sell" the land in the white man's meaning of that term. All they could do was lease it.) When prisoners were brought in, the women decided those who were to be adopted into the tribe.

The families were made up of clans but no one was allowed to marry into his own clan. These clans had hereditary chiefs and sometimes sachems who were chosen for their outstanding powers in war, such as Joseph Brant. These clans were named after animals—Wolf, Bear, Beaver, Tortoise.

We first learn the importance of the Iroquois when Champlain chose to support the Huron tribe against the Iroquois. The latter, in consequence, became the bitter enemies of the French for, unlike the Hurons, they refused to respond to the missionary efforts of the Jesuit priests. In the end, the Iroquois wiped out the Hurons at Georgian Bay in 1749, together with the Petuns (Tobacco Indians) immediately south of them, and the Neutrals along the north shore of Lake Erie in 1751. This was done as a matter of self-defense.

It was during the Seven Years' War of 1755–1763 that the Iroquois reached a new importance to the British. William

Johnson, who later became Sir William, was certainly one of Britain's early empire builders. He identified himself with the Six Nations by winning their confidence by honest dealing, learning to speak their language, dressing on occasion like them, and being accepted as a chieftain of their nation. During the struggle with the French in the 1750's he was able to assure their allegiance and hold it for the British Crown, and it was probably through the support of the Six Nations that Britain was able to defeat the French and conquer Canada.

This allegiance held good for the Mohawks, Cayugas, Onondagas and Senecas during the American Revolutionary War. Unfortunately, when the treaty was signed between Britain and the Americans, no provision was made for the Six Nations tribes who had remained loyal. However, General Haldimand promised them a home in Canada and this was accepted and acted upon.

In 1784 the Six Nations settled in Canada. Some went to the area reserved for them on the Bay of Quinte, but the bulk of them settled near the Grand River, south of what is now Brantford. Actually, they were given land six miles on either side of the Grand River from its source to its mouth —from Fergus to Lake Erie. These Indians should be regarded as agricultural settlers, since it was for them as well as white settlers that many saw- and grist-mills were built at that time by white settlers. Actually, the Indians far outnumbered the white settlers. If proof is required to show that these Indians were agriculturists, one can point to the fact that it took General Sullivan two days to destroy the crops of the Senecas in the year 1779.

Again, the contribution of Joseph and Molly Brant and the Six Nations towards keeping Canada intact cannot be over-estimated. After the death of Sir William Johnson in 1774, it was Molly Brant, his wife by Indian practice, who was able, almost single-handed, to retain the allegiance of the Six Nations for Britain and it was her brother, Joseph, the protégé of Sir William, who fought for the rights of his people and secured for them land in Upper Canada and later looked after their settlement on that land.

When we come to the war of 1812–1814, we find that, had it not been for the Indians, the battle of Queenston Heights might well have been lost by the British. Historian G. F. G.

Stanley points out the role they played during that struggle. Perhaps their numbers were not large but the Indian mode of fighting increased their importance many times. Stanley ends his appraisal in these words: "If the Raiders failed at Queenston Heights and on the Niagara frontier, it was in part, and in large part, owing to the participation on the British side of those descendants of the League of the Hodenosaunce, whom the fortunes of war and revolution brought to Canada nearly two hundred years ago."[3]

What Stanley has said in regard to the Battle of Queenston Heights is equally true for the balance of the war. Once again Ontario owes the Six Nations a debt of gratitude.

It should be self -evident that the Six Nations have played a strategic part in the life of Canada. For this reason, if for no other, there should be a reappraisal of them as people. Only as we understand their nature and aspirations and recognize the contributions they have made in the past, can we successfully co-operate with them for their future.

VIII

SOME CONCLUSIONS

As stated at the beginning, this has been a study in understanding an ethnic group which has become unaware of its background (except the religious) and is unwilling to make any claims for itself as having made any special contribution to the body politic.

From the facts that we have been able to discover certain conclusions may be drawn:

1. The very earliest settlers in Upper Canada were mainly Palatinate and Swiss Germans, French Huguenots, or English Quakers who came for the most part from New York State.

2. A much closer relationship existed between the settlers in the Colonies and Canada than history has suggested. Because of this relationship, information (largely through the fur-trade) was available for anyone wishing to migrate.

3. There were more settlers in Upper Canada than those of whom we have accurate knowledge. There were squatters who came to Canada before there were government officials to even grant them location tickets. (Robert Gourlay makes a significant statement after giving the population of the Newcastle district as 4734. He says: "... and admit that poor persons, *who are not on the roll* [italics mine], amount to 266.") [1]

4. Many of those who migrated did so because they had fought against the revolting Colonists or because they wished to remain neutral (Quakers, Mennonites, Dunkards). To be neutral was always interpreted as being *against* the Colonists. There were many, however, who went north because of the promise of cheap land and because they were impelled by the spirit of adventure; besides, the Indians were friendly.

5. As one studies the development of the different sects one is impressed by the fact that in each period there was a *Zeitgeist* which operated in the different countries throughout Europe, taking the form appropriate to the psychology of

each race. Names for these movements differed but the basic principles were the same.

6. Democracy was kept alive by the sects we have been studying, since they, without exception, championed the right of the individual to live and worship according to his way of thinking, unobstructed by Church or State.

7. There were few persons of Scottish background among the early settlers in Upper Canada largely because as Scotch-Irish they were much opposed to Britain and had fought against her during the Colonial War. This point of view is borne out by Hall: "It has often seemed strange that the States that fought most fiercely to free the West from the influences of France, and to make the Mississippi Valley English, should thirteen years later have been not one bit behind New England in fighting England. The reasons lie largely in the influence of this Scotch-Irish group. When in 1719 the Scotch-Irish began to come to America they were the bitter enemies of England, and particularly of the Anglo-Catholic tradition of England as established in Ireland. It was French Catholicism that they fought in America, and when the battle was over they were as eager as ever to fight the English; especially when the threat of a bishop and a really active Anglo-Catholicism seemed to be on the horizon. For the Scotch-Irish grew up in bitter opposition to all Catholicism, in both its Roman and Anglican forms. Its hatred of the papacy and of Episcopal Catholicism amounted to a passion...." [2]

"Without any doubt the Scotch-Irish Presbyterian ministry was almost to a man on the side of the Revolution, and the General Synod that had been meeting since 1717 was in 1776 one of the most thoroughly interstate associations the colonies possessed." [3]

What is more, their numbers were not great. According to the Beards: "The Scotch-Irish and Scotch were about one-sixth of the population of the colonies, most of it having passed through Pennsylvania to Virginia, Maryland, North Carolina, and even Tennessee." [4] As recent an historian as Donald Creighton claims that the Scots formed no important part of the original Loyalist settlement and that they did not begin to come in increasing numbers until the conclusion of the War of 1812. [5]

8. There were five main areas of settlement. These were in

order of time: Niagara, 1776; Essex, 1780; Eastern Ontario, 1784; York County, 1793; and Waterloo, 1800. Fifteen of the thirty-two counties of lower Ontario had settlers by 1780 or earlier.

9. Financially, there were two classes of immigrants: soldiers and settlers who had lost everything in the United States and who had to be financed for three years for they brought no assets with them, and the Pennsylvania Germans and Quakers who brought money, livestock, and equipment.

10. The land, climate, and farm practices required were similar to what were to be found in New York or Pennsylvania—or in the Palatinate or Switzerland. For this reason the same methods were employed, thus giving the pattern of agriculture to the province. This pattern in the main was the building of bank barns as soon as possible for the purpose of storing feed and housing the livestock during the winter months; the proper care of the land and the development of the family farm which was more or less financially self-contained; and the knowledge of and interest in the growing of fruits of all kinds.

11. With the exception of the County of Waterloo, settlers in other parts of the province belonging to this ethnic group have been assimilated to such an extent that many of their descendants are entirely unaware of their background. However, in the assimilative process, the characteristics of this group—a pioneering spirit, an unwillingness to compromise for selfish ends, integrity, persistence, and willingness to work hard—are quite apparent in those who definitely can trace back their ancestry to this group.

Religiously, again the process of assimilation has taken place, except in Waterloo County where the Mennonite group are increasing in numbers. This is equally true of the Amish who with few exceptions came directly from Europe.

12. Culturally this ethnic group has made a major contribution but one which is seldom appreciated. Our language has been enriched by many words, phrases, and sayings which were brought here by them. Many arts and crafts can be traced to the Pennsylvania German, such as the making of rugs, quilts, and furniture. Our food menus have been enriched by many dishes and our landscape by many an attractive bank barn, a stone house, or a brick house set in a carefully kept yard with a vegetable and fruit garden close by.

In view of the fact that so many residents of Ontario and many other parts of Canada can trace their ancestry to members of this ethnic group, it is only fitting that some appraisal be made of them and their contribution not only as religious sects but as groups which have built their racial characteristics into the warp and woof of our national life, adding variety and richness. "Queer" they may have been (perhaps "different" would be a better term), but it is significant that in two particulars they have given leadership to the United Nations. The Plain Folk anticipated the Marshall and Colombo plans, because since the close of World War II they have sent supplies of food and clothing amounting to millions of dollars to the stricken parts of the world. Their "Heifer Plan" has meant and will mean a great deal to backward countries where a well-bred animal is almost unknown.

The relief work done by the Mennonites and Brethren in Christ (Dunkards) in Canada has reached amazing proportions. Mr. Cornelius J. Rempel, Manager of the Mennonite Central Committee, which handles all the relief activities of these two church bodies, has given the following information:

During past years, thousands of tons of clothing, shoes, bedding and mending material; flour, meats, fats, fruits, and vegetables; Christmas bundles, school books, and other books, toys, etc., have been sent throughout the world to persons in need. The value of the foregoing has been estimated in millions of dollars. In addition, many thousands of dollars has been contributed in cash.

Friends and relatives have also contributed large sums to help their co-religionists settle in Canada. Most of this amount will be repaid by the immigrants. Mr. Rempel estimates that, in addition to the above, supplies of clothing, various utensils, and cash have been sent during the past three years to Europe and South America to the value of $100,000 each year.

Bishop E. J. Swalm advises that the Brethren in Christ in Canada have contributed to the "Heifer" project for relief carried on through the Church of the Brethren in the United States. During past years they have sent several heifers each year to Europe; these have been registered pure-bred animals, blood-tested and meeting other government requirements. Each family which receives a heifer is expected to give the calf to another family. If the calf is a heifer, it may be raised to produce milk for them; if a bull calf, it is raised to sire dairy herds.

To the Quakers must go the credit for originating relief work. As far back as 1917, Albert S. Rogers acted as the Canadian representative for the American Friends Service Committee, and during the period from 1917 (when the organization was formed) until 1922, funds came in which were channelled through the Philadelphia office and used for relief work in such countries as Germany, Austria, and France.

The Canadian Friends Service Committee was officially established in 1931 and in the sphere of relief it has been coöperating with the Canadian Save the Children Fund until the present day. The Committee also has its own relief appeal for foreign service and the funds received by it are used for the purchase of relief supplies in Canada. Receiving countries have been Austria, Finland, France, Germany, Hungary, Poland, India, China, Japan, and Syria. In addition to this work it has also participated in the work of the Friends Ambulance Unit in China, which later became the Friends Service Unit. Also, aside from personnel serving in China, young people from Canada served with the Friends Service Units in Germany, Poland, and India. The funds for these came in the main from other Canadian sources although the Committee did make a cash contribution. G. M. White writes: "They [Quakers] are probably the world's most-respected minority group. Far more non-Quakers than Quakers work for and support the American Friends Service Committee. Quakers are a minority. Many friends of Friends see in them the practice of the essentials of first-century Christianity. . . . Those who know Friends, honor them." [6]

The Quakers too are once more gaining recognition for their technique of settling their differences, especially by the United Nations to which it is becoming more clear as time goes on that majority decisions often settle nothing, in fact, create greater problems. It is no wonder then that the old Quaker technique, where the sense of the meeting may be arrived at by unanimous agreement and where no one individual or group of individuals is permitted to dominate the situation, is admired.

However, the Quakers in Ontario (like other Plain Folk)

have had their greatest problems in the religious sphere. The first seceders became the Children of Peace; then came the Separation of 1812 as a result of the Hicksite-Orthodox Controversy; then the Separation of 1881, which was really a split between the Conservative and Liberal groups. Then, too, they have had the common difficulties of pacifist groups during two world wars, but the government has somewhat moderated its attitude towards "conscientious objectors." As previously mentioned, the Quakers have served on many occasions in non-combatant services in the field of war.

"Because of never having been primarily interested in recruiting membership, they have depended almost entirely on birthright membership and membership by convincement." [7] For this reason their numbers have decreased rather than increased.

The Mennonites, on the other hand, have increased their membership, although throughout the nineteenth century this was not the case. A struggle went on in regard to the use of English rather than German in their church services, with English finally winning out. Then too, because of the opposition of many groups to higher education, many young people drifted into other church affiliations. Persecution of any kind was lacking until World War I, when a stand had to be taken in regard to enlistment. A considerable number of Mennonite youth enlisted in both world wars and this caused Mennonite principles to be resurveyed (including a change of attitude on the part of certain groups to a more liberal interpretation of life and education), resulting in an increase in interest and membership.

But the Mennonite basic practices have not really changed much from those laid down by their founder, Menno Simons, and true to their individualism, Ontario Mennonites have divided into six main groups, although some of these have split again. They are as follows:

1. Conservative Mennonites—(a) Martin: wear long dresses, very plain, no light colors; hooks and eyes. They won't use a motor car even to ride in; no tractors, but will use stationary engines.
   (b) Old Order: less conservative than Martin. They won't use a car but will ride in one. A telephone for business only; tractors but no trucks. Dress not so plain.

(c) Markham: will use cars and telephones; quite progressive but do not believe in higher education or in Sunday Schools. These three groups have no missionary effort.

2. The Ontario Mennonite Conference—they have thirty congregations in Waterloo County. They are active in missionary effort and believe in education and are increasing in numbers.

3. Mennonite Brethren—Russian background; came to Kansas in 1874. Seven churches in Ontario; strong interest in education, music, and missionary work; practise single immersion, backwards.

4. United Missionary—formerly known as Mennonite Brethren in Christ. Active in missionary work; interested in education; also increasing in numbers. This group practises single immersion, backwards.

5. Sterling Avenue—General Conference Mennonites. Quite liberal; very active in education and missionary effort.

6. Amish—this is the most conservative of all the groups and is divided into: (a) Old Order; (b) Conservative. The Old Order Amish usually wear beards whereas the Mennonites no longer do. A few of the Amish wear garb which is of the plainest, hooks and eyes replacing buttons. They wear broadfall trousers and cut their hair in a straight line about level with the lobe of the ear. They are furthermore definitely opposed to education beyond the eighth grade and their community life is very in-bred. Their church services are carried on in High German and they use the hymn book written in Germany. The Conservative groups have modern conveniences in their houses, curtains on their windows and use telephones and motor cars. Their dress resembles that of the moderate Mennonites.

In brief, these Palatinates and others belonging ideologically to the same ethnic group, have at one time or another been considered heretics and treated as such. Although throughout the centuries they have been persecuted for their beliefs as they have usually been a minority group, yet they have always stood for the rights of the individual, a principle basic to democracy. Upholding the Four Freedoms, they have felt that it was their duty to alleviate the sufferings of other human beings regardless of their race, color, or religion. Almost fanatically individualistic, they have always believed that every person should live and worship as his conscience dictated. They have in peace times organized to promote peace and prevent war. Not only have they thought that war never settled any world problems, but they have considered that to kill one's fellow-man was sinful, even in self-defense. The United Nations Organization has recognized the great need of alleviating the sufferings of stricken peoples if peace is ever to be achieved. The great unpublicized efforts of the Plain Folk during the past years are a concrete way of putting into practice the principles advocated by the United Nations.

Ralph Waldo Emerson once said, "Whoso would be a man, let him be a non-conformist." The Palatinate or Swiss German is a non-conformist. By the same token he is an individualist and it would be difficult to say which preceded the other. To explain what brought about this non-conformity and individualism one must go back, not to Pennsylvania, but to Europe. Furthermore, one cannot find the genesis in the seventeenth century but in the twelfth; that is, his progenitors in thought at least were the Waldenses.

The Palatinate or Swiss German furthermore does not take any particular pride in his individualism nor does he get much satisfaction from it, except for the fact that he has been true to himself. Seldom does he come to conclusions by the emotional route. Wrong he may be, yet he has reasons which appeal to him and once oriented he proceeds in that direction regardless of the opposition he may encounter.

On this account he has often been considered as pig-headed yet, if his stubbornness be analyzed, it will be found that it is based on moral conviction. Because of his courage he makes a good leader for the cause he represents since he will follow through. He will not deliberately offend, but he is not given to showing too much tact. His very frankness will command respect but not increase his popularity. Throughout the centuries he has had to pay dearly for his forthrightness and allegiance to what he believed to be the right objective.

Paradoxically, outwardly he may seem very docile, easily led, and one not likely to stand up for himself. However, this demeanor is deceptive, since he is only easily led when he has confidence in the leadership. Whenever this confidence ceases, he immediately asserts his prerogative to choose his own direction. This explains the many sects these people have broken into.

Two more outstanding characteristics are the large part religion plays in his life and his love for the soil. To him the soil is sacred and he is its custodian. Although often unwilling to follow new patterns of living, he is usually most receptive to new ideas concerning agriculture. Manually he has always been expert and his home and his barn bear testimony to his ingenuity with tools.

He makes an excellent pioneer for several reasons: in the first place he has an "itchy heel" and is eager to seek out new lands, hence is a born explorer; secondly, he adjusts to new situations because he has an inventive mind. Lastly, he has never been afraid of physical hardship, and his constitution, rugged because of the plain living of his ancestors, stands him in good stead.

The German housewife too must not be overlooked. She has long been expert in growing flowering plants, fruits, and vegetables; also in their preparation for the table. She has been just as dexterous with her fingers, as is shown by her rugs and quilts. Although quiet in manner, she has ruled her family in an effective way and instilled in them the tenets of her beliefs, sacred and secular. At all times she has been a helpmate in the true sense of the word for her husband.

Altogether the Palatinates or Swiss Germans, whether male or female, have been an asset to any country that has offered them asylum.

More study and recognition should also be given to the Huguenots and the Six Nations Indians who fled to Canada after the American Revolutionary War.

APPENDIX A

LOCATIONS AND DATES OF FIRST SETTLEMENTS IN UPPER CANADA

From *Report of Ontario Agriculture Commission*, 1881

County	Township	First Settled	First Recorded Settlers	Nationality	Religion
I *Counties entered by settlers in 1780 or earlier*					
Essex . .	Sandwich W.	1700	Army Settlers (1700)	French	
	Sandwich E.	1760	Baby Family (1796)	English	
	Gosfield	1782	Army Settlers (1760) Kratz, Weigeli, Iler, Fox (1782)	German	Lutheran (?)
Prince Edward .	Colchester S.	1782–85			
	Marysburg North	1760	Hessians (1784)	German	Lutheran
	Hallowell	1770	Conrad Bongard	English	
	Sophiasburg	1780	Quakers (1784)	English	Quaker
	Athol	1783	Quakers (1784)		Quaker
	Hillier	1783			
	Marysburg South	1808			
Grenville . .	Edwardsburg	1775	Jessop's Corps (1784)	German, Scotch	Lutheran, Reformed
	Watford	1789			
	Bastard	1795			
	Augusta	1796	Paul & Barbara Heck (1778)	German, Scotch	Lutheran, Reformed
	Oxford	1800	Jessop's Corps (1784)		
	Gower South	1802			
Lennox and Addington .	North Fredericksburg	1776			
	South Fredericksburg	1783	Col. Rogers' Corps (1784)	German, English, French	Lutheran, Quaker, Reformed
	Ernestown	1784	Miller, Mabee, Huff (1784)	German	Lutheran

County	Township	Date	Settlers	Nationality	Religion
	Adolphustown	1784	Van Alstine, Dorland (1784)	English	Quaker
			Rutton	French	Huguenot
	Camden and Richmond	1800	Moravians (?)	German	Moravian
Haldimand ·	Seneca	1776			
	Rainham	1791	Jacob Hoover & Sons (1791)	German	Mennonite
	Walpole	1791	Peter Klinger Smith (White Peter) (1788?)	German	
	Canboro	1802			
	Nelson	1804			
	Trafalgar	1805			
Stormont ·	Cornwall	1776			
	Osnabruck	1784			
	Finch	1805			
Lincoln ·	Caistor	1778	John Dochstader (1778)	German	Lutheran (?)
	Clinton	1780	John Beam (1788)	German	
	Louth	1780	Andrew Bradt	German	
	Grimsby	1780	Kulps, Albright, Hahn, Tufford (1786)	German	Mennonite
	Gainsboro	1782	John Greene (1782)	German	Quaker
	Grantham	1783	John Dochstader (1782)	French	
	Niagara	1784	John DeCou (1788)	German	Lutheran
Leeds ·	Elizabethtown	1779	Peter Lampman (1783)		
	Escott Front	1780			
	Yonge Front	1790	Jacob Baker (1797)		
	Leeds and Lansdowne	1805			
Hastings	Sidney	1780			
	Thurlow	1788			
Welland ·	Bertie	1780	Quakers	English	Quaker
	Pelham	1780	John Winger	German	Dunkard
	Thorold	1781	Quakers	English	Quaker
	Willoughby	1784	Sherk (1789)	German	Mennonite

LOCATIONS AND DATES OF FIRST SETTLEMENTS IN UPPER CANADA—*cont.*

County	Township	First Settled	First Recorded Settlers	Nationality	Religion
Welland ·	Stamford	1784			
	Humberstone	1785			
	Crowland	1788			
	Wainfleet	1790			
Prescott and Russell ·	Hawkesbury East	1780			
	Clarence	1780			
	Hawkesbury West	1800	Simeon Vankleek (1786)		
Kent ·	Longueuil	1800			
	Camden	1780			
	Howard	1795			
	Dover	1800			
	Chatham	1810			
Frontenac ·	Wolfe Island	1780			
	Kingston	1783	Capt. Grass' Corps	German	Lutheran
	Loughboro	1800			
	Storrington	1804			
	Portland	1806			
II *Counties entered by settlers in 1785 or earlier*					
Glengarry ·	Charlottenburg	1783	Highlanders	Scottish	Roman Catholic
	Lancaster	1786			
	Kenyon	1790			
	Lochiel	1794			
Dundas ·	Williamsburg	1784	Merkley, Casselman, Becker, Shell, Williamsburgh	German	Lutheran
	Matilda	1800(?)			
	Mountain	1803			

218

III *Counties entered by settlers in 1790 or earlier*

County	Township	Year	Settler	Nationality	Religion
York .	Markham	1790	Michael Quantz (1793)	German	Lutheran
			W. Stiver (1793)	German	Lutheran
	York	1792	Nicholas Miller (1793)		
	Whitchurch	1795	Nathaniel Hastings (1796)		
	Vaughan	1796			
	Scarborough	1798	Jeremiah Annis (1793)	English	Puritan
			Sarah Ashbridge (1793)	English	Quaker
	Gwillimbury E.	1798			
	King	1799	Benjamin Pearson (1797)	German	
			Adam Kaake (1796)	German	
	Etobicoke	1800	Philip Bartholomew (1800)		
	Gwillimbury North	1803			
Lanark	Montague	1790			
Durham and Northumberland	Murray	1790			
	Clark	1792	Germans from Pa. (1792)		
	Hope	1793			
	Darlington	1794	Roger Conant (1778)	English	Puritan
	Cramahe	1796	Joseph Keeler (1789)		
	Haldimand	1797			
Wentworth .	Saltfleet	1790	Jean Baptiste Rousseau (1780)	French	Huguenot
	Ancaster	1790			
	Glanford	1793	McGregor VanEvery (1783)	English	
	Flamboro West	1793	Gilbert Family (1782)		Quaker
	Flamboro East	1800			
	Beverley	1800			
	Binbrook	1814			

IV *Counties entered by settlers after 1790*

County	Township	Year	Settler	Nationality	Religion
Norfolk .	Walsingham	1791	William Smith (1785)	German	Dunkard
	Woodhouse	1792	John Troyer (1789)	German	
	Windham	1795			

LOCATIONS AND DATES OF FIRST SETTLEMENTS IN UPPER CANADA—*cont.*

County	Township	First Settled	First Recorded Settlers	Nationality	Religion
Norfolk	Townsend	1796	Culvers (1798) Slaght (1796)		
Brant	Middleton Burford Brantford	1810 1793 1806	Thomas Horner (1793)		
Oxford	Oxford West Blenheim Oxford East Norwich South Norwich North	1796 1798 1800 1807 1810	Abraham Nelles (1797)		
Ontario	Pickering Uxbridge	1800 1807	Thos. Hilborn and Pa. Quakers (1798)		
Elgin	Whitby East Whitby Bayham Dunwich Aldborough Malahide	1800 1810 1800 1803 1804 1809	Ben Wilson (1794)		
Waterloo	Waterloo	1800	John Bean George Bechtel } (1800)		
Middlesex	Woolwich Delaware	1806 1801	First settlers (1799) B. Allan & Jasper Crow (1801)		
Halton	Nelson	1804	Peter Ghent (1805)	English	
Peel	Trafalgar Toronto	1805 1808	Asabel Davis (1792) Bates (1800)		
Simcoe	Tecumseh	1810	Andrew Cook (1808)		

ADDITIONAL NAMES OF PERSONS OR FAMILIES MIGRATING FROM THE COLONIES
TO UPPER CANADA

I THE SQUATTERS' ERA (1776–1792)

Name	Migrated from	Date	Migrated to	Other Information
Beam, John	New Jersey	1788	Founded Beamsville	Parents, German.
Boughner (Buchner), Henry, John, Matthias, Martin	Maryland	1789	Lyons Creek	
Bower (Baumwart), Henry		1791	Walsingham	
Cohoe, Ambrose (wife, Deborah Heacock)	Bucks Co., Pa.	1788	Fonthill	Father, Daniel, born in Ireland of Huguenot descent, married Mary Cutter of England before migrating to Pa. All were Quakers.
Cohoe, Andrew (wife, Lydia Wesley)		1788	Norwich	
Cohoe, John (wife, Mary Moore)		1788	Thorold	
Gonder, Jacob	Pa.	1787		Michael (his son) Gonder's house set on fire during war; fined £1000 for not carrying arms against the King.
Hansler, George	Pa.	1786	Twelve Mile Creek	Married Rosanna Slough as second wife.
Lampman, Peter	New York	1783	Niagara Tp.	Died 1834, aged 86, Lutheran.
Lampman, Frederick	New York	1784		
Plato (Platow) family	Mohawk Valley, N.Y.			A member of Butler's Rangers, buried in Plato burying-ground with other German families such as Rohr, Huffman, Jansen, Beam, Benner.
Lundy, Samuel		1786	Niagara (later Yonge St., York Co.)	Quaker.
Lundy, William		1786	Niagara	Quaker.

APPENDIX B

ADDITIONAL NAMES OF PERSONS OR FAMILIES MIGRATING FROM THE COLONIES TO UPPER CANADA—THE SQUATTERS' ERA (1776-1792)—cont.

Name	Migrated from	Date	Migrated to	Other Information
Rohrer, Chris.	Maryland	1791	Walsingham	
Sloughs	Pa.	1789		
Young (Mrs. Anna Beamer)	Huntingdon Co., Pa.	1790	Grimsby (1791)	Daughter of John William and Anna Maria Young, who emigrated from Germany in 1753.
Barker, David (wife, Lydia Shore)	New York	1784	Adolphustown	Came with Van Alstine—attended Quaker meetings.
Bonisteel Family	New York	1797	Sidney	
Bowerman Family (Thomas) (wife, Maturah Bull)		ca. 1792	Hallowell Tp.	Quakers.
Bull, Josiah (wife, Tripp of Dutch family)			Prince Edward Co.	
Burdett Family	Rochelle			Huguenot.
Blanchard Family	New York	1815	Sidney	Ancestors came from Holland.
Cole Family	New York	1810	North Marysburg	Low German background.
Cronk Family	New York	1784	Sophiasburgh	Holland background.
Demike Family	New York	ca. 1784	North Marysburg	Huguenot.
Demille Family	Vermont	1792	Northport	Huguenot (born in Scotland).
Doane (five brothers)	Bucks Co., Pa.			Quakers.
Doxsee Family	Long Island	1800	Prince Edward Co.	
Fraleck Family	New York	1784	Ernesttown	Originated in Prussia.
Fraleigh Family	New York	1784	Adolphustown	Came with Van Alstine.
Farley, James	New York	1799	Sidney	Quaker.
Demorest Family	Dutchess Co., N.Y.	1794	Prince Edward Co. (1794)	Huguenot background.
Flagler Family	Dutchess Co., N.Y.	ca. 1784	Adolphustown	Palatinate background.
Fox Family	Dutchess Co., N.Y.	1791	Sophiasburg	Quaker (?)

Family	Origin	Year	Settlement	Notes
Dulmage Family	New York	1784	South Bay	Germans from Limerick.
Gorssline Family	Long Island	1802	Prince Edward Co.	Ancestry from Holland.
Huff Family	New York	1784	Adolphustown	Huguenot.
Hagerman Family	New York	1784	Adolphustown	Came with Van Alstine.
Huyck Family	New York	1784	Adolphustown	Came with Van Alstine. Low German stock.
Lazier Family	New York	1792	Prince Edward Co.	Huguenot.
Meyers, John Walten	New York	1787	Thurlow	Born in Prussia, married Polly Kruger. Founded Belleville; built first mills in Hastings Co.
Niles Family	Pa. and N.Y.	ca. 1800	Prince Edward Co.	Quaker (?)
Ostrander Family	Albany, N.Y.	1796	Prince Edward Co.	German.
Parliament Family	New York	1784	Adolphustown	Huguenot.
Pearsall Family	Long Island			
Ruttan Family	New York	1784	Adolphustown	Huguenots. (Came with Van Alstine.)
Rose, Peter	New York	ca. 1802	Prince Edward Co.	Quaker.
Schermehorn, Captain	Dutchess Co., N.Y.	ca. 1787	Bay of Quinté	
Solmes Family	New York	1787	Sophiasburg	German.
Steckle Family	New York	1784	Sidney	German.
Valleau Family	New York	1800	Prince Edward Co.	French Huguenot.
Vanblack Family	New York	1800	Prince Edward Co.	Holland Dutch.
Vandervoorte Family	New York	1795	Hay Bay	Holland Dutch.
Vandewater Family				Holland Dutch.
Vandusen Family (Conrad and Caspar)	New York	1784	Adolphustown	Came over in Major Van Alstines' party.
Waldron Family } Weller, Asa }	New York	1790	Prince Edward Co.	Dutch descent.
Young, Stephen	Vermont		{ Carrying Place, first in Murray.	
Williamsburgh, Fred, Frank	Banks of Susquehanna River	1802	Williamsburg	Owned 1000 acres in Pa., escaped to Canada.

APPENDIX B

ADDITIONAL NAMES OF PERSONS OR FAMILIES MIGRATING FROM THE COLONIES TO UPPER CANADA—cont.

II THE SIMCOE REGIME (1792–1796)

Norfolk County

Name	Migrated from	Date	Migrated to	Other Information
Backhouse, John .		1793	Long Point, Norfolk Co.	The Backhouse family are descended from an old and distinguished Quaker family of England. In 1812 John Backhouse built the first grist-mill in Walsingham. He became a member of Church of England.
Cosad, Abigail .	New Jersey	1800	Waterford, Norfolk Co.	She was wife of Samuel Barber and the daughter of Jacob and Elizabeth Cosad, who came from Holland to New Jersey.
Buchner, Jacob .	Pa.	1796	Woodhouse	A surveyor who began his surveys in that township.
Hazen, Daniel .			Walsingham	One of founders.
Johnson, Lawrence .	Pa.	1799	Charlotteville	German background.
Kern (Karn), Christopher .	New Jersey (?)	1799	Forrestville	
Miseners .	New Jersey	1800		
Potts, Jacob .	Maryland	1800	Lyons Creek	Born in Maryland in 1761 of German parents. Later went to Woodhouse with Miseners and Slaghts.
Schlact (Slaght), Hendrick, sons —Job, John, Richard .	German Valley, Morris Co., N.J.	1796	Forrestville	German background.
Sovereign, Frederick and sons .	New Jersey		Waterford	Soldier in Germany; came to New

Name	From	Date	Location	Notes
Steinhoff Brothers (seven sons)	New Jersey (?)			German background.
Woodley, George	New Jersey	1800	Long Point Oakland Tp.	Three Woodley brothers came from Germany to N.J. in 1750. George, after fighting in Revolutionary War, went first to St. John, N.Y., then to Stoney Creek settlement.
Forses Family	New Jersey	ca. 1797	New Brunswick, then Woodhouse	Of German descent.

Wentworth County

Name	From	Date	Location	Notes
Cope	Long Island, N.Y.	1794	Copetown	A German after whom Copetown was named.
Gustin, John	New York	1794	Copetown (?)	Built first mill.

Lincoln County

Name	From	Date	Location	Notes
Wyckoff, Peter		1794	St. Catharines, Foot of Mountain	

III THE GREAT MIGRATION (1796-1812)

York County

Name	From	Date	Location	Notes
Burkholder, William	Pa.	ca. 1800	York Tp., Con. 4	German descent.
Crosson, John	Pa.	1801	York	The elder Crosson returned to Pa.; then brought his family and household goods on back of a two-year-old colt. He owned the first wagon in that part.
Crosson, John	Pa.	1805	Lot 22, Con. 5	
Holley, Joseph	Pa.	1794	Weston, York Tp.	Of Mennonite faith.
Kaiser, Peter Erlen	Pa.	ca. 1800	York Tp., Con. 4	German descent.
Mulholland, Henry	Pa.	1806	York Tp.	From Ireland, of German descent.
Saunders, Henry	Pa.	1800	York Tp., Lot 6, Con. 6	German descent. Noted shipbuilder.

225

APPENDIX B

ADDITIONAL NAMES OF PERSONS OR FAMILIES MIGRATING FROM THE COLONIES TO UPPER CANADA—THE GREAT MIGRATION (1796–1812)—*York County*—*cont.*

Name	Migrated from	Date	Migrated to	Other Information
Shunk, Jacob	Pa.	ca. 1800	York Tp. Con. 4	German descent.
Snyder, John	Pa.	ca. 1800	York Tp., Con. 4	German descent.
Stong, Daniel	Pa.	ca. 1800	York Tp., Con. 4	German descent.
Storey, David	Pa.		York Tp.	German descent.
Barkey Family	Pa.		Markham Tp., Con. 8	Intermarried with Hoover Family.
Bartholomew, Henry	Pa.	1800	Markham Tp., Lot 35, Con. 7	Born in Pennsylvania in 1779.
Button, Major		1799	Buttonville, Markham Tp.	Lived two years at Niagara and settled in Markham in 1801, founding Buttonville.
Heise, Christian (Mary Keefer)	Pa.	1804	Heise Hill, Markham Tp.	He was the first deacon of the Dunker Church in that area.
Heise, Jacob	Pa.	1805	Heise Hill, Markham Tp.	His log house, built in 1810, covered with clapboard, is still in use.
Heise, Joseph	Pa.	1806	Heise Hill, Markham Tp.	
Hoover, John and Daniel	Lancaster Co., Pa.	1804	Markham Tp.	Swiss German background.
Horner, Daniel } brothers Horner, Emanuel	Pa.		Markham Tp.	German descent; built first steam saw mill in township.
Kindy, Eyer, Troyer, Wismer	Pa.	1804–1807	Markham Tp.	German descent.
Kreider, Strickler, Hare (Herr)	Pa.	1804–1807	Markham Tp.	German descent.
Lehman, Schunk, Burkholder	Pa.	1804–1807	Markham Tp.	German descent.
Marr Family	Pa.	1801	Markham Tp., Lot 14, Con. 9	

Name	Origin	Date	Location	Notes
Miller, Jacob	Erie Co., Pa.	1750	Markham Tp., Lots 21, 22, Con. 9	...Badgerow, they formed the first Baptist Church in Markham Tp. A Mennonite minister.
Musselman, Peter	Pa.	1803	Markham Tp.	
Oberholzer, Mishler, Snyder	Pa.	1804–1807	Markham Tp.	A brother of Joseph Schoerg, pioneer of Waterloo Co. German descent.
Sherk (Schoerg), Casper	Pa.	1804	Markham Tp.	
Stover, Boyer (Byer), Steckley	Pa.	1804–1807	Markham Tp.	
Tipp, Daniel (father and mother)	Pa.	1799	Markham Tp.	His father was given 300 acres of land at Chippewa, which he sold, later moving to Markham.
Wideman, Henry	Montgomery Co., Pa.	1803	Markham Tp.	A Mennonite minister.
Wideman, Ludwig	Northampton Co., Pa.	1801	Markham Tp.	Born in 1781.
Keffer, Peter	Somerset Co., Pa.	1806	Vaughan Tp., Lot 12, Con. 3	Peter was the son of Jacob Keffer. He owned 150 acres of land in Brothersvalley Tp., Somerset Co., Pa., in 1779.
Snider, John	Pa. (near Susquehanna River)	1800	Vaughan Tp., Lot 17, Con. 5	Lutheran by religion.
Clubine, Andrew	New Jersey	1801	Yonge St., Vaughan Tp.	Later he moved to Whitchurch Tp., Lot 88, Con. 1. Quaker (?).
Stong, Joseph	Pa.	1805	Vaughan Tp., Lot 23, Con. 3	Son of Daniel Strong.
Troyer, Christian	Somerset Co., Pa.	1804	Vaughan Tp., Lot 5, Con. 3	A Mennonite preacher, probably a brother of "Dr." Troyer.
White, Hiram Sr.	Vermont	ca. 1800	Vaughan Tp., Lot 8, Con. 3	Descended from an English family who settled in Vermont before Revolutionary War. Came to Canada, settled on Humber River, later moving to Vaughan, where he was one of first settlers in that section; only three houses there.

APPENDIX B

ADDITIONAL NAMES OF PERSONS OR FAMILIES MIGRATING FROM THE COLONIES TO UPPER CANADA—THE GREAT MIGRATION (1796-1812)—*York County—cont.*

Name	Migrated from	Date	Migrated to	Other Information
Dennis, Nathan	Pa.	1806	King Tp., Lot 31, Con. I	
Doan Family (Charles)	Bucks Co., Pa.	1806	King Tp.	Quaker.
Irwin, Charles	Pa.	1800	King Tp.	
Pearson, Peter Pentz	Pa.	1808	King Tp.	
Proctor, Gresham	Vermont	1800	King Tp.	Son of Henry Proctor.
Rouse, John	Pa.	1812	King Tp.	
Gould (Gold), Joseph	Pa.	ca. 1804	King Tp.	His father, Michael, of German descent, came from Ireland to Philadelphia in 1720. Joseph changed his name from Gold to Gould. Later settled in Uxbridge.
Armitage Family (Seth)	Bucks Co., Pa.	1804	Whitchurch Tp., Lot 92, Con. I	Quaker.
Bogart, John	New York	1803	Whitchurch Tp.	
Hartman, John	Pa.	1809	Whitchurch Tp., Lot 80, Con. I	Of German extraction.
Lloyd, James	Pa.	1810	Whitchurch Tp.	Quaker (?)
Lundy, John	Bucks Co., Pa.	1801	Whitchurch Tp.	Quaker.
		Waterloo County		
Bear, Michael	Lancaster Co., Pa.	1800		He arrived a few months after Joseph Sherk but did not stay permanently until 1801. He became one of the first Mennonite ministers, being ordained by Bishop Moyer of The Twenty.

228

Name	Location	Year		Notes
Benners, George, Abraham, Joseph, George B.	Montgomery Co., Pa.	1802		
Betzner, Samuel	Franklin Co., Pa.	1800		Born in Württemberg, 1738; came to Penn. in 1775; changed from German Reformed to Dunkard; married Detweiler.
Biehn (Bean), John	Lancaster Co., Pa.	1800	Bean's Tract	He was born in Switzerland in 1737; came to America in 1742.
Brech, Catharine	Dauphin Co., Pa.	1806		John Brech married Catharine Sherk. She came to Canada, a widow.
Bricker, John and Sam	Lancaster Co., Pa.	1802		Their father, Hans, came from Zweibrücken in 1718.
Detweiler, Jacob	Pa.	1822		
Detweiler, Rudolf	Pa.	1810		Detweiler Family were Swiss.
Eby, Benjamin	Lancaster Co., Pa.	1806		Born 1785; married Mary Brubacher; 1807; ordained 1809; taught school as well as preached.
Eby, David	Lancaster Co., Pa.	1807		Theodosus Eby, born Canton Zurich, came to America. Three grandsons settled at Lititz; David, son of John, came to Canada.
Erb, Abraham	Pa.	1806		He founded Waterloo by building mills.
Erb, John	Pa.	1805		He founded Preston by building mills.
Brubacher, Susannah	Pa.			She, an Erb, was the widow of Hans Brubacher, who left Zurich in 1710 for Lancaster. Her daughter, Mary, married Ben Eby.
Fordney Family	Pa.	1802		
Fordney, Michael	Lancaster Co., Pa.	1802		A Huguenot who went first to Virginia, then to Lancaster Co, later to Canada. He married Catharine Baker.

ADDITIONAL NAMES OF PERSONS OR FAMILIES MIGRATING FROM THE COLONIES
TO UPPER CANADA—THE GREAT MIGRATION (1796-1812)—*Waterloo County—cont.*

Name	Migrated from	Date	Migrated to	Other Information
Gingerich, Abraham	Pa.	1801		His father, Michael, left Alsace for America in 1747. Abraham brought ten children to Waterloo.
Kinzie, Dilman	Pa.	1800		Married Catharine Mylin in Lancaster County.
Livergood, John	North Carolina	1802	East Bank, Grand River	He was a Moravian who was born in N. Carolina in 1754. He came north with his wife and six children with Fordney Family.
Pannabecker, Cornelius	Montgomery Co., Pa.	1810	Hespeler	
Reichard, Christian	Pa.	1799–1800	Opposite Doon	Moravian background. Daniel Reichard emigrated to America in 1753.
Reichard, John	Pa.	1799–1800	Opposite Doon	
Reichard, Samuel	Pa.	1799–1800	Opposite Doon	
Rosenberger, Benjamin	Pa.	1801	Preston	
Schneider, Christian	Pa.	1806	Doon	
Shantz, David, Isaac, Veronica	Montgomery Co., Pa.	1808		These came with their mother, Barbara Reif, the widow of Isaac Shantz, the son of Jacob Shantz, who left Switzerland and went to live in Holland for fifteen years. The latter migrated to Montgomery Co. in 1737.
Stauffer, Samuel	Pa.	1808		

Name	From	Date	Location	Notes
Hilborn, Thomas	Pa.	1804	Uxbridge, Lot 35, Con. 6	His daughter, Anna, was the mother of Joseph Gold.

Welland County

Name	From	Date	Location	Notes
Smith, Abraham		1785	Fort Erie	His wife was a Dutch woman; they moved to Charlotteville in 1793.

IV AFTER 1812

Waterloo County

Name	From	Date	Location	Notes
Bearsinger, David	Pa.	1815	Hespeler	
Bingeman, John	Pa.	1825	Bridgeport	
Burkholder, Christian	Lancaster Co., Pa.	1818		His grandfather emigrated from Geneva in 1730. His ancestors came to Lancaster Co. from Switzerland in 1755.
Good, John	Pa.	1818		The Good Family came from Switzerland in 1737.
Groh, Michael	Pa.	1804		
Martin, Peter	Lancaster Co., Pa.	1819		His grandfather, David Martin, came to Lancaster Co. from Switzerland in 1727.
Moyer, Henry	Lancaster Co., Pa.	1825		He was born in Montgomery Co. in 1778, settled in Lancaster Co.
Musselman, David	Pa.	1819	Woolwich Tp.	
Musselman, Frederick	Pa.	1819	Woolwich Tp.	
Winger, Isaiah	Lancaster Co., Pa.	1825		Winger Family arrived from Switzerland in 1748.
Winger, Joseph	Lancaster Co., Pa.	1825		Winger Family arrived from Switzerland in 1748.
Ziegler, Dillman	Montgomery Co., Pa.	1816		Ziegler Family came from Switzerland to Montgomery Co.

231

APPENDIX B

ADDITIONAL NAMES OF PERSONS OR FAMILIES MIGRATING FROM THE COLONIES TO UPPER CANADA—AFTER 1812—*cont.*

Name	Migrated from	Date	Migrated to	Other Information
		Perth County		
Fryfogle, Sebastian . .	Germany	1829	Easthope Tp.	
Kastner, Michael . .	Germany		Kastnerville	
Sebach, John . .	Germany	1828	Ellice Tp.	He built a tavern.
Sebring, John . .	Germany	1834	Downie Tp.	He founded Sebringville.
		Prescott County		
Vankleek, Simeon .	Dutchess Co., N.Y.	1798		Was the first settler and founded Vankleek Hill.

APPENDIX C

THE FOLLOWING IS A LIST OF NAMES ON
SURVEY OF RIVER THAMES, 1793

Robert Surplet
John Peck
Widow Gamline
Anthony Dequinder
Col. McKee
Remmy Gampeair
Fontenay Dequinder
George Jacobs
Madam Goane
Charles Goane
Alex LeBute
Sissney
Thomas Parsons
Thomas Duggan
Richard Merry
Thomas Clarke
Meldrum and Park
Thomas Williams
Mrs. Willson
Daniel Field
John Donalson
Widow Newkirk
Thomas Smith
John Welch
Isaac Dolsen
John Dodemead
Daniel Dolsen Jr.
Andrew Hamilton
James Forsith
Richard Earpe
David McGregor
William Baker
Capt. Ford
Capt. Loughton
John Carpenter
Samuel Nall
Nathan Miller
William Searle
Charles Bolange

Jasper Brown
Thomas McCrea
Peter Shunk
Hezekiah Willcocks
Hugh Holmes
Matthew Dolsen
John Goose
Joseph Springfield
William Dugan
John Barbo
Godfrey Corbus
Wendell Wigley
Robert Bedford
Peter Trackley
Frederick Hardboard
James Jackson
Frederick Arnoldie
Robert Emson
Michael Shannon
Lewis Arnoldie
John Arnoldie
Matthew Gibson
W. Chambers
Christopher Arnoldie
John Wheaton
John Flynn
Patrick O'Flaherty
Jacob Quaint
Edward Watson
Peter Fouchette
Edward Turner
James McDonnel
Frederick Ravelly
Julius Ravelly
John Whitehead
Thomas Kelly
Charles Gascoyne
Joseph Row
Gabriel Charon

Survey of the River Thames (formerly River La Tranche) from its Entrance or Confluence with Lake St. Clair to the upper Delaware Village. From the Entrance to the 12th Lot of the 3rd township was surveyed Two years since, from the 12th Lot of the 3rd township to the upper village surveyed in April and May 1793, delineated by a scale of Forty Gunter's Chains to one Inch.

By

Patrick McNiff

Detroit 25 June (1793)

(Lands & Forests Survey Records, Map No. 018–7)
  (RML: 10/4/51)

233

APPENDIX D

Sample Assessment Statistics in 1802 of property in Somerset County, Pa., belonging to settlers, some of whom came to Canada about that time and settled in Vaughan Township, York County.

	Taxes $	Rate	Acreage	Cleared	Occupation	Horses	Horn Cattle	Houses	Value $
Stoney Creek Tp.:									
Baker, Andrew	.15	3	300	2	Tavern stillery	1	1		7.00
Baker, Jonathan	.15	3	30(	2	Tavern stillery	1	1		7.00
Keefer, Jacob	.65	3	150	20	Shoemaker	1	1		202.00
Reaman, John	.91	1	129	20	Weaver	1	2		302.00
	.08	4	50	20	Weaver	1	2		25.00
Reaman, George	1.43	3	435	2	Weaver	1	1		476.00
Reaman, Charles	1.00	1	109	60	Cabinet Maker	1	1		335.00
	.07	4	50	60	Cabinet Maker	1	1		25.00
Addison Tp.:									
Keefer, Michael	1.11	3	183	35	Tailor	1	1	1	369.00
Keefer, Abraham	.15	3	183	35	Tailor	1	1	1	369.00
Somerset Tp.:									
Baker, Michael	1.25	2	240	60	Grist Mill	2	2	1	416.00
Brothersvalley Tp.:									
Baker, Henry	2.61	1	173	30	Shoemaker	2	4	1	870.00
Baker, Peter	2.26	2	100	20	Cooper	2	3	1	720.00
Baker, Phillip	2.01	2	100	20	Cooper	2	1		670.00

APPENDIX E

A comparison of family names of the earliest settlers in Waterloo Township, Waterloo County, as recorded in:

Ezra Eby, *A Biographical History of Waterloo Township and other Townships of the County* (Berlin (Kitchener), 1895), and Arthur D. Graeff *The Pennsylvania Germans in Ontario, Canada.*
Vol. XI of the Year Book of the Pennsylvania German Folklore Society (Allentown, Pa., 1946);

and the Kaiserslautern-Pfalz district, Germany, as prepared by Dr. Fritz Braun.

Waterloo County, Canada	Stadt Kaiserslautern Pfalz (1949)	Pfalz
Albright	Albrecht	Albrecht
Bauman (Bowman)	Baumann	Baumann
Bear (Baer)	Baer	Baer
Bearinger (Boehringer)	Beringer	Böhringer
Bechtel	—	Bechtel
Bergey		—
Betzner	(Betzer)	Betzner
Biehm (Beam)	Böhm	Böhm
Bhehm (Boehm)	Böhm	Böhm
Block (Bloch)	Block	Block, Bloch
Bock	Bock	Bock
Bower (Bauer)	Bauer	Bauer
Break	(Brück)	(Brück)
Bretz	Bretz	Bretz
Bricker (Brucker)	Brucker	Brucker, Brücker
Brower (Brauer)	Brauer	Brauer
Brubacher (Brubaker)	—	Brubacher
Burkhard (Burkhart)	Burkhard, Burkhart	Burkhard, Burkhart
Burkholder	Burkholder	Burkholder
Cassel	Cassel	Cassel
Christener		—
Clemens	Clemens	Clemens
Cober (Kober)	Kober	Kober
Cress (Kress)	Kress	Kress
Cressman	—	—
Detweiler	Dettweiler	Dettweiler
Dewitt	—	—
Eby		Eby, Ewy
Erb	Erb	Erb
Ernst	Ernst	Ernst
Eshleman	—	Eschelmann
Fordney	—	—
Fried	Fried	Fried
Gehmann		Gehmann
Geiger	Geiger	Geiger
Gingerich	—	Gingerich

Waterloo County, Canada	Stadt Kaiserslautern Pfalz (1949)	Pfalz
Gole	Göhl(?)	Göhl (?)
Good (Guth)	Guth	Guth
Goudie	—	Gouthier
Groff (Graff-Graeff)	Graf, Gräf(f)	Graf, Gräf(f)
Groh	Groh	Groh
Haas	Haas	Haas
Hagey	—	(Haege)
Hallman	Hallmann	Hallman
Hammacher		Hamacher
(Hoimacher)	Hamacher	Hagedorn
Heckedorn	—	
Hembling	—	—
Herner (Harner)	Hörner	Hörner
Hiestand	—	Hiestand
Hilborn	—	Heilbrunn
Hoffman	Hoffmann	Hoffmann
Hohn	Höhn	Höhn
Honsberger		
(Hunsberger)	—	—
Horst	Horst	Horst
Hostetler	(Hochstätter)	(Hochstättler, Hochstetter)
Huber (Hoover)	Huber	Huber
Janzen (Johnson)	Jansen, Jansohn	Jansen, Jansohn
Jones	Jonas	Jonas
Kaufman	Kaufmann	Kaufmann
Keller	Keller	Keller
Kinzie	—	(Kintsy)
Kinzinger	—	Kinzinger
Koch	Koch	Koch
Kolb (Culp)	Kolb	Kolb
Kraft	Kraft	Kraft
Latschaw (Latschar)	—	Latscha
Levan	—	Lava (?)
Lichty (Light)	Licht	Lichti, Licht
Livergood (Livingood)	—	Leibengut
Lutz	Lutz	Lutz
Martin	Martin	Martin
Master (Meister)	Meister	Meister
Musselman	—	Muselmann
Myers	(Meyer, Mayer)	(Meyer, Mayer)
Nahregang	—	Nargang
Oberholtzer	—	—
Pannebacker, Pennypacker	—	Pfannebecker
Reichert (Reichard)	Reichert, Reichard	Reicher, Reichard
Reist	—	
Reitzel	—	Reitzel
Rife (Reiff)	Reiff	Reiff
Ringler	(Ringle)	Ringler
Rosenberger	—	Rosenberger
Rudell	—	—

Waterloo County, Canada	Stadt Kaiserslautern Pfalz (1949)	Pfalz
Rudy	—	Rudy
Saltzberger	—	—
Schantz	Schanz	Schantz
Scheidel	Scheidel	Scheidel
Schlechter	—	Schlechter
Schmidt	Schmidt	Schmidt
Schneider	Schneider	Schneider
Schuh	Schuh	Schuh
Schwartz	Schwartz	Schwartz
Seibert	Seibert	Seibert
Shelly	—	—
Shoemaker	Schumacher	Schumacher
Shoup	Schupp	Schupp
Sitler	—	—
Souder	Sautter	Sauter
Springer	(Sprenger)	Springer
Stauffer	—	Stauffer
Stoeckle	—	Stöckle
Strickler	—	Strickler
Strome	Strohm	Strohm
Tohman	Thomann	Thomann
Tyson	Thyson	Thyson
Unger	Unger	Unger
Urmy	—	—
Wanner	Wanner	Wanner
Weber	Weber	Weber
Winger	(Wingert)	Winger
Weideman	Weidmann	Weidmann
Wile (Weil)	Weil	Weil
Wissler	—	Wissler
Witmer	Wittmer	Wittmer
Yost	Jost	Jost
Zeller	Zeller	Zeller
Ziegler	Ziegler	Ziegler

BIBLIOGRAPHY

Introduction

1. Bryant, Arthur: *English Saga*, p. 11. New York, William Collins Sons & Company, 1940.
2. Mencken, H. L.: *The American Language*, Supplement I, p. 599. New York, Alfred A. Knopf, 1945.
3. Currie, A. W.: *Economic Geography of Canada*, p. 148. Toronto, The Macmillan Company of Canada, 1945.

I. Backgrounds in Europe

1. McCabe, James D., Jr.: *From Cross to Crown*, p. 23. Philadelphia, Jones Brothers & Company, 1874.
2. Muston, Alexis D. D.: "The Trail of the Alps; a Complete History of the Waldenses and their Colonies," Vol. I, trans. by Rev. John Montgomery, in James D. McCabe, Jr., *From Cross to Crown* (Philadelphia, 1874), pp. 25–6.
3. Randall, Henry John: *The Creative Centuries*, p. 298. New York, Longmans, Green & Company, 1947.
4. Niebuhr, Reinhold: *Encyclopædia of Social Sciences*, Vol. XIII, p. 628. New York, The Macmillan Company, 1930.
5. Bender, Harold S.: "The Anabaptist Vision," pp. 7–8. Reprinted, 1940, from *The Mennonite Review* (April 1944).
6. ——, ——: *ibid.*, p. 9.
7. ——, ——: *ibid.*, p. 21.
8. Niebuhr: *op. cit.*, p. 630.

II. Migration to and Settlement in America

1. Dorland, Arthur Garrett: *A History of the Society of Friends (Quakers) in Canada*, p. 114. Toronto, The Macmillan Company of Canada, 1927.
2. Anon.: *The Denominational Reason Why*, rev. ed., p. 280. London, Houlston and Wright, 1866.
3. Graeff, Arthur D.: *This History of Pennsylvania*, p. 30. Philadelphia, John C. Winston Company, 1945.
4. Smith, C. Henry: *The Story of the Mennonites*, p. 537. Berne, Indiana, Mennonite Book Concern, 1941.
5. ——, ——: *ibid.*, p. 537.
6. ——, ——: *ibid.*, p. 539.
7. Smith, Abbot Emerson: *Colonists in Bondage*, p. 207. Chapel Hill, North Carolina, University of North Carolina Press, 1947.
8. ——, ——: *ibid.*, p. 216.

9. O'Callaghan, E. B., and others: *Documentary History of the State of New York*, Vol. III, p. 338. New York, New York State Library, 1849–51.
10. ——, ——: *ibid.*, p. 391.
11. Croll, P. C.: *Conrad Weiser and his Memorial Park*, p. 9. Womelfdorf, Penn., private printing, 1926.
12. Cronmiller, C. R.: "Dundas County Lutherans," *Lutheran Gleanings*, Vol. I, No. 1, pp. 14–15.
13. ——, ——: *ibid.*, p. 16.
14. ——, ——: *ibid.*, p. 17.
15. Climenhaga, A. W.: *History of the Brethren in Christ Church*, p. 45. Toronto, Evangelical Publishers, 1942.
16. Bevier, Katherine: *The Bevier Family*, pp. 15–16. New York, Tobias A. Wright, 1916.
17. Curzon, S. A.: *The Story of Laura Secord*, p. 10. Niagara Falls, Lundy's Lane Historical Society, 1898.
18. Graeff, Arthur D.: *The Pennsylvania Germans*, p. 13. Princeton, N.J., Princeton University Press, 1942.
19. Klees, Frederic: *The Pennsylvania Dutchman*, p. 72. Toronto, The Macmillan Company of Canada, 1951.
20. Wood, Ralph: *The Pennsylvania Germans*, pp. 93–4. Princeton, N.J., Princeton University Press, 1942.

III. MIGRATION TO AND SETTLEMENT IN UPPER CANADA

1. Smith, Abbot Emerson: *Colonists in Bondage*, p. 50. Chapel Hill, North Carolina, University of North Carolina Press, 1947.
2. Hall, Thomas Cuming: *The Religious Background of American Culture*, pp. 178–9. Boston, Little, Brown & Company, 1930.
3. Dorland, A. G.: *A History of the Society of Friends (Quakers) in Canada*, p. 59. Toronto, The Macmillan Company of Canada, 1927.
4. Canniff, William: *History of the Province of Ontario*, p. 187. Toronto, A. H. Hovey, 1872.
5. Cruikshank, E. A.: "Records of Niagara," *Niagara Historical Society Publication*, No. 39, pp. 7–11.
6. Canniff, *op. cit.*, p. 56.
7. "Champlain Series": *Champlain Society Publications*, No. 27 (1946), p. 315.
8. Green, Ernest: "Some Graves on Lundy's Lane," *Niagara Historical Society Publication*, No. 22, p. 52.
9. Owen, E. A.: *Pioneer Sketches of Long Point Settlement*, p. 409. Toronto, William Briggs, 1898.
10. Cruickshank, E. A.: "Ten Years of the Colony of Niagara," *Niagara Historical Society Publication*, No. 17, p. 3.
11. *Haldimand Papers*, Ottawa, Public Archives of Canada, B100, p. 226.
12. ——: *ibid.*, B62, p. 259.
13. ——: *ibid.*, B104, pp. 24–5.
14. ——: *ibid.*, B169, p. 1.

15. Stanley, F. G.: "The Indians in the War of 1812," *Canadian Historical Review*, Vol. 31, No. 2, p. 145.
16. Middleton, J. E., and Landon, F.: *The Province of Ontario, a History*, Vol. I, p. 31. Toronto, The Dominion Publishing Company, 1927.
17. *Haldimand Papers*, Ottawa, Public Archives of Canada, B115, p. 160.
18. Brown, Ralph H.: *Mirror for Americans; the Inlands of New York*, p. 168. New York, American Geographical Society, 1943.
19. Graham, Lloyd: *Niagara County*, p. 71. New York, Duell, Sloan & Pearce, 1949.
20. Fitzgibbon, Mary Agnes: "The Jarvis Letters," *Niagara Historical Society Publication*, No. 8, p. 26.
21. Land, John H.: "Record of Robert Land, U.E.L.," *Wentworth Historical Society Papers and Records*, Vol. 7 (1916), p. 6.
22. Crysler, John M.: *History of that Branch of the Crysler Family who Settled in the Township of Niagara*, pp. 115–18. Niagara-on-the-Lake, Printed for John M. Crysler, 1936.
23. Cruikshank: *op. cit.*, p. 5.
24. ——: *ibid.*, p. 10.
25. Robertson, John Ross, ed.: *The Diary of Mrs. Simcoe*, p. 294 Toronto, William Briggs, 1911.
26. Fitzgibbon: *op. cit.*, p. 34.
27. Kirby, William: *The Annals of Niagara*, p. 69. Niagara Falls, Lundy's Lane Historical Society, 1896.
28. ——, ——: *ibid.*, p. 74.
29. ——, ——: *ibid.*, p. 75.
30. Paterson, G. C.: "Land Settlement in Upper Canada," from Report of the Ontario Department of Records and Archives for 1920. Quoted by W. Spragge in *Ontario Historical Society Papers and Records*, No. 39, p. 93.
31. Hadfield, Joseph: *An Englishman in America*, p. 92. Toronto, Hunter Rose Company, 1933.
32. ——, ——: *ibid.*, p. 92.
33. Johnson, H. C: *The Martin Settlement*, p. 59. Brantford, Brant Historical Society, 1908.
34. Canniff: *op. cit.*, p. 86.
35. Servos, Alexander: "Historic Houses," *Niagara Historical Society Publication*, No. 5, p. 8.
36. ——, ——: *ibid.*, p. 9.
37. Robinson, Percy James: *Toronto during the French Regime*, pp. 212–15. Toronto, Ryerson Press, 1933.
38. Sherk, M. G.: "Reminiscences of the Upper Part of the Old Niagara River Road," *Ontario Historical Society Papers and Records*, Vol. 25 (1929), p. 423.
39. *Origin and History of the Tunker Church in Canada*, p. 5. M. V. Fisher, Ridgway, 1918.
40. Green, Ernest: "Frey," *Ontario Historical Society Papers and Records*, Vol. 33, p. 50.
41. Robertson: *op. cit.*, p. 222.

42. Robertson: *ibid.,* p. 290.
43. "Prominent Americans of Swiss Origin," *Swiss American Historical Society Publication* (1932), p. 3.
44. *Hoover Family History.* Private printing.
45. Laidler, George: "John Troyer of Long Point Bay," *Ontario Historical Society Papers and Records,* No. 39, pp. 15–40.
46. Owen: *op. cit.,* p. 544.
47. Dorland: *op. cit.,* p. 52.
48. "Journal of Joseph Moore," *Friends' Miscellany Publication,* Vol. 6, p. 289.
49. Kirby: *op. cit.,* p. 88.
50. Canniff: *op. cit.,* p. 182.
51. Fraser, Alexander, ed.: *Sixteenth Report of the Department of Archives for the Province of Ontario, 1920,* pp. 15–16. Toronto, Clarkson W. James, 1921.
52. Herrington, W. S.: *History of the County of Lennox and Addington,* p. 27. Toronto, The Macmillan Company of Canada, 1913.
53. Croil, James: *Dundas,* pp. 127–8. Montreal, Dawson & Sons, 1861.
54. Cronmiller, C. R.: "Dundas County Lutherans," *Lutheran Gleanings,* Vol. I, No. 1, p. 14.
55. Canniff: *op. cit.,* p. 461.
56. ——: *ibid.,* p. 462.
57. Herrington: *op. cit.,* p. 61.
58. ——: *ibid.,* p. 141.
59. ——: *ibid.,* p. 414.
60. Dorland: *op. cit.,* p. 51.
61. Canniff: *op cit.,* p. 120.
62. Talman, J. J., ed.: *Loyalist Narratives from Upper Canada,* pp. 297 ff. Toronto, Champlain Society, 1946.
63. Canniff: *op. cit.,* p. 443.
64. ——: *ibid.,* pp. 315–16.
65. Dorland: *op. cit.,* p. 50.
66. Canniff: *op cit.,* p. 279.
67. ——: *ibid.,* p. 275.
68. *Census of Canada, 1870–71,* Vol. IV, p. 13. Ottawa, I. B. Taylor, 1876.
69. Burch, Mary J.: *A Family Record.* Private printing, 1880.
70. ——, ——: *ibid.*
71. Brown, James R.: *Views of Canada and the Colonists,* p. 276. Edinburgh, A. & C. Black, 1844.
72. Hamil, Frederick Coyne: *The Settlement of the Lower Thames,* p. 346. Toronto, University of Toronto Press, 1950.
73. ——, ——: *ibid.,* p. 14.
74. Bangs, Nathan: *A History of the Methodist Episcopal Church,* Vol. II. 166. New York. Private printing, 1840.
75. Quaife, M. M.: *Moravian Papers,* pp. 9–16. Burton Historical Collection, Detroit Public Library, 1809.

76. Campbell, J. V.: *Campbell Papers*. Burton Historical Collection, Detroit Public Library.
77. *Claus Papers*. Burton Historical Collection, Detroit Public Library.
78. Fuller, Robert M.: *Radio Broadcast*. Station CKLW, Windsor, Ontario, July 7, 1949.
79. Askin, John: *Papers*, Vol. I, p. 222. Burton Historical Collection, Detroit Public Library.
80. "Early Settlements and Surveys," "Kentiana," *Kent Historical Society Papers and Addresses*, Vol. 6, p. 33.
81. ———: *ibid.*, p. 33.
82. Dorland: *op. cit.*, p. 54.
83. Canniff: *op. cit.*, p. 189.
84. Tasker, L. H.: "Dedrick," *Ontario Historical Society Papers and Records*, Vol. 2, p. 70.
85. Ryerson, Adolphus Egerton: *The Loyalists of America and their Times*, Vol. II, p. 227. Toronto, William Briggs, 1880.
86. ———, ———: *ibid.*, p. 227.
87. ———, ———: *ibid.*, p. 232.
88. ———, ———: *ibid.*, p. 233.
89. Sissons, C. B.: *Egerton Ryerson; His Life and Letters*, Vol. I, p. 1. Toronto, Clarke, Irwin & Company, 1937–47.
90. Graeff, Arthur D.: "Transplants of Pennsylvania; Indian Nations in Ontario," *Pennsylvania Historical Association Quarterly Journal*, Vol. 4, No. 3 (July 1948), pp. 1–14.
91. Bliss, Eugene F., ed.: *Diary of David Zeisberger*, pp. 250 ff. Cincinnati, R. Clarke & Company, 1885.
92. Heriot, George: *Travels Through the Canadas*, p. 76. London, Printed for Richard Phillips, 1807.
93. Graeff: *op. cit.*, p. 11.
94. *The History of the Moravian Mission Among the Indians in North America From its Commencement to the Present Time, by a Member of the Brethren's Church*, p. 287. London, T. Allman, 1838.
95. Hamil, Frederick Coyne: "Fairfield," "Kentiana," *Kent Historical Society Papers and Addresses* (1939), p. 21.
96. Bruce, A. D.: *Historical Sketch of Markham Township, 1793–1850*, p. 11. Markham, Markham Centennial Committee, 1950
97. Fraser: *op. cit.*, p. 185.
98. *The Province of Ontario, a History*, Vol. I, p. 29. Toronto. The Dominion Publishing Company, 1927.
99. *History of Toronto and County of York, Ontario, containing a History of the City of Toronto and the County of York*, Vol. I, p. 116. Toronto, C. Blackett Robinson, 1885.
100. Cassaday, John C.: *The Somerset County Outline*, pp. 124–63. Scottdale, Pa., Mennonite Publishing House, 1932.
101. Cober, A. A.: *Cober Genealogy*, p. 2. Private printing, 1933
102. *Record of Cummer Family*. Private printing, 1911.
103. History of Toronto and County of York, Vol. II, *op. cit.* p. 218.
104. ———: *ibid.*, p. 180.

105. Robertson: *op. cit.*, pp. 213–14.
106. Cassaday: *op. cit.*, p. 164.
107. *Illustrated Historical Atlas of the County of York, and the Township of West Gwillimbury and Town of Bradford in the County of Simcoe, Ontario, comp., drawn and published from personal examinations and surveys.* Toronto, Miles & Company, 1878.
108. Fraser: *op. cit.*, pp. 187–8.
109. Wood, W. R.: *Past Years in Pickering*, p. 40. Toronto, William Briggs, 1911.
110. *Letter* from Miss Lenora Starr, Newmarket, Ontario.
111. Dorland: *op. cit.*, p. 110.
112. Sherk, A. B.: "The Pennsylvania Germans in Waterloo County," *Ontario Historical Society Papers and Records*, Vol. 7, pp. 100–101.
113. Eby, Ezra E.: *A Biographical History of Waterloo Township and other Townships of the County, being a History of the early settlers and their descendants*, Vol. I, pp. 20–1. Berlin, 1895–6.
114. *Moyer Family History*. Private printing, 1896.
115. ———: *ibid.*
116. Burkholder, Lewis J.: *A Brief History of Mennonites in Ontario*, p. 31. Toronto, Livingstone Press, 1935.
117. Dorland: *op. cit.*, p. 66.
118. Fraser: *op. cit.*, p. 189.
119. ———: *ibid.*, p. 89.
120. Ermatinger, Charles Oakes: *The Talbot Regime*, pp. 36–7. St. Thomas, Municipal World, 1904.
121. Gourlay, Robert Fleming: *Statistical Account of Upper Canada*, Vol. I, p. 336. London, Simpkin & Marshall, 1822.
122. *The Statutes of the Province of Upper Canada, 1791–1831*, p. 228. Kingston, Francis M. Hill, 1831.
123. Fraser: *op. cit.*, p. 113.
124. Swalm, E. J. *Manuscript* loaned author.

IV. Contributions to Canadian Agriculture

1. Carrier, Lyman: *Beginnings of Agriculture in America*, p. 41. New York, McGraw-Hill Company, 1923.
2. Brown, Ralph H.: *Mirror for Americans*, pp. 164–5. New York, American Geographical Society, 1943.
3. Hudson, S. C., and others: "Types of Farming," *Farmer's Bulletin* 157, Publication 825, p. 5.
4. ———: *ibid.*, p. 10.
5. James, Henry F.: *The Agricultural Industry of Southeastern Pennsylvania; a Study in Economic Geography*, p. 37. Philadelphia, Geographical Society of Philadelphia, 1928.
6. Huber, Levi B.: *Two Hundred Years of Farming in Lancaster County. Papers and Addresses of the Lancaster County Historical Society* (1931), p. 108.
7. Brown: *op. cit.*, pp. 197–9.

8. Correll, Ernst H.: *Das Schweizerische Taufermennoniten-tum*, pp. 110–20. Mohr, Tubingingen, 1925.
9. Randall, H. J.: *The Creative Centuries*, p. 361. New York, Longmans, Green & Company, 1947.
10. Seebohm, Frederic: *The Evolution of the English Farm*, p. 282. London, George Allen & Unwin, 1927.
11. ——, ——: *ibid.*, p. 309.
12. ——, ——: *ibid.*, p. 317.
13. Fordham, Montague: *A Short History of English Rural Life*, p. 127. London, George Allen & Unwin, 1916.
14. Shryock, R. H.: "British Versus German Traditions in Colonial Agriculture," *Mississippi Valley Historical Review*, Vol. 26 (1939–40), pp. 39–54.
15. Meynen, Emil: *Das Pennsylvanien Deutsche Bauerland*, pp. 268–9. Leipzig, O. Harrassowitz, 1939.
16. ——, ——: *ibid.*, p. 269.
17. Graeff, Arthur D.: "The Influence of the Pennsylvania Germans," *The Pennsylvania Forum* (January 9, 1950), p. 9.
18. Kollmorgen, Walter M.: *The Pennsylvania Germans*, p. 33. Princeton, N.J., Princeton University Press, 1942.
19. Hollenbach, Raymond E.: Quoted from "The Morning Call," (June 25, 1949), Allentown, Pa.
20. Edwards, E. E.: "The Settlement of Grasslands," *Year Book of Agriculture*, p. 18. U.S. Department of Agriculture, 1948.
21. McCoy, Charles Francis, and others: *One Hundred Years Progress of the U.S.*, Hartford, L. Stebbins, 1872.
22. Benson, Adolph B., ed.: *Peter Kalm's Travels into North America, trans. by J. R. Forster.* London, Wilson-Erikson, 1771.
23. Hollenbach: *op. cit.*
24. Fletcher, S. W.: *Pennsylvania Agriculture and Country Life, 1640–1840*, p. 134. Harrisburg, Pennsylvania Historical and Museum Commission, 1950.
25. Edwards: *op. cit.*, p. 18.
26. Carrier: *op. cit.*, p. 176.
27. Graeff, Arthur D.: "The Influence of the Pennsylvania Germans," *The Philadelphia Forum* (January 1950), p. 9.
28. Omwake, John: *Conestoga Six-Horse Bell Teams, 1750–1850*, pp. 82–3. Cincinnati, The Ebbert & Richardson Company, 1930.
29. ——, ——: *ibid.*, p. 85.
30. ——, ——: *ibid.*, p. 15.
31. ——, ——: *ibid.*, p. 45.
32. ——, ——: *ibid.*, p. 88.
33. Kennedy, W. J.: *Selecting and Judging Horses.* Year Book of the U.S. Department of Agriculture, 1902, p. 455.
34. Evans, Lewis: "Dutch Settlements in Pennsylvania," *Mississippi Valley Historical Review*, Vol. 26 (1939–40), p. 3.
35. Shryock: *op. cit.*, pp. 39–54.
36. Russell, Robert: *North America; Its Agriculture and Climate*, pp. 45–6. Edinburgh, Adam & Charles Black, 1857.

37. Hopkins, J. Castell: *Canada, An Encyclopædia of the Country,* pp. 24–6. Toronto, Linscott Publishing Company, 1898–1900.
38. Dunlop, William: *Statistical Sketch of Upper Canada for the use of Immigrants, by a Backwoodsman,* p. 78. London, John Murray, 1832.
39. Bruce, A. D.: *Historical Sketch of Markham Township,* 1793–1850, p. 6. Markham, Markham Centennial Committee, 1950.
40. Robertson, John Ross, ed.: *The Diary of Mrs. Simcoe,* p. 199. Toronto, William Briggs, 1911.
41. Jones, Robert Leslie: *History of Agriculture in Ontario, 1613–1880,* Chapters 2, 5, 6. Toronto, University of Toronto Press, 1946.
42. ——, ——: *ibid.,* p. 81.
43. Robertson: *op. cit.,* pp. 277–88.
44. Canniff, William: *The Medical Profession of Upper Canada, 1783–1850,* pp. 440–2. Toronto, William Briggs, 1894.
45. Gourlay, Robert Fleming: *Statistical Account of Upper Canada,* Vol. I, pp. 170–1. London, Simpkin & Marshall, 1822.
46. Jones: *op. cit.,* Chapters 2, 5.
47. Croil, James: *Dundas,* p. 194. Montreal, Dawson & Son, 1861.
48. ——, ——: *ibid., pp. 194–5.*
49. Conant, Thomas: *Upper Canada Sketches,* p. 42. Manchester, William Briggs, 1898.
50. Warrington, C. J. S., and Nicholls, R. V. V.: *History of Chemistry in Canada,* pp. 77–8. Toronto, Sir Isaac Pitman & Sons (Canada), 1949.
51. Gray, Hugh: *Letters from Canada,* p. 215. London, printed for Longmans, Hurst, Rees & Orme, 1809.
52. Croil: *op. cit.,* p. 132.
53. Canniff: *op. cit.,* pp. 595–6.
54. Eby, Ezra E.: *A Biographical History of Waterloo Township and other Townships of the County, being a History of the early settlers and their descendants,* Vol. I, pp. 20–1. Berlin, 1895–6.
55. ——, ——: *ibid.,* p. 33.
56. ——, ——: *ibid.,* p. 22.
57. *Illustrated Historical Atlas of the County of Halton, Ontario, comp. and drawn from Official Plans and Special Surveys.* Toronto, Walker & Miles, 1877.
58. Jones: *op. cit.,* p. 147.
59. Evans, William: "Editorial," *Agricultural Journal and Transactions of the Lower Canada Agricultural Society* (October, 1850), p. 304.
60. Gourlay: *op. cit.,* p. 169.
61. Russell: *op. cit.,* p. 49.
62. Reaman, George Elmore: *The Holstein-Friesian Breed in Canada,* p. 15. Toronto, William Collins Sons & Company (Canada), 1946.
63. Gourlay: *op. cit.,* p. 474.
64. Fletcher: *op. cit.,* p. 176.
65. ——: *ibid.,* p. 192.

66. Fergusson, Adam: *Tour of Canada, 1832*, p. 278. London, William Blackwood & Son, 1834.
67. ——, ——: *ibid.*, p. 281.
68. ——, ——: *ibid.*, p. 277.
69. Jones: *op. cit.*, pp. 75–6.
70. Baker, Jonathan: *A Brief History of Early Settlers on this Line, including Langstaff P.O., Yonge Street and as far West as the Fifth Concession, gotten up by Henry Horne from Facts Collected by a Resident of Concord.* Pamphlet, private printing., p. 3.
71. Sherk, M. G.: *Pen Sketches of early Pioneer Life in Upper Canada by a "Canuck" (of the Fifth Generation)*, p. 170. Toronto, William Briggs, 1905.
72. Hind, H. Y., and others: *Eighty Years of Progress of British North America, showing the Wonderful Development of its Natural Resources*, p. 40. Toronto, L. Stebbins, 1863.
73. Le, Chun-Fen: "Land Utilization in the Middle Grand River Valley of Western Ontario," *Economic Geography*, Vol. 20 (April 1944), p. 137.

V. Contributions to Canadian Cultural Life

1. Hall, Thomas Cuming: *The Religious Background of American Culture*, p. 41. Boston, Little, Brown & Company, 1930.
2. ——, ——: *ibid., passim.*
3. ——, ——: *ibid.*, pp. 278–9.
4. Conant, Thomas: *Upper Canada Sketches*, p. 57. Manchester, William Briggs, 1898.
5. ——, ——: *ibid.*, p. 30.
6. *Aylesworth Family History.* Private printing, 1929.
7. *Centennial of Canadian Methodism*, p. 57. Manchester, William Briggs, 1898.
8. Clark, S. D.: *Church and Sect in Canada*, p. 107. Toronto, University of Toronto Press, 1948.
9. Tolan, Mrs. Stanley C.: "Christian Warner, a Methodist Pioneer," *Ontario Historical Society Papers and Records*, Vol. 37, p. 75.
10. Carroll, John: *Case and his Contemporaries*, p. 11. Toronto, Samuel Rose, 1867–77.
11. ——, ——: *ibid.*, p. 19.
12. ——, ——; *ibid.*, p. 79.
13. Canniff, William: *History of the Province of Ontario*, pp. 292–3. Toronto, A. H. Hovey, 1872.
14. Dunlop, William: *Statistical Sketch of Upper Canada for the use of Immigrants, by a Backwoodsman*, p. 102. London, John Murray, 1832.
15. Clark: *op. cit.*, p. 144.
16. ——: *ibid.*, p. 144.
17. Shortt, Adam, and Doughty, A. G., ed.: *Canada and its Provinces*, Vol. I, p. 265. Toronto, Publishers' Association of Canada, 1914.

18. Gregg, W.: *History of the Presbyterian Church in the Dominion of Canada from the Earliest Times to 1834*, p. 175. Toronto, Presbyterian Publishing Company, 1885.
19. ———, ———: *ibid.*, p. 175.
20. ———, ———: *ibid.*, p. 180.
21. ———, ———: *ibid.*, p. 181.
22. Mead, Frank S.: *Handbook of Denominations in the United States*, pp. 25 ff. Nashville, Abingdon-Cokesbury Press, 1951.
23. Graeff, Marie Knorr: *Pennsylvania German Quilts*, Vol. XIV, p. 15. Published by Mrs. C. Naaman Keyser, Kutztown, Pa., 1946.
24. Kurath, Hans: *A Word Geography of the United States, passim*. Ann Arbor, Michigan, University of Michigan Press, 1949.
25. Fogel, Edwin Miller: *The Proverbs of the Pennsylvania Germans*, p. 1. Philadelphia, Pennsylvania-German Society, 1929.
26. ———, ———: *ibid.*, p. 1.
27. Wintemberg, W. J.: *Folk-Lore of Waterloo County, Ontario*. Bulletin No. 116 of the Anthropological Series, No. 28, p. 23.
28. Gibbons, Phebe Earle: *Pennsylvania Dutch and Other Essays*, p. 22. Philadelphia, J. B. Lippincott Company, 1882.

VI. HUGUENOTS

1. Garneau, F. X.; *op. cit.*, Vol. I. Chapter 11, pp. 156–57.
2. Reaman, G. Elmore: *The Trail of the Huguenots*, pp. 65–69. The Book Society of Canada, 1965.
3. Canniff, William: *History of the Province of Ontario*, p. 6. Toronto. A. H. Hovey, 1872.

VII. SIX NATIONS INDIANS

1. Wright, J. V., Head, Eastern Canada Section, Archaeology Division, National Museum of Canada. Personal letter to author.
2. April 5th, 1960.
3. Stanley, G. F. G.: *Six Nations in the War of 1812*, Ontario History, Volume IV, No. 4, 1963, pp. 215–231.

VIII. SOME CONCLUSIONS

1. Gourlay, Robert: *Statistical Account of Upper Canada*, Vol. I, p. 469. London, Simpkin & Marshall, 1822.
2. Hall, Thomas Cuming: *The Religious Background of American Culture*, p. 125. Boston, Little, Brown & Company, 1930.
3. ———, ———: *ibid.*, p. 170.
4. Beard, Charles A. and Mary R.: *The Rise of American Civilization*, Vol. I, pp. 83 ff. New York, The Macmillan Company, 1927.
5. Creighton, Donald M.: *The Young Politician*, p. 16. Toronto, The Macmillan Company of Canada, 1952.
6. White, G. M.: "Editorial," *Ladies' Home Journal* (July 1951).
7. Mead, Frank S.: *Handbook of Denominations in the United States*, p. 95. Nashville, Abingdon-Cokesbury Press, 1951.

INDEX

Aargau Canton (Switzerland), 61, 106
Adair, family, 63
Adams, John, 35
Addington County, *see* Lennox and Addington
Addison, Rev. Robert, 178
Adolphustown Tp., 68, 69, 70, 71, 72, 217, 222–3
Agriculture, 79, 126–65; animal husbandry, 135, 138–9, 141, 146, 147, 153–6, 158; animals, 153–6, 209; buildings, 132, 148–50, 164, 209; conservation, 129–30, 134, 147, 164, 209; crop rotation, 130, 134, 158, 164, 209; crops, 79, 118, 126–36, 141, 152, 157–8, 165, 209; harvesting, 159–63; implements, 137–40, 151, 160–3; —in Ontario, 126 ff.; —in Pennsylvania, 128–37, 209; —in Western Europe, 129 ff.; influence of climate and topography, 127–9, 209; irrigation, 164; practised by Indians, 126–7; practised by Moravians, 90–4; —and folklore, 141–2
Agricultural Society, 51
Ainse, Sarah, 76
Albany (New York), 20, 21, 22, 29, 31, 68, 76, 105, 117, 223
Albertson, family, 118; William, 119
Albigenses, *see* Cathari
Albrecht, *see* Albright
Albright, family, 63, 114, 115, 217, 235; Amos, 113; Francis, 115
Aldborough Tp., 115, 116, 219
Allan, B., 220
Alleghanies, 72, 88, 101, 132
Allen, Capt., 71
Alsace, 8, 31
Althouse, family, 114, 115
America, xix, 6, 7, 9, 10, 11, 16, 18, 19, 26, 27, 32, 35, 39, 40, 41, 44, 45, 46, 55, 67, 69, 78, 122, 131, 142, *et passim*

Amherst, General, 28 n.
Amherstburg, 73, 76, 82
Amish, xx, 23, 27, 35, 37, 63, 123, 159, 168, 209, 218; customs, 37–8
Amman, Jacob, 8
Amsterdam, 8, 56
Anabaptism, 5–6
Anabaptists, 4, 7, 8, 129, 179
Ancaster, 59, 74, 75, 108, 109, 118, 119
Ancaster Tp., 75, 229
Ancrum, Maj. William, 77
Anderson, Charles, 47
Anne, Queen, 19–22, 36, 45, 47, 172
Annis Jeremiah, 219
Armitage, family, 228; Seth, 228
Arnold, Frederick, Sr., 75
Arnoldie, Christopher, 233; Frederick, 233; John, 233; Lewis, 233
Arts and Crafts, 179–81, 209, *see also* Handicrafts
Ashbaugh, family, 114
Ashbridge, family, 100; John, 100; Jonathan, 100; Sarah, 219
Ashbridge's Bay, 98, 100
Askin, John, Jr., 77; John, Sr., 77, 82
Athol Tp., 216
Aubrey, Capt., 49
Augusta Tp., 68, 171, 216
Aurora, 104
Austria, 5, 6, 28, 211
Awrey, family, 119
Aylesworth, family, 170–1; Sir Allen, 171; Arthur, 171; Job, 171; Philip, 171

Bâby, family, 216; Duperon, 77
Backhouse, family, 224; John, 224
Backus, Stephen, 116
Baden County (Germany), 74
Badgerow, Hezekiah, 227; Joshua, 227; Phoebe, 227
Baer, *see* Bear
Bahl, *see* Ball

248

Bogart, family, 104; John, 104, 228; Martin, 104; Mary, 104; Mary Opp, 104
Bohemia, 3
Bolange, Charles, 233
Bolton, Col., 47, 49, 53, 54
Bongard, Conrad, 69, 216
Bonisteel, family, 222
Bonheur, see Bonnar
Bonnar, Mrs. ——, 45
Book, family, 63
Boomer, see Bulmer
Bossuet, Bishop, 11
Boston (Massachusetts), 26, 34, 170
Botanical garden, first American, 136
Boughner, see Buchner
Bower, family, 235; Henry, 221
Bowerman, Thomas, 222
Bowman, see Bauman
Bowman, Abraham, 112; Christian, 112; Daniel, 112; Dr. Isaiah, 124; Jacob, 45; John, 112; Joseph, 112; Peter, 45
Boyer, family, 114, 215
Bradt, Albert Andriessen, 56; Andrew, 56, 222; Arent, 56
Brant, Joseph, 59, 78, 93
Brant County, 128, 220
Brantford Tp., 220
Brauer, see Brower
Break, family, 235
Brech, Catherine, 229; John, 229
Bremen, Hanover, 46
Brethren in Christ (Canada), see Dunkards
Bretz, family, 235
Brice, Sarah, 119
Bricker, family, 235; Annie, 111; Hans, 229; John, 111, 112, 229; Sam, 111, 112, 229
Bridgeport, 110, 124, 231
Brigham, family, 116
British Claims Commissioners, see Land Boards
Brockville, 177
Broeffle, Rev. John Ludwig, 177, 178
Brothersvalley Tp. (Pennsylvania), 227
Brower, family, 235
Brown, family, 235; Hans, 229; Jacob, 112; John, Jr., 112; John, Sr., 112; Maria, 229; Mary, 229; Susannah, 229
Brubaker, see Brubacher
Brucker see Bricker
Bruderhofs, 28

Brunner, family, 82
Buchner, family, 63; Henry, 221; Jacob, 224; John, 221; Martin, 221; Mathias, 221
Buck, Mrs. ——, 45
Bucks County (Pennsylvania), 31, 35, 63, 65, 104, 221–2, 228
Buffalo, 51, 123
Buffalo Creek, 64
Bull, Maturah, 222
Bulmer (Boomer), family, 124
Burdett, family, 222
Burford Tp., 60, 220
Burgoyne, General John, 73
Burk, John, 171
Burkhard, family, 235
Burkhart, see Burkhard
Burkholder, family, 226, 235; Christian, 231; William, 225
Burlington, 55
Burlington Bay, 51, 61
Burnett, William, 20–2
Burril, Adam, 114; Sarah, 114
Burwell, Adam, 64
Butchering, 184
Butler, Col. John, 48, 49, 50, 53, 54, 60, 75
Butler's Rangers, 23, 43, 45, 48, 54, 55, 56, 58, 59, 60, 65, 75, 82, 221
Button, Major, 226
Buttonville, 226
Byer, see Boyer
Byers, family, 115
Byllinge, Edward, 16, 30

Cainsville, 58
Caistor Tp., 217
Calais, 26
Calvin, John, 5, 170
Calvinism, 9
Camden Tp., 217, 218
Canada, 14, 22, 28, 32, 40, 41, 42, 45, 47, 49, 51, 59, 60, 65, 69, 70, 72, 73, 74, 77, 96, 104, 119 et passim
Canada Company, 157
Canadian Friends' Service Committee, 211
Canajoharie, 61, 177
Canborough Tp., 227
Canby, Benjamin, 64
Captivetown, 89
Card, Rev. Peleg, 179
Carleton, Sir Guy, 48 n., 54, 56, 57, 85
Carleton Island, 66
Carolinas, xvii, 10, 20, 26, 28, 29

Green's Mills, 61
Greisler, Johan Philip, 55
Grenville County, 85
Gressman, John, 113
Greyfelt, *see* Crefeld
Grimsby (Ontario), 47
Grist mills, 49, 51, 59, 63, 65, 87, 98, 119, 224, 234
Grobb, family, 63, 114
Groff, family, 236
Groh, family, 236; Michael, 231
Grossdawdy house, 133
Grosse Isle, 73, 74
Guelph, 156
Guinea fowl, 158
Gustin, John, 225
Guth, *see* Good
Gwillimbury Tp., 103, 104, 107, 219
Gypsum, 135–6

Haas, family, 236
Hadfield, Joseph, 58
Hager, family, 118; Lawrence, 118
Hagerman, family, 222; Nicholas, 69
Hagey, family, 236
Hahn, family, 114, 217
Haldimand, Gen. Frederick, 47, 48 n., 49, 50, 53, 54, 56
Haldimand County, 61, 115, 178, 217
Haldimand Tp., 219
Hall, family, 96
Hallman, family, 236; Wendell, 113
Hallowell Tp., 171, 216, 222
Halton County, 118–19, 220
Hamburg (Germany), 96
Hamilton, 61, 119
Hamilton, Andrew, 233
Hammacher, family, 236
Hand, Sally, 90
Handicrafts, 152
Hanover (Germany), 46
Hans, George Schmidts-dorf, 21
Hansler, George, 221
Hardboard, Frederick, 233
Hare, family, 63, 226
Harlem (Ontario), 179
Harner, *see* Herner
Harris, Amelia, 87; Daniel, 118
Harrisburg (Pennsylvania), 82
Harrison, Gen. William Henry, 94
Hartman, John, 228
Hartmans-dorf, 21
Hartshorne, Richard, 16
Hasbrouck, Abraham, 26

Hasle, ——, 89
Hastings, Nathaniel, 219
Hastings County, 85, 217, 223
Hatt, ——, 109
Haven, Joseph, 114
Havens, Joseph, 64
Hawkesbury Tp., 218
Hawn, family, 63
Hay Bay, 72, 223
Hazard, John, 77
Hazen, Daniel, 224
Heacock, Deborah, 221; Jonathan, 104
Heath, Sir Robert, 29
Heck, Barbara, 171, 216; Paul, 17, 216
Heckedorn, family, 236
Heckwelder, ——, 88
Heidelberg, 59
"Heifer project," 210–11
Heilbronn, 19
Heise, Christian, 226; Jacob, 226; Joseph, 226
Heise Hill, 226
Helmke, ——, 97
Hembling, family, 236
Henry, Bill, 93
Herd, John, 136
Herner, family, 236
Herr, *see* Hare
Herrit, John, 114; Mary, 114
Herschberg, family, 114
Hersche, Benjamin, 114
Hesky, family, 114
Hespeler, 113, 123, 230–1
Hespeler, Jacob, 123
Hess, family, 115
Hesse, District, *see* Western
Hesse (Germany), 10, 66
Hesse-Cassel (Germany), 124
Hesse, family, 109
Hesse-Hamburg (Germany), 69
Hessian mercenaries, 34, 66, 69, 73, 76, 96, 105, 107, 216
Hex signs, 191–2
Hick, Elijah, 72
Hicksite-Orthodox controversy, 212
Hiestand, family, 236
High, *see* Hoch
Highlanders, *see* Scottish
Hilborn, family, 236; Anna, 231; Thomas, 220, 231
Hill, Benjamin, 64, 114; Jacob 77; John, 64, 114
Hillier Tp., 216
Hilltown (Pennsylvania), 113
Hipple, family, 63, 114

Hitchcock, family, 63
Hoch, family, 114
Hoemacher, *see* Hammacher
Hoffman, family, 236
Hog Island, *see* Belle Island
Hohn, family, 236
Holland, xvii, xx, 5, 6, 7, 8, 9, 10, 17, 19, 20, 25, 35, 56, 66, 104, 110, 119, 155, 170, 179, 222–3, 230
Hollanders, Reformed, *see* German Reformed Church
Holly, Joseph, 225
Holm, Neil P., 113
Holmes, family, 76; Asa, 63; Hugh, 77, 233; Rev. William, 178
Holstein-Friesian cattle, 155
Home district, 47, 52, 57, 85, 117, 153
Honey, 91, 158
Honsberger, *see* Hunsberger
Hooper, William, 76
Hoover, family, 62, 217, 226; Abraham, 62; Benjamin, 62; Daniel, 62, 226; David, 62; Herbert, 61; Jacob, 62; Jessie Clark, 61; John, 226
Hope Tp., 219
Horner, Daniel, 226; Emmanuel, 226; Thomas, 220
Horning, family, 109, 110
Horning's Tract, 110
Horst, family, 236
Horticulture, *see* Agriculture
Hostetler, family, 236
House, family, 63, 115; Harmonius, 49
Housser, family, 114
Howard Tp., 218
Howe, General, 34
Huber, family, 236; Jonas, 61, 62, *see also* Hoover
Hudson, Henry, 30
Huff, family, 216, 223; Joseph, 70
Huffman, family, 82, 221; Henry, 82
Huguenots, xvii, xx, 9 and n., 10, 25–6, 29, 31, 32, 34, 35, 36, 43, 45, 46, 56, 59, 60, 66, 87, 106, 116, 119, 147, 167, 169, 170, 207, 217, 219, 221–3, 229
Hugues, Besançon, 9 n.
Humber River, 95, 107, 227
Humberstone Tp., 218
Hungary, 3, 211
"Hungry Year," 64
Hunsberger, family, 63, 114, 246

Hunter, Gen. Robert, 21, 69
Huntingdon County, Pa., 222
Huron, Lake, 78
Huron Church (Sandwich), 78
Huron Indians, 95
Huron River, *see* Clinton River
Hurst, David, 113
Huss, John, 3
Hutter, Jacob, 28
Hutterites, 28, *see also* Mennonites
Huyck, family, 223

Île aux Noix, 68
Iler, family, 216; Jacob, 74
India, 211
Indian Department, 49, 50, 54, 58, 82
Indian lands, 58, 72, 74
Indian ponies, 154
Indians, 22, 28, 32, 36, 44, 48, 49, 50, 51, 54, 55, 56, 58, 61, 62, 72, 73, 74, 77, 82, 87, 88–95, 117, 118, 126–7, *see also* tribal names
Ingersoll, Laura, 46; Col. Thomas, 118
Intolerable Acts, 34
Ireland, 20, 67, 119, 208, 221
Irish, xviii, 17, 32 n., 40, 116, 117, 118, 166
Iroquois, 22
Irrigation, *see* Agriculture
Irwin, Charles, 228; Eli, 153
Italy, 10

Jackson, James, 233
Jacobs, George, 233
Jamestown, 29
Jansen, family, 221; *see also* Johnson
Janzen, family, 236
Japan, 211
Jarvis, William, 57; Mrs. William, 56
Jessop, Major Edward, 68 n.
Jessop's Corps (Loyal Rangers), 68 and n.
Jesuits, 11
Johns Hopkins University, 124
Johnson, family, 63; Asa, 98; E. Pauline, 58; George H. M., 58; Col. Guy, 50, 56, 59, 60; Hanna, 98; Sir John, 22–3, 50, 67, 68, 70, 98; Lawrence, 212; Sally, 98; Sir William, 47, 49, 50, 58
Jones, family, 246
Jones, Augustine, 115; Augustus. 57, 83, 96, 112; Rev. Peter, 57

256

257

New Orleans, 122
New Paltz, 26
"New Purchase," 55
New Rochelle, 26, 46, 70
"New Settlement," 77
New-Schoenbrun, 88
New Survey, 117
New York City, 21, 29, 48 n., 67, 70, 97, 117, 118, 122
New York Confiscation Act, 68 n.
New York State, xvii, xix, xx, 10, 18, 20, 21, 22, 24, 26, 29, 31, 35, 43, 44, 45, 51, 56, 61, 62, 63, 65, 70 and n., 71, 96, 98, 99, 100, 101, 102, 107, 110, 115, 117, 119, 122, 123, 153, 154, 155, 177, 207, 209, 221–3, 225, 232
Newark, see Niagara-on-the-Lake
Newburgh, 29
Newcastle district, 207
Newkirk, family, 76; widow ——, 233
Newmarket, 104
Niagara, 64, 66, 72
Niagara district, 51, 53–61, 64, 65, 74, 75, 84, 86, 101, 102, 103, 106, 107, 118, 121, 167, 168, 171, 209
Niagara Falls, 87, 109, 122, 146
Niagara River, 46, 50, 54, 56, 58, 108, 109, 114
Niagara-on-the-Lake, 44, 46, 47, 51, 54, 55, 56, 57, 59, 61, 64, 72, 85, 91, 92, 96, 100, 112, 116, 119, 177, 178, 226
Nichol Tp., 124
Nicholson, Col. ——, 20
Niles, family, 70, 223
Nine Partners (Dutchess County, N.Y.), 72
Nith River, 123
Non-resistance, xx, 7
Norfolk County, 63, 83, 85, 86, 119, 127, 128, 153, 177, 219–20, 224
North Carolina, 29, 119, 208, 230
Northampton County (Pennsylvania), 27, 35, 227
Northport, 222
Northumberland County, see also Durham and Northumberland counties
Northumberland County (Pennsylvania), 75
Norwich, 61
Norwich Tp., 117, 220, 221
Northwest Company, 76
Nottawasaga, 124–5
Nova Scotia, 34, 117, 136

Oakes, Garrett, 116
Oakland Tp., 225
Ober Weisers-dorf, 21
Oberholzer, family, 227, 236; Martin, 112
Oberkulen, 61
O'Flaherty, Patrick, 233
Ohio, 72, 77, 88, 93
Ohio River, 27
Old Fairfield, see Schoenfeld
"Old Survey," 117
Ontario, see also Upper Canada, xix, xx, 20, 42, 83, 108, 123, 127–8
Ontario, Lake, 50, 55, 72, 102, 103, 128, 177
Ontario County, 85, 104, 220, 231
Oronhyehtaka, 58
Osnabruck Tp., 177, 217
Ostracism, see Meidung
Ostrander, family, 223
Oswego, 44, 52, 66
Oyerholt, family, 63, 114
Oxford County, 117, 128, 220
Oxford Tp., 216, 219

Pacifism, 3, 37, 88
Palatinates, see Palatine Germans
Palatine Germans, 19, 20, 22, 23, 27, 29, 31, 33, 42, 55, 66, 69, 83, 131, 207, 213–15
Palermo, 119
Pannabecker, family, 236; Cornelius, 230
Papermill, first in America, 18, 31
Park, family, 76, 233
Parliament, family, 223
Parsons, Thomas, 76, 233
Pastorius, Francis Daniel, 18
Patterson, family, 116
Patterson's Creek, see Port Dover
Paulin, Benjamin, 64
Pearce, family, 116
Pearsall, family, 223
Pearson, Benjamin, 219; Peter Pentz, 228
Peasants' War, 6
Peat, Adam, 70
Peck, family, 76; John, 233
Peel County, 117, 220
Pelham Tp., 60, 64, 65, 217
Penn, William, 16–18, 30, 31, 33, 34, 83, 138
Pennsylvania, xvii, xix, xx, 10, 17, 18, 22, 23, 24, 26, 27, 28, 29, 30–9, 42, 47, 48 n., 52, 59, 60, 61, 62, 64, 71, 74, 76, 81, 83, 84, 88–9, 99, 100, 101, 102, 104, 105,

Reichard, Christian, 230; Daniel, 230; John, 230; Samuel, 230
Reichert, family, 236
Reidesel, Gen. Baron de, 69
Reif, Barbara, 230
Reiff, see Rife
Reist, family, 236; Adam, 112; John, 112
Reitzel, family, 236
"Resisters," xx
Revolutionary War, xix, 26, 29, 32 n., 33, 34, 35, 37, 41, 42, 44, 45, 46, 47, 49, 55, 58, 60, 64, 65, 66, 67, 68, 72, 83, 86, 94, 107, 119, 171, 177, 178, 225, 227
Rhine River, 129
Rhode Island, 171
Rice, Moses, 116; Thomas, 64
Richelieu River, 68
Richert, Christian, 111
Richmond Hill, 100, 106
Richmond Tp., 217
Rickart, family, 114
Rideau River, 120
Rife, family, 236
Ringler, family, 236
Ringwood, 160
Riseby, family, 114
Risser, see Reesor
Rittenhouse, family, 114; William, 18, 31
Ritter, Edward, 96
Riverside, 70
Roaring Creek Valley, 104
Robertson, Jane, 124
Robinett, Allen, 118
Rochefoucault-Liancourt, Duc de La, 146
Roger's Rangers, 216
Rogers, Col. Robert, 68; Timothy, 103–4
Rohr, family, 221
Rohrer, Chris, 224
Rollston, Catharine, 58
Romeran, Juliana, 73
Roman Catholic Church, 4, 6, 7, 8, 10, 11, 70
Roman Catholics, 20, 30, 32 n., 67, 123, 168, 208, 218
Rome, 11
Root, family, 119
Rose, Peter, 223
Rosenberger, family, 236; Benjamin, 111, 128
Ross, Major ——, 68
Rotan, see Rutton
Rotterdam, 56

Rouge River, 97, 105
Rouse, John, 228
Rousseau, Jean Baptiste, 59, 108, 219
Row, Joseph, 221
Rowe, Daniel, 49; John, 60
Roy, family, 115
Royal Yorkers, see King's Royal Regiment of New York
Rozel, family, 119–20
Rozell, family, 115
Rudell, family, 236
Rudy, family, 237
Rumania, 28
Russia, 7, 28
Ruttan, see Rutton
Rutton, family, 70, 217, 223; Henry, 70; Jean Baptiste, 70; John, 70; Peter, 69, 70
Ryerse, family, 63, 86, 87; George J., 86, 87; Col. Samuel, 87
Ryerse Creek, 87
Ryerson, family, 87; Egerton Adolphus, 45, 86
Ryertz, see Ryerse, also Ryerson
Ryerzoon, Adrian, 87; Martin, 87

Sackrider, Sol., 117
Sailer, family, 114
St. Bartholomew's Day Massacre, 10, 26
St. Catharines, 104, 225
St. Clair, Lake, 233
St. Clair River, 78
St. David's, 56
St. Francis, Lake, 72
St. John (New York), 225
St. Lawrence River, 68, 72
St. Michel parish (Montreal), 59
St. Thomas, 89, 116
Salem, see Winston
Saltfleet Tp., 115, 119, 219
Saltzberger, family, 236; Philip, 112
Samuel (Indian), 89
Sand, David, 72
Sandwich, 65, 78
Sandwich Tp., 216
Saratoga, 69, 73
Sauer, Christopher, 24, 38
Saugeen River, 118
Sault Ste Marie, 79
Saunders, Henry, 225
Save the Children Fund, 199
Sawmills, 49, 51, 59, 65, 78, 87, 97, 98, 119, 124, 152
Saxony, 66, 96 n.
Sayler, see Sailer
Scarborough Tp., 103, 219

Schaeffer, John, 113
Schantz, family, 237
Scheidel, family, 237
Schenectady, 21, 31
Schermhorn, Capt. ——, 223;
    John, 224; Richard, 224
Schiller, Corporal John, 118
Schlacht, *see* Slaght
Schlacht, Henrick, 224; Job, 224
Schlechter, family, 237
Schmidt, family, 237
Schneider, family, 237; Christian,
    153, 218; Jacob, 153
Schoenbrunn, 88, 93
Schoenfeld, *see* Fairfield
Schoerg, *see* Sherk
Schoharie County, 20, 21, 22, 31,
    47, 55, 177
Schooley, Asa, 64, 114
Schörg, *see* Sherk
Schuh, family, 237
Schulter, David, 64
Schunk, family, 226
Schuykill River, 31, 136
Schuyler, Peter, 20, 22
Schwartz, family, 237
Schwenkfelder, Casper, 28, 32
Schwenkfelders, 28, 32
Scotch-Irish, 29, 32 and n., 33, 34,
    131, 134, 142, 170, 208
Scotland, 142
Scottish, xviii, 17, 40, 68, 121, 166,
    177, 208, 216, 218
Scottish Highlanders, 67, 218
Scratch, *see* Kratz
Searle, William, 233
Sebach, John, 232
Sebring, John, 232
Sebringville, 232
Secor, Marquis de, 26, *see also*
    Secord
Secord, family, 45–6, 51; Ambroise, 45; David, 116; James,
    46, 49; Laura (Ingersoll), 26;
    Peter, 49, 86; Mrs. ——, 51
Seibert, family, 237
Selkirk, 62
Seneca Tp., 217
Sensemann, Gottlob, 88, 92, 93
Serigley, Enoch, 64
Servos, Daniel, 56
Servos House, 56
Seven Years War, 22, 34, 35, 36,
    45, 49, 67
Seventh Day Baptists, 24–5
Sevits, *see* Zavitz
Seykott, Richard, 21
Shade, Absalom, 122

Shank (Mennonite preacher), 62,
    115
Shannan, Michael, 233
Shantz, David, 230; Isaac, Jr., 230;
    Isaac, Sr., 230; Jacob, 230;
    Veronica, 230
Sharon, 107
Shay's Rebellion, 35
Sheiffelin, Jacob, 77
Shell, family, 69, 218
Shelly, family, 237
Shenk, Christian, 112; Martin, 112
Sherck, Peter, 112
Sherick, family, 116
Sherk, family, 59, 114, 217; Casper, 227; Joseph, 108–9, 111,
    228
Sherwood, 107
Shoemaker, family, 237
Shonk, Peter, 76, 233
Shore, Lydia, 222
Short Hills, 64
Shorthorn cattle, 154
Shoup, family, 114, 237
Showers, Michael, 49
Shunk, *see* Shonk
Shunk, Jacob, 226
Shupe, Ben, 113; George, 113
Sidney Tp., 217, 222–3
Sievenpipher, family, 114
Silesia, 28, 32
Silverthorn, John, 118; Joseph, 118
Simcoe, John Graves, 44, 51, 61,
    83–8, 90–3, 95, 97, 99, 100, 101,
    102, 115–16, 145, 177
Simcoe, Mrs. J. G., 56, 61, 100,
    101, 102, 145
Simcoe, Lake, 96
Simcoe County, 95, 124–5, 220
Simons, Meno, 7, 212
Sissney, ——, 233
Sitler, family, 233
Six Nations Indians, 49
Sixth Line German settlement
    (Simcoe County), 124–5
Skippack Creek, 19
Slaght, family, 220
Slavery, 23, 29, 33
Sloat, Michael, 69
Slough, family, 222
Slough, Rosanna, 221
Smith, Abraham, 63, 231; Charles,
    69; David William, 85; Henry,
    69; John, 109, 110; Molly
    Klinger, 62; Peter Klinger, 62,
    205; Thomas, 57, 77, 233; William, 219

Smith's Bay, 69
Snider, John, 227
Snyder, family, 82, 115, 227; Elizabeth, 74; John, 74, 226
Soap making, 150–1
Society of Friends, *see* Quakers
Society for the Propagation of the Gospel in Foreign Parts, 71
Solmes, family, 223
Somerset County (Pennsylvania), 99, 100, 105, 106, 227, 234
Somerset (England), 105
Sommerfield, Frederic, 96
Sophiasburg Tp., 216, 222–3
Sorel, 68
Souder, family, 237
South America, 42
South Bay, 223
South Carolina, 29
South Dakota, 28
Southwold Tp., 116
Sovereign, family, 118, 153; Frederick, 224; Philip, 119
Spain, 10
Speed River, 112
Spener, Philip Jacob, 11
Spohn, Mrs. Elizabeth Bowman, 45
Sprangle, Michael, 62
Springer, family, 109, 116, 119, 237; David, 119; Richard, 119
Springfield, Joseph, 233
Sproat, family, 118
Stamford (Connecticut), 68 n.
Stamp Act, 41
Starr, James, 104
Stauffer, family, 237; Christian, 112; Samuel, 230
Steckle, family, 223
Steckley, family, 227
Stegmann, John, 107
Stephens, family, 96
Stevens, Abel, 179; Anne, 114; Joseph, 114
Stewart, Benjamin, 62
Stienhoff, family, 225
Stiver, W., 97, 219
Stoeckle, family, 237
Stolzfusz, Christian, 113
Stoney Creek Road, 61
Stoney Creek Tp. (Pennsylvania), 225, 234
Stoney Island, 78
Stong, Daniel, 226, 227; Joseph, 227
Stony Arabia, *see* Maqua country
Storey, family, 116

Storme, family, 114
Stormont County, 85, 177, 217
Storrington Tp., 218
Stoutenberg, family, 124
Stover, family, 227; Adam, 117; Fred, 117; Michael, 117
Stoves, 133
Street, Margaret, 70
Strickler, family, 115, 226
Stouffer, Abraham, 105
Stouffville, 105
Strome, family, 237
Stuart, George; Rev. John, 178
Suffolk County, 85
Sully's house, Nantes, 70
Sultz, family, 63
Summerfeldt, ——, 97
Sunnidale Corners, 124
Surphlet, family, 76
Surplet, Robert, 233
Susquehanna River, 25, 45, 64, 76, 129, 223, 227
Sussex County (New York), 63
Swabians, 22
Swalm, family, 124–5; Conrad, 124–5; Bishop E. J., 125, 210
Swatz, family, 114, 115
Swedes, 30
Swedish West India Company, 30
Swine, 155
Swiss Brethren, *see* Mennonites
Swiss Germans, 19, 23, 33, 35, 42, 60, 61, 83, 131, 207, 214–15
Switzer, Harvey Morris, 119
Switzerland, xx, 5, 6, 7, 9, 10, 17, 26, 32, 37, 106, 122, 124, 131, 170, 209, 229–31
Syple, John, 117
Syria, 211

Talbot, Thomas, 115–16
Talbot Road, 116
Talbot Settlement, 115–16
Taufscheins, 36
Taylor, John, 64, 114; Samuel, 64
Tecumseh Tp., 220
Teeple, Peter, 86
Teeter, family, 63
Telner, Jacob, 18
Temple, family, 96
Tennessee, 208
Tewits, *see* Zavitz
Thames River, 71, 74, 75, 76, 82, 83, 85, 89–95, 116, 233
Thirty Mile Creek, 63
Thirty Years' War, 46
Thornhill, 100, 106

York Pioneer and Historical Society, 107
York Tp., 103, 107, 219, 225-6
Yorkshire (England), 30
Yost, family, 237
Young, Mrs. ——, 45; Mrs. Anna Beamer, 222; Anna Maria, 222; Stephen, 223; William, 224
Young's Creek Valley, 63
Youngstown (New York), 46

Yung, Michael, 88, 93, 95

Zavitz, family, 114
Zeisberger, David, 71, 88-93
Zeller, family, 237
Ziegler, family, 231, 237; Dillman, 231
Zimmerman, family, 63, 114
Zinzendorf, Count von, 12, 27, 36
Zurich, 5, 229
Zwingli, 4, 5, 6